Daniela Obradovic, Heiko Pleines (Eds.)

The Capacity of Central and East European Interest Groups to Participate in EU Governance

CHANGING EUROPE

Edited by Dr. Sabine Fischer, Dr. Heiko Pleines and
Prof. Dr. Hans-Henning Schröder

ISSN 1863-8716

Daniela Obradovic, Heiko Pleines (eds.)

The Capacity of
Central and East European Interest Groups
to Participate in EU Governance

ibidem-Verlag
Stuttgart

Bibliografische Information der Deutschen Nationalbibliothek
Die Deutsche Nationalbibliothek verzeichnet diese Publikation in der
Deutschen Nationalbibliografie; detaillierte bibliografische Daten sind im
Internet über http://dnb.d-nb.de abrufbar.

Bibliographic information published by the Deutsche Nationalbibliothek
Die Deutsche Nationalbibliothek lists this publication in the Deutsche Nationalbibliografie;
detailed bibliographic data are available in the Internet at http://dnb.d-nb.de.

∞

Gedruckt auf alterungsbeständigem, säurefreien Papier
Printed on acid-free paper

ISSN: 1863-8716

ISBN-10: 3-89821-750-7
ISBN-13: 978-3-89821-750-7

© *ibidem*-Verlag
Stuttgart 2007

This publication has been produced as part of

NewGov

NEW MODES OF GOVERNANCE PROJECT
Project no. CIT1-CT-2004-506392, Integrated Project, www.eu-newgov.org
Priority 7 – Citizens and Governance in the Knowledge-based Society
Funded by the European Union under the Sixth Framework Programme

Reference number: 24/D8a
Lead contractor for this deliverable:
Forschungsstelle Osteuropa (Research Centre for East European Studies), Bremen

Language editor: Hilary Abuhove
Technical editor: Matthias Neumann

This book presents results of a research team which examines the impact of the EU eastern enlargements on EU governance structures involving the participation of civil society organisations. In this context, the focus is on questions of capacity and accountability in a multi-level perspective.

The research team is part of the NEWGOV Integrated Project, led by the European University Institute (Florence, Italy). It belongs to NEWGOV project 24, which is directed by Daniela Obradovic, Amsterdam Center for International Law. The research team is headed by Heiko Pleines, Research Centre for East European Studies (Forschungsstelle Osteuropa) at the University of Bremen. Further NEWGOV partners in the research team are Michał Federowicz (Institute of Philosophy and Sociology, Polish Academy of Sciences, Warsaw), David Lane (University of Cambridge, UK) and Zdenka Mansfeldová (Institute of Sociology, Academy of Science of the Czech Republic, Prague).

Contents

List of Tables

List of Figures

Part I. Introduction

Daniela Obradovic and Heiko Pleines

1. The Capacity of Civil Society Organisations to Participate in EU Multi-Level Governance. An Analytical Framework

1.1. Introduction

The European Union (EU) is a special case of independent states transferring considerable powers to a supranational body in order to meet the challenges of changing societies and globalisation. As policy-making powers are transferred to the supranational level, groups representing societal interests have to become active at the supranational level, too. Recent research on the role of interest groups at the EU level has focused on two topics. First, it has been broadly discussed whether the integration of interest groups (or 'civil society organisations' in EU parlance[1]) can help compensate for the perceived deficit of democracy at the EU level. Second, issues of multi-level governance, i.e. of the division of policy-making powers between the EU, national and regional/local levels, have been widely examined.

Attempts to reform the system of EU governance have given rise to new modes of governance, which cover a wide range of different policy processes. These include the open method of co-ordination, voluntary accords, standard setting, regulatory networks, regulatory agencies, regulation 'through information', bench-marking, peer review, mimicking, policy competition and informal agreements. At the same time, more traditional modes of governance continue to play an important role in EU decision-making processes.

The efficiency of the traditional decision-making model, originally developed in the EU-15, was increasingly questioned in the run-up to the 2004 enlargement. Accordingly, the Nice Treaty of 2003 and the European constitution, signed in 2004, recommended far-reaching reforms of the system of EU governance. Since the French and Dutch populations rejected the new constitution in a referendum in 2005, the reforms have been stalled.

---

1   As the EU refers to all collectively organised non-state actors as "civil society organisations", this term will be used synonymously with "interest groups". According to the European Commission's definition, civil society includes the following groups: (1) trade unions and employers' organisations (social partners); (2) organisations representing social and economic players that are not social partners in the strict sense of the term (such as business sector associations); (3) non-governmental organisations that bring people together in a common cause, such as environmental or human rights organisations, charities, professional associations and grass roots organisations; (4) institutions or sectors that involve citizens in local and municipal life, such as churches or religious communities (Commission 2001).

However, the new EU Treaty will contain the provisions agreed upon at the 2004 Intergovernmental Conference on participatory democracy.[2] Those provisions are as follows:

'Article I-47, The principle of participatory democracy

1. The institutions shall, by appropriate means, give citizens and representative associations the opportunity to make known and publicly exchange their views in all areas of Union action.

2. The institutions shall maintain an open, transparent and regular dialogue with representative associations and civil society.

3. The Commission shall carry out broad consultations with parties concerned in order to ensure that the Union's actions are coherent and transparent.

4. Not less than one million citizens who are nationals of a significant number of Member States may take the initiative of inviting the Commission, within the framework of its powers, to submit any appropriate proposal on matters where citizens consider that a legal act of the Union is required for the purpose of implementing the Constitution. European laws shall determine the provisions for the procedures and conditions required for such a citizens' initiative, including the minimum number of Member States from which such citizens must come'.[3]

Within this framework the direction of governance reforms within the EU continues to be the subject of heated debates, and the 2004 and 2007 eastern enlargements of the EU have only added complexity. On the one hand, the number of member states has risen from 15 to 27, thus making consensus more difficult to reach and increasing the number of interest groups active at the EU level considerably. On the other hand, representatives of the new member states, including their interest groups, deserve equal representation in EU decision-making processes.

1.2. The EU and Civil Society Organisations

From the very beginning of European integration, informal consultations with interest groups have been a constant and distinct feature of the decision-making process of the European Commission. The Council of Ministers, however, is not directly exposed to the lobbying activities of interest groups at the EU level, as the participants in the decision-making process at the Council level are national actors, representing their respective national governments. The European Parliament, meanwhile, was initially ignored by interest groups because of its mostly symbolic role in EU decision-making. It

---

2 Brussels European Council 21/22 June 2007, Presidency Conclusions, http://www.eu2007.de/en/News/download_docs/Juni/0621-ER/010conclusions.pdf, p.17.

3 Conference of the Representatives of the Governments of the Member States, Treaty establishing a Constitution for Europe, Brussels, 29 October 2004, http://www.consilium.europa.eu/igcpdf/en/04/cg00/cg00087-RE02.en04.pdf, pp. 51-52.

has gained more attention in recent years due to the broadening of its powers in the political process (see e.g. Christiansen/Piattoni 2004; Greenwood 2007).

Following the Sutherland Report in 1992, the European Commission systematically increased the number of recognised interest groups with the proclaimed aim of making the consultation process more open and transparent. When the first post-socialist states joined the EU in 2004, the Commission had contact with around 1,500 interest groups, two thirds of which represented business interests. Additionally, an estimated 350 large firms and 200 regions were active in EU politics. The consultations took place on an ad hoc basis through various channels, such as participation in the formation of Green and White papers, communications, advisory committees and informal working groups.

Although the Commission claims to follow a policy of open access, the ownership of resources determines which interest groups gain access to EU institutions (see e.g. Bouwen 2002; Michalowitz 2004 a+b). At the same time, there is no Commission-wide approach on how to undertake consultations with interest groups. Each department has its own mechanisms and methods for consulting its respective sectoral interest groups.

In its White Paper on Governance (Commission 2001), published in July 2001, the European Commission acknowledged the need to reform European governance in the wake of debates about a perceived democracy deficit at its highest levels. The White Paper called for the greater involvement of two constituencies – regional/local actors and civil society organisations – in order to bolster its democratic legitimacy. The emphasis is clearly upon EU-level civil society actors. The Paper's authors envisaged improvements that would ultimately take the form of more structured processes of consultation, which would supposedly evolve via the closer relationship between these transnational organisations and EU institutions (more particularly, the Commission) (see also Armstrong 2002). The prime forms of structured consultation processes are the civil dialogue and the social dialogue.

1.3. The Civil Dialogue

The oldest institutionalised avenue for the participation of civil society organisations in the EU decision-making process is the European Economic and Social Committee (EESC). The EESC is a non-political body that gives representatives of member states' economic, social and civic organisations a formal platform on which to express their views on EU issues and to play an integral part in decision-making. Set up by the Rome Treaties in 1957, the EESC has since then seen its role confirmed and strengthened. It brings together representatives of employers' organisations, including public-sector corporations (Group I) and employees (Group II), but also – and this is the EESC's distinguishing feature – other sectors of organised civil society (Group III).

The EESC's 317 members are drawn from these three groups. Members are nominated by national governments and appointed by the European Council for a renewable 4-year term of office. Consultation with the EESC by the Commission or the Council is mandatory in certain cases but is otherwise optional. The EESC may, however, also issue opinions unilaterally. The Single European Act (1986) and the Maastricht Treaty (1992) extended the range of issues that must be referred to the Committee, in particular the new policies (regional and environmental). The Amsterdam Treaty (1997) further broadens the areas for referral to the EESC and allows it to be consulted by the European Parliament.

In 2001, the Commission signed a protocol with the EESC[4] effectively recommending that the Commission invite the EESC to issue exploratory opinions as well as rely on it to deepen its relations with organised civil society. The protocol provides for the Commission to consult the Committee on certain issues on an exploratory basis prior to drawing up its own proposal, thus allowing the Committee to play a consultative role at an earlier stage in the decision-making process. However, the EESC operates in a strictly advisory capacity and has to reach an internal consensus on any issue before it can make itself heard in the decision-making process in Brussels.

Newer elements of the civil dialogue, which aim to increase the involvement of civil society in EU governance, are based on a range of consultation forums. These include the Dialogue with Business,[5] Dialogue with Citizens,[6] European Round Table on Democracy, Green and White Papers and Internet consultations via the Web portal Your Voice in Europe.[7] These are conducted between the Commission and interest groups in the pre-drafting phase of European legislation or via the open method of co-ordination (OMC)[8] guidelines preparation process.

Your Voice in Europe is the Commission's single access point offering citizens, consumers and business an opportunity to play an active role in the process of shaping

---

4   Protocol governing arrangements for co-operation between the European Commission and the Economic and Social Committee, 24 September 2001, CES 1253/2001.
5   http://europa.eu.int/business/en/index.html
6   http://europa.eu.int/citizens/en/index.html
7   http://europa.eu.int/yourvoice
8   The OMC is not designed to produce legislation at the European level. It aims to co-ordinate the actions of the member states in a given policy domain and to create conditions for mutual learning that are intended to introduce some degree of voluntary policy convergence. It also helps member states to develop their own policies through the discussion and dissemination of best practises, with the aim of identifying common goals. The OMC is concretised through the production of guidelines drafted by the Commission and issued by the Council of Ministers, to be translated into national policy through national action plans (NAPs), combined with periodic monitoring by the Commission, evaluation and peer review organised as mutual learning processes and accompanied by indicators and benchmarking as means of comparing best practises. The OMC is applied as an instrument for the development of budgetary, economic, employment and social inclusion policy, and also as a strategy in pension reform, information society, research and innovation, education and training and youth policy.

Commission policy. This Internet site is to be replaced in the near future by a more encompassing contact centre, Europe Direct, which will promote 'one-stop shopping'
access for EU citizens. For an overview of the different forms of the civil dialogue, see
Obradovic (2006).

1.4. The Social Dialogue

The Commission's dialogue with representatives of management and labour organised at the EU level constitutes the so-called 'social dialogue'. It is based on law, namely
Articles 138 and 139 of the Treaty establishing the European Community, which en-
dow the social partners with law-making and implementation powers. The European
Commission is required to automatically accept as a legislative initiative any legislative proposal jointly submitted by all of the social partners. The Commission must
then transmit the proposal to the EU Council. Formally, EU institutions cannot take
action in the area of social policy without consulting the social partners. In the event
that the social partners abstain from negotiations, however, legislative competence
reverts back to the EU institutions.

The European Trade Union Confederations (ETUC), along with the European Centre
of Public Enterprises (CEEP – Centre européen des entreprises à participation publi-
que et des entreprises d'intérêt économique général, European Centre of Enterprises
with Public Participation and of Enterprises of General Economic Interest) and the
Union of Industrial and Employers' Confederations of Europe (UNICE – Union des
Confédérations de l'Industrie et des Employeurs de l'Europe), are recognised by the
European Commission as social partners and are involved in the social dialogue.

However, industrial relations in the EU are still very much divided along national
lines. Due to the conflicting national interests that still dominate the decision-making
process, consensus among the social partners is difficult to achieve. Additionally, the
national interest groups are reluctant to transfer resources to transnational umbrella
organisations. This assessment is supported e.g. by Greenwood (2007), Rojot (2004),
Grande (2003), Hartenberger (2001) and Falkner (2000).

1.5. The Specifics of EU Multi-Level Governance

By definition, EU governance is a specific form of multi-level governance. As the EU
consists of sovereign nation states, the decision-making powers of EU bodies are necessarily limited. Based on the subsidiarity principle, decisions within EU governance
should ideally be made at the lowest appropriate level. In addition, responsibility for
the implementation of these decisions rests foremost with national (and sub-national)
executive bodies. As a result, most policy decisions involve several levels, and regulation for most policy fields includes the EU and national levels on a regular basis.

Accordingly, civil society organisations dealing with specific policy issues have to be active at several levels simultaneously.

Nearly all civil society organisations in EU member states are founded on the national (or sub-national) level; they later expand their activities to the EU level. As a result, at the EU level, civil society organisations active in a specific policy field are often not only divided by their issue-specific position but also along national lines. In many policy fields, the result has been a rather chaotic mass of civil society organisations trying to gain access to EU decision-makers. That is why another of the European Commission's efforts to structure consultations with civil society organisations has focused on the creation of supra-national umbrella organisations uniting all civil society organisations representing a specific interest. The Commission has encouraged national civil society organisations to form umbrella organisations by promising preferential access to decision-making processes and substantial financial support for such umbrella organisations.

However, the degree of support furnished by the Commission varies widely. Some organisations, like the European Women's Lobby, receive substantial financial support from the EU, whereas others, especially among the social partners, are strong enough to represent their interests without any financial support from the EU and some, like for example Greenpeace, reject EU funding by principle.

At the same time, some umbrella organisations, such as the European Women's Lobby, have come close to establishing a consultation monopoly concerning representation of their specific interest at the EU level. Other groups, despite being formally united, like the Green 10, which bring together environmental NGOs, struggle to find a common position. Meanwhile, other umbrella organisations, especially among business interests, are often side-lined by the direct engagement of individual members or national member organisations.

Accordingly, the structure of civil society at the EU level varies widely depending on the policy field and the specific interests involved. The system of multi-level governance further complicates the picture: the relationship between the Commission and the interest groups (organised in umbrella organisations) does not simply consist of two parties, but also involves national and sub-national state actors and civil society organisations. In such a complex setting, links extend in all directions.

One common pattern found, for example, in the agricultural policy field, is the strong co-operation of national governments and national interest groups in the defence of common "national" interests at the EU level. In this case, national interest groups often leave a large part of the negotiation activities at the EU level to national state actors. Another pattern typical, for example, in the environmental policy field, is strong co-operation between the Commission and national environmental interest groups. The Commission relies on the interest groups to pressure for and monitor the implementation of EU regulation at the national and sub-national levels. However, in most policy fields, the constellations are more complex. An overview of the different patterns of relations between interest groups and the European Commission is offered by Greenwood 2007.

1.6. Capacity to Engage in EU Governance

The capacity to engage in EU governance is distributed very unevenly among civil society organisations, varying according to policy fields and nationality. For example, interest representation in industrial relations is much better organised than in most other policy fields. At the same time, civil society is in most respects more developed in the central western and northern EU member states than in the southern and central eastern ones.

Three major prerequisites determine the capacity of civil society organisations to successfully engage in EU governance. The first is a general ability to engage in political decision-making processes. The second is the capacity to engage at the EU level and the third is the fulfilment of EU eligibility criteria regulating access to different consultation processes in EU governance.

In chronological order, most civil society organisations first develop the general capacity to engage in political decision-making processes. In most cases, they start at the national or sub-national level and develop a policy-related position that they wish to communicate to political decision-makers. They then have to identify the relevant decision-makers and suitable modes of communication, i.e. they have to develop a basic understanding of political processes. Common strategies for gaining access to political decision-makers include the provision of expertise, public protest actions and media attention. All of these tactics require specific resources, ranging from expertise to an active membership base and from financial resources to public relations skills.

Engagement at the EU level demands additional personnel and financial resources as well as new competencies. The latter include basic skills, such as knowledge of English and of EU decision-making structures, as well as more refined ones, such as the ability to network in a multi-national arena. The difficulties of multi-level governance are illustrated by the inability of almost all civil society organisations to organise protest actions at the EU level (in contrast to the national level). This means that engagement at the EU level cannot simply be treated as a logical continuation of national activities in policy fields that are becoming increasingly regulated by the EU. Engagement in EU governance demands new capacities. Civil society organisations are continually striving to overcome barriers to access and are engaged in learning processes.

The European Commission has (at least on paper) erected another barrier to access via the imposition of minimum requirements for civil society organisations wishing to participate in EU governance. The corresponding Code of Conduct, adopted in 2002 (Commission 2002), makes civil society organisations active at the EU level subject to the principles of good governance, which include transparency, accountability and representativeness.

With respect to transparency and accountability, the Commission wants to know (1) which interests a group represents and (2) how inclusive that representation is. Interested parties wishing to submit comments on policy proposals by the Commission must therefore be ready to provide the Commission and the public at large with the requisite information. Representativeness in the social dialogue is predominantly determined in terms of membership.[9] How these criteria can be applied to the civil dialogue has not yet been elaborated, as NGOs are almost never representative in terms of membership.

Many civil society organisations definitely lack the capacity to organise a "representative" membership base. At the same time, the eligibility criteria themselves remain very abstract, vague and unintelligible. It thus cannot be determined with certainty which organisations actually fulfil them. Accordingly, the actual implications for the capacity of civil society organisations to engage in EU governance remain unclear, as the chapter by Obradovic and Vizcaino in this volume elaborates.

1.7. The Normative Dimension

The European Commission believes that greater civil society participation in EU governance through early consultations will not only make the European integration process more inclusive and ensure that EU issues are debated by a wide range of interested parties, but will also contribute to a more effective shaping of policy in the Union (Commission 2001). The fact that the Commission advocates the involvement of civil society in the debate on the future of Europe (Commission 2005b) illustrates its commitment to inclusion. The promotion of citizen participation in EU governance is another of the Action Plan's strategies to improve communication within the Union (Commission 2005a). The commitment to greater opportunities for active stakeholder participation in EU policy-shaping is one of the 'Strategic Objectives 2005–2009' with which the European Commission launched its 'Partnership for European Renewal.'

With reference to new modes of governance, it has been argued that the public/ private border has disappeared, since the real decision-making process now continually involves, and combines, public and private actors. The government's job is not to govern but to mediate. In other words, negotiation and mediation are to play the

---

9   Commission of the European Communities (12/1993); Case T-135/96, Union Européenne de l'Artisanat et des Petites et Moyennes Entreprises (UEAPME) vs. Council, [1998] ECR II-2334, consideration 85. The representativeness of the social partners measures membership density, both of the candidate organisations themselves and of each of their members.

same central role in modern systems of governance as the prerogatives of authority and sovereignty did in the classical system. Under this approach, the Commission's task is not to present policies to a European electorate, but rather to act as a policy entre- preneur, collecting views and recommending policies for action, and then acting as a watchdog of EU interests to see that those policies are implemented at the national level. In this way, the Commission should assume the role of facilitator (or regulator) of a public/private network with a duty to create, foster and maintain relationships in this network (Harlow 2005, Schapiro 2001).

However, the European Commission's method of engaging civil society organisa- tions in EU governance does little to dispel the perceived democratic deficit at the EU level. First, even though civil society organisations are granted access to the consul- tation process, they are not accorded any decision making powers in EU governance. Second, even if the criterion of representativeness is extended, civil society organisa- tions can never act as a substitute for an electorate. For an overview of different lines of argument on this issue see Smismans 2006.

Moreover, with the introduction of eligibility standards for interest groups wish- ing to take part in EU governance, the Commission has partly changed the direction of accountability in the relationship between politics and civil society. Historically, the very idea of civil society was to hold state actors accountable. Engagement in civil so- ciety organisations was meant to offer citizens more permanent and more competent control over state actions than the simple election process. Now the Commission tries to hold civil society organisations accountable, or, more precisely, attempts to define who is allowed to hold *it* accountable.

Accordingly, it has been argued that "the more the European institutions count on civil society organizations to provide links to the citizenry and, therefore, help to bolster the legitimacy of EU rule, the more they will demand that they are represent- ative of interests which are, in turn, defined by the institutions. The relationship be- tween 'state' and civic organizations is a very difficult and fragile one, especially if the latter become more and more dependent on funding and power resources provided by the former. Almost since the inception of the then European Economic Community, the Commission has created or helped to build up a raft of civil society organizations, some of which receive important funding resources from the Commission (if they are not financed entirely by it). The attempts to involve NGOs in an institutionalized con- text have therefore been criticized by several authors working in this field. They warn against the danger that such efforts might lead to the creation of a false civil society by European institutions" (Goehring 2002, 123).

1.8. Conclusions

In summary, research on the capacity of civil society organisations to participate in EU multi-level governance has to take into account a multitude of aspects. In our view, the most important ones, which will be examined in this book, are:

- The regulation of EU governance concerning the involvement of civil society (and the normative justification attached to it);
- The general capacity of civil society organisations to engage in politics;
- The specifics of multi-level governance;
- The strategies employed by civil society organisations to engage in EU policy-making processes.

The following chapter will give a general overview of recent literature dealing with these topics. The third chapter will then tailor the questions to the new Central and East European member states, which joined the EU in 2004 and 2007. It will also lay out the research strategy employed to analyse these questions and thereby explain the structure of this book.

References

Armstrong, Kenneth A. (2002): *Rediscovering Civil Society: The European Union and the White Paper on Governance*, European Law Journal, 8(1), pp. 102–132.

Borragán, Nieves Pérez-Solórzano (2002): *Coming to terms with European Union lobbying. The Central and East European experience*, in: Warleigh, A. / Fairbrass, J. (eds.), *Influence and interests in the European Union. The new politics of persuasion and advocacy*, Europa, London, pp. 160–184.

Bouwen, Pieter (2002): *Corporate Lobbying in the EU: the Logic of Access*, Journal of European Public Policy, 9(3), pp. 365–390.

Christiansen, T./ Piattoni, S. (eds) (2004): *Informal Governance in the European Union*, Edward Elgar, Cheltenham.

Commission of European Communities (2001): *European Governance: White Paper*, COM(2001) 428, Brussels, 25 July 2001, 14.

Commission of European Communities (2002): *Towards a Reinforced Culture of Consultation and Dialogue. General Principles and Minimum Standards for Consultation of Interested Parties by the Commission*, COM(2002) 704 final, Brussels, 11 December 2002.

Commission of the European Communities (2005a): *Communication to the Commission: "Action plan to improve communicating Europe by the Commission"*, SEC 985.

Commission of the European Communities (2005b): *Communication from the Commission to the Council, the European Parliament, the European Economic and Social Committee and the Committee of the Regions: "The Commission's contribution to the period of the reflection and beyond: Plan-D for democracy, dialogue and debate"*, COM 494.

Falkner, Gerda (2000): *The Council or the social partners? EC social policy between diplomacy and collective bargaining*, Journal of European Public Policy, 7(5), pp. 705–724.

Goehring, Rebekka (2002): *Interest representation and legitimacy in the European Union. The new quest for civil society formation*, in: Warleigh, A. / Fairbrass, J. (eds.), *Influence and interests in the European Union. The new politics of persuasion and advocacy*, Europa, London, pp. 118–137.

Grande, Edgar (2003): *How the Architecture of the EU Political System Influences Business Associations*, in: Greenwood, J. (ed.), *The Challenge of Change in EU Business Associations*, Palgrave, Basingstoke, pp. 45–59.

Greenwood, Justin (2007): *Interest Representation in the European Union. 2nd ed.*, Palgrave, New York.

Harlow, C. (2005): *Deconstructing government*, Yearbook of European Law 2004, pp. 57–89.

Hartenberger, Ute (2001): *Europäischer Sozialer Dialogue nach Maastricht. EU-Sozialpartnerverhandlungen auf dem Prüfstand*, Nomos, Baden-Baden.

Michalowitz, Irina (2004a): *Analysing Structured Paths of Lobbying Behaviour: Why Discussing the Involvement of 'Civil Society' Does not Solve the EU's Democratic Deficit*, European Integration, 26(2), pp. 145–170.

Michalowitz, Irina (2004b): *Lobbying as a Two-way Strategy: Interest Intermediation or Mutual Instrumentalisation?*, in: Warntjen, A. / Wonka, A. (eds), *Governance in Europe: The Role of Interest Groups*, Nomos, Baden-Baden, pp. 76–93.

Obradovic, D. (2006): *Civil and social dialogue in European governance*, Yearbook of European Law 2005, pp. 261–327.

Rojot, Jacques (2004): *European Collective Bargaining: New Prospects or Much Ado About Little?*, in: Neal, A. (ed.), *The Changing Face of European Labour Law and Social Policy*, Kluwer, The Hague, pp. 13–38.

Schapiro, M. (2001): *Administrative law unbounded*, Indian Journal of Global Legal Studies, 8, p. 369.

Smismans, Stijn (ed.) (2006): *Civil Society and Legitimate European Governance*, Edward Elgar, Cheltenham.

Kristina Charrad and Gudrun Eisele

2. What Role for Civil Society in EU Governance? A Review of the Relevant Literature

For a European Union that finds itself in a full-blown midlife crisis (The Economist 2007), civil society involvement has been welcomed as an rejuvenating elixir, infusing new ideas into established patterns of decision-making and providing new energy to deal with the challenges at hand. Particularly after the 2004 enlargement that increased the heterogeneity of economic and institutional conditions as well as normative preferences in the member states, the integrating potential of civil society is seen as a centripetal remedy counteracting the risks of a centrifugal coming apart of the Union. Civil society is referred to in nearly all recent publications by the European institutions as well as academia. In this multitude of references, the meaning and role of civil society become blurred.

Despite this ubiquitous talk, there is still a lack of research and understanding of the specific capacities of civil society organisations, especially in the context of EU enlargement. What hopes are linked to civil society involvement in the political process? After pointing out different aspects of the civil society concept and its analytical usage, our contribution gives an overview of the roles associated with civil society organisations. These functions will then be set in the larger context of research on governance and Europeanisation. Overall, we aim to present an extract of current research trends at the interface of European studies and civil society research.[1]

2.1. Nailing a Pudding to the Wall: What is Civil Society?[2]

When it comes to the precise meaning of the term 'civil society', scholars issue warnings:

> Talk of civil society in the context of EU governance has become popular among diplomats, civil servants, parliaments, non-governmental organizations and others, to the point where the words themselves (and their synonyms) are as fickle as they are fashionable (Curtin 2003, 56).

> The social arrangements found huddling under the umbrella of 'civil society' are so diverse that the danger of conceptual stretching becomes very real (Kubik 2000, 181).

---

1   We would like to thank Regina List, an editorial consultant, for smoothing out our non-native English. Our thanks also go to Dörthe Niedorf for helpful comments.
2   Trying to define civil society was compared to nailing a pudding to the wall more than 15 years ago by Brumlik (1991). The attempt to grasp civil society is nevertheless current, as recent publications demonstrate.

Despite the growth of a cottage industry among political theorists bent on tracing the roots of the concept and providing a definite reading of its meaning, the precise meaning of 'civil society' remains elusive (White 2004, 8).

Nevertheless, we will in this part briefly trace the understandings of 'civil society' that are present in current research.[3] Two dimensions of the term 'civil society' can be distinguished: Civil society in a normative sense and civil society in an analytical sense.

The normative dimension of the term can entail, on the one hand, 'a kind of political *laissez-faire*, as a way of minimizing the role of the state in society – both as a mechanism for restraining state power and as a substitute for many of the functions of the state'. On the other hand, the political project linked to civil society can be about 'increasing the responsiveness of political institutions' and cover 'the idea of an active citizenry who take an interest in public affairs and share a commitment to common human values' (Curtin 2003, 56).

As an analytical concept, civil society attracts scholars from very different disciplines such as political science, sociology, history, philosophy, law, ethnology, and economics. This attraction can be explained by the normative radiance emanating from this term as well as by the multitude of organisations that can – depending on the point of view – be subsumed under 'civil society': Associations – including even business interest associations not directly aimed at profit –, non-governmental organisations, local communities, volunteer programmes, religious communities, foundations, and interest groups.

Cohen and Arato understand civil society as 'a sphere of social interaction between economy and state, composed above all of the intimate sphere (especially the family), the sphere of associations (especially voluntary associations), social movements, and forms of public communication' (Cohen and Arato 1992, IX). Generally, the following elements are considered essential for civil society: Civil society is a sphere of societal self-organisation, opposed to the state. It addresses the public and aims at communicative action. Associations of civil society do not apply violence – at least not against living beings – to promote their causes as part of a certain minimal consensus on values. And the issues, causes and actions of civil society stand in relation to what is called the common weal or the *res publica* (Gosewinkel et al. 2004, Merkel and Lauth 1998).

A significant characteristic is civil society's dynamic interaction with the state: Civil society is often defined in contrast to the state, as an autonomous societal sphere distinct from the state order. On the other hand, 'states may play an important role in shaping civil society as well as vice-versa' (White 2004, 11). Civil society associations regularly address not only the general public, but also the state. Depending on the

---

3   For a more detailed account on the historical development of the term 'civil society' including its relation with democratic theory, see e.g. the writings of Klein (2001), Beyme (2000), Kocka (2000) and Schade (2002).

various conceptions of the state as a constitutional state, cooperative state, welfare state ('Gewährleistungsstaat') or activating state, different and changing roles are ascribed to civil society organisations, as Schuppert points out (quoted in Anheier and Freise 2004, 133).

For analytical purposes, scholars often resort to using the term 'third sector' when studying civil society. This concept distinguishes a third sector apart from the societal spheres of state and market, and commonly (unlike Cohen and Arato above) also from family and the private sphere. Each of these sectors follows a different functional logic. The third sector constitutes the infrastructure of civil society (Mansfeldová et al. 2004, 99) and is composed of a multitude of different organisations. As these are not oriented towards profit (non-profit organisations) and do not distribute their profits to stakeholders or members, this sector is also called the non-profit sector. Due to the fact that membership and engagement in this sector are voluntary, it is also called the voluntary sector.

The third sector can further be classified and differentiated along organisational lines: For the research project 'Future of Civil Society' (Zimmer and Priller 2004), Sachße suggested the – analytical, not empirical – classification into membership organisations, interest organisations, service organisations, and support organisations, with most organisations being 'mixed-type' (Sachße 2004). Research focusing on the third sector sometimes restrictively seems to identify the third sector solely with non-profit social service providers and to adopt a perspective framed by supply and demand, industrial societies' and organisational structures (e.g., Anheier 2002).

Other strands of research describe associations of civil society as having positive impacts on political attitudes and behaviour in many respects: They generate trust, instil social and political virtues, produce social ties and provide opportunities for mobilisation and collective action. The concept of social capital, in today's research coined by Robert Putnam, suggests that social networks represent an important capital that can be enjoyed for its own sake as well as used for material advantage by individuals and social groups (e.g., Putnam 2001). This concept evoked a rich body of research that generally suggests a positive association between civil society and democracy. In their macro perspective, however, these studies – which are sometimes accused of being too idealistic – tend to focus on the 'strength rather than the composition of civil society' (Bermeo 2000, 237) and neglect the specific character of the particular body of associations.

A contrasting perspective on civil society is adopted by critical approaches stating that civil society cannot be equated with a healthy democratic society. Publications on 'real civil societies' and 'uncivil societies' (Alexander 1998, Kopecký and Mudde 2003) put forward that civil society is not in all respects an autonomous sphere, but subject to ambiguous influences from the other societal spheres, and that associations also

have their dark sides (Roth 2003). Thus, they may enhance social segregation and foster uncivil attitudes like racism (Dimitrov 2003). The idealistic concept that civil society
organisations give voice to the poor and integrate the underprivileged is contrasted by
empirical findings of the third sector's strong middle class bias and of the correlation
between economic well-being and civic engagement. Furthermore, the – often implicitly referred to – 'perfect' 'legal transparent civil society' does not subsume all forms
of civil society that help citizens to try to solve their problems (Kubik 2000, 198).

The renaissance of the term 'civil society' is closely connected to the recent political upheavals in the former Eastern Bloc in which it was rediscovered and brought to
life by dissidents and protest movements. Civil society played a key role in the transformation processes in Central and Eastern Europe, and there is an important body
of literature emphasising the role of civil society in democratisation and transformation processes in European as well as in African, Latin American and East Asian world
regions (e.g., Burnell and Calvert 2004, Pietrzyk 2003). The development of a strong
civil society is mostly seen as a condition for the democratic und cultural development of societies: 'The successful future of Central and Eastern Europe's communities is based on a dynamic civil society from which emanates a decisive impulse for
empowerment, democracy, cultural exchange, and mutual understanding' (Zimmer
2004, 11). Therefore, external support for civil society is provided to foster democratisation (Freise 2004).

Eastern European dissidents embraced the term civil society as the counter-ideal
opposed to socialist repression, as the public space open for free political articulation
and activity opposed to state surveillance. In many Eastern European conceptions
of civil society, there persists a strong idealistic moment (Havel and Klaus 1996) and
often a strict dichotomy between civil society and the state, a remnant of 'anti-poli-
tics' (Mazowiecki 1998). These divergent perspectives are rooted in different historical developments (Bunce 2000). Obviously, these divergences can bring about conflict – thus, there have been claims that a Western model of civil society is imposed on
Eastern European countries where a different grasp of civil society prevails.[4]

Before the historic EU accession round of 2004, the state of civil society in the
applicant countries, especially in those with post-socialist background, was of special interest to the European Union. In fact, the White Paper on European Governance
highlighted the EU's efforts to encourage 'the development of civil society in the applicant countries as part of their preparation for membership' (European Commission
2001, 14).

---

4   To be sure, there exists no 'western model of civil society' stricto sensu since also among Western
     European countries as well as between Western Europe and the USA, there is no single con-
     ception of civil society. Quite to the contrary, strong national traditions continue to impact on
     the respective roles attributed to civil society and on the organisational forms of third sector
     organisations.

With regard to European governance, the importance of civil society organisations as well as awareness about and debates on them have gained momentum in recent years. Besides rather functional aspects of private actors' contributions to European governance that are traditionally interwoven with European policy-making, there are aspects of a more normative nature, and it is this category that was recently brought to the fore: Addressing citizens' diagnosed distrust, disinterest and lack of confidence in the European Union, the White Paper on European Governance aimed to 'connect Europe with its citizens' and therefore called for the Commission's 'stronger interaction with [...] civil society' (European Commission 2001, 3–4). Under the heading of 'participatory democracy', the draft constitutional treaty was to oblige the European institutions to 'maintain an open, transparent and regular dialogue with representative associations and civil society'. It further stated that '[t]he Commission shall carry out broad consultations with parties concerned in order to ensure that the Union's actions are coherent and transparent' (art. I-47 §2-3). Much has been talked and written about the way these developments – already now and irrespective of the further process of renewing the EU's foundations – 'reshaped the political debate on "EU democracy"' (Smismans 2003, 484).

In the EU context, the most current – if not uncontested – understanding of civil society is reflected in a definition first written down by the European Economic and Social Committee and later adopted by the Commission. According to it, the following groups are counted among civil society: 'trade unions and employers' organisations ("social partners"); nongovernmental organisations; professional associations; charities; grass-roots organisations; organisations that involve citizens in local and municipal life with a particular contribution from churches and religious communities' (European Commission 2001, 14, FN 9). This is the definition from which we will proceed in our subsequent discussion.

Now that we have looked more closely at what is meant by civil society, we will in the next part examine the functions civil society organisations are said to fulfil. This will help to understand the potential role for civil society in European governance.

2.2. Functions of Civil Society Organisations

From the normative attractiveness of the term civil society to the positive impacts of civil society organisations discussed in the social capital debate and elsewhere to the key role of civil society not only in the peaceful unification of Europe, but also in current EU debates: it already has become clear that civil society is a topic of exceptional interest. Ultimately the roles civil society can play and the functions it can fulfil are what make it so interesting.

In the following, we will highlight each of the different functions civil society organisations can play. A special focus will lie on interest representation since the articulation of interests historically has formed the cradle in which civil society on the European level grew and developed (2.2.1). Civil society's potential to provide societal integration (2.2.2) is closely linked with the participatory promise inherent in it (2.2.3). The public space spanned by civil society deserves consideration especially in times when communication ranks high on the public agenda (2.2.4). Last but not least, civil society organisations can serve as partners in governance tasks (2.2.5).

2.2.1. Interest Representation

The articulation, aggregation, and intermediation of interests in the national contexts are central themes in political science, and they have been broadly researched. During the last decades, research has more and more addressed interest representation on the European level due to the deeper and wider European integration. With the dynamic development of the reach and areas of competence of European institutions simultaneously rose the amount of interest organisations at the European level (Kohler-Koch et al. 2004, 231, Eising 2001, 473, Greenwood 2007, 10). Moreover, the legitimacy and transparency pressures on the institutions, especially the Commission, grew, so that civil society in its function as interest representative, supplementary to the elected MEPs, became very en vogue.

   Research on the European interest groups' activities is very fragmented. Most research literature on the role of interest groups on the EU level focuses on empirical studies (e.g. Claeys et al. 1998, Greenwood 1995, Greenwood et al. 1992, Aspinwall and Greenwood 1998a, Greenwood 2003, Mazey and Richardson 1993, Van Schendelen 1993, Pedler and Van Schendelen 1994, Pedler 2002, Van Schendelen 2005, Greenwood 2007). Theoretical works are rare (Kohler-Koch 1994, Grande 1996, Bouwen 2002c). Academic literature differentiates between various categories of interest groups – such as business, professional, labour, public, social and territorial interests – and describes their activities on the EU level. Business groups are widely seen as being dominant both numerically and politically in the EU arena (Jordan 1998, 31, Kohler-Koch et al. 2004, 234, Greenwood 2002). They are also the most analysed in the academic literature. In recent years, however, research has focused ever more intensely on non-business interest groups (Wallace and Young 1997, Pollack 1997, Balme et al. 2002, Warleigh 2000, Warleigh and Fairbrass 2002). As Pedler states, '[p]layers who have clearly gained influence since the first case studies are the issue groups – NGOs, often known collectively as civil society' (Pedler 2002, 3).

   The European institutional environment encourages civil society organisations to engage on the EU level (Eisele forthcoming). The European Commission – an initiator of policies in the institutional setting of the EU – depends on information and expertise from outside due to its limited resources in light of its wide field of competences. Hence, it is very open to civil society[5]. What is more, '[a] number of groups, particularly in public interest fields, have been kick-started directly by Commission departments in search of allies, and sustained through functions delegated to them by the Commission' (Greenwood 2003, 9–10).

Greenwood describes the relation between interest groups and EU institutions as an interdependency, which explains the parallel growth of interest groups and EU competencies: 'Special to the EU is its multi-level context and the way in which this shapes EU interest representation, and the intensity of the dependency of central EU institutions upon outside interests as a whole' (Greenwood 2003, 27). To sum up: While the institutions need to draw on external expertise, interest groups seek access to them in order to promote their interests.

2.2.1.1.   Interest Intermediation System: Pluralism, Corporatism or Network?

The framework for interest group activities on the European level – the interest intermediation system – is a much discussed topic throughout the research literature. To explain interest intermediation patterns on the European level, researchers resorted to pluralist as well as corporatist concepts. Both theoretical approaches were developed in comparative studies of interest groups on the national level (cf. Czada 1994).

Pluralism assumes the existence of a huge variety of non-hierarchically organised interests competing to influence the state and its decisions. The state is here regarded as a neutral arbiter with a rather passive role. It is claimed that all interests have equal opportunities to provide input to the decision-making process (Schmitter 1979, 15–16). The competing groups lobby for their issues – lobbying is an essential element of pluralist structures (Nollert 1997, 113). The focus of this approach is definitely on the input side of the political process.

The corporatist model, in contrast, assumes that there are only a small number of hierarchically organised and functionally divided organisations. They are representative for their respective categories and enjoy preferential treatment on the part of the state in the decision-making process (Schmitter 1979, 13). These interest groups do not have to lobby in order to be included; instead, they are integrated in public decision-making by the state. Corporatists focus on steering and output aspects and attribute an active role to the state.

Most interest intermediation patterns in nation-states could quite aptly be characterised by either the corporatist or the pluralist model. However, these models reach

---

5   Of all the European institutions, the Commission is of particular importance to groups wishing to influence European decision-making, as is underlined by the following statement by the director of the European Citizen Action Service (ECAS): 'Unless this is done with the Institution which has the right of initiative and is at the start of the legislation or policymaking, it is impossible to have any meaningful process of consultation let alone participation at a later stage' (Venables 2004: 158).

their limits when applied to interest intermediation on the European level. The decision-making process there is much more complex than in any national state, with its
shared power through different institutions and its multitude of veto points (Scharpf
2004, 319), multi-level and multi-arena governance context, and the huge diversity of
interest groups. Due to the lack of strong peak associations as well as the existence
of less hierarchically organised and internally competitive interest groups, Schmitter
and Streeck conclude that at the European level, pluralist patterns of interest intermediation are more likely to be established than corporatist patterns (Schmitter and
Streeck 1991, 185–186). Evidence for pluralism is without doubt provided by the high
number of interests competing freely in the European arena as well as by the high
degree of lobbying (e.g., Mazey and Richardson 1993). Researchers with a corporatist background, on the other hand, point to the preferential treatment of some interest groups by the Commission, to the existence of consultative bodies including interest groups (e.g., Gorges 1996, 10–1), and to the financial support some groups receive
from the Commission.

As Michalowitz points out, a major problem of applying these concepts is that one
basic condition of both theories, i.e., the state, is in this form non-existent (Michalowitz
2002, 37). She suggests instead that research should concentrate on single decision-
making stages: Patterns of interaction could be at some stages pluralist, at some stages
corporatist (Michalowitz 2002, 42–3). A general application of either pluralist or corporatist approaches to the whole system of interest intermediation on the European
level seems fruitless. This led researchers to speak about mixed models of interest
intermediation (Schmidt 1999, Hix 1999) or a 'patchwork of representation modes'
(Saurugger 2002, 2).

A third approach, developed in the debate on pluralism, is to define the patterns
of interest intermediation as policy networks. This approach overcomes the cleavage
between pluralism and corporatism (Saurugger 2002). The usage of the term 'network',
very much en vogue in recent years, is, however, rather problematic. It has a threefold
meaning: first, as a mode of interest intermediation, second, as a governance form,
and finally, as a method of analysis.[6] The policy network approach is characterised by
power dependency relationships between government and interest groups as well as
by resource exchange (Börzel 1997). Multiple interest groups – as in the pluralist model
– and the government are linked to each other by resource dependencies (Marsh and
Rhodes 1992). Resources are dispersed among several actors making cooperation the
best strategy for effective policy-making (see Börzel 1998). According to Kassim, the
state actors receive information; the interest groups that provide information have the
opportunity to influence the content of policy (Kassim 1994, 17).

---

6   A good overview on the problematic of the term 'network' is given by Börzel, 1997, and Börzel,
      1998.

This approach is better suited to grasp the reality of European policy-making than pluralism or corporatism. The EU decision-making process involves a multitude of actors, both public and private – institutions and national or European associations as well as professional lobbyists –, dispersed resources, flexible, informal collaborations, and informal bargaining (cf. Peterson 1995, 390). Various case studies illustrate the policy network approach, e.g., in the fields of European environmental policy (Bomberg 1998) and telecommunications policy (Schneider et al. 1994).

2.2.1.2. Sub-Field of Interest Group Research: Lobbying

One of the sub-fields in research on interest groups is lobbying. The word 'lobbying' has acquired some negative connotations, i.e., that 'lobbying confers an unfair advantage on those that can afford to carry it out and therefore runs counter to the notion of democracy' (Warleigh and Fairbrass 2002, 2).

What does lobbying actually mean? The Latin word 'labium' means entrance hall, lounge. And here, a link to policy-making today can be seen: Political decisions are nowadays often made in the pre-parlamentarian phase of balancing the various interests. The oldest research definition is given by Milbrath, who perceived lobbying primarily as a communication process: 'Communication is the only means of influencing or changing a perception; the lobbying process, therefore, is totally a communication process' (Milbrath 1960, 32).

Van Schendelen adds a new aspect to the definition of lobbying: 'Lobbying is the informal exchange of information with public authorities, as a minimal conception on the one hand, and as trying informally to influence public authorities, as a maximal description on the other hand' (Van Schendelen 1993). The most comprehensive definition is formulated by Koeppl: 'Lobbying is the attempted successful influence of legislative-administrative decisions by public authorities through interested representatives. The influence is intended, implies the use of communication and is targeted on legislative or executive bodies' (Koeppl 2001, 71).

While Brussels may not be considered the centre of the world, it is 'the centre for European lobbying' (Biliouri 1999, 173). The growing number of lobbyists and their activities have attracted the attention of research only since the 1990s; European lobbying research is thus quite a new research field. Lobbying is mainly studied from three perspectives: as a form of transnational collective action (e.g., Aspinwall and Greenwood 1998a), as an economic exchange (e.g., Henning 2000, Bouwen 2002a), and as a special type or pattern of political protest mobilisation (social movements research). Corresponding to the different angles of observation, a variety of approaches to lobbying emerged.

The first studies on European lobbying were based on Olson's logic of collective action (1965) and discussed the difficulties associated with organising collective action and mobilising national organisations to participate in the EU networks (Greenwood et al. 1992, Aspinwall and Greenwood 1998a). Those studies aimed to determine the factors for success or failure of collective action.

Later analyses put forward the exchange approach on the basis of economic theories of exchange (e.g., Salisbury 1969) regarding supply, demand and transaction costs. They describe the relationship between the EU institutions and private actors as political exchange. One example of such an approach is Bouwen's 'Theory of Access', in which Bouwen relates the organisational characteristics of business interest associations to their respective capacity to provide access goods as well as to their capacity to gain access to the EU institutions (Bouwen 2004, 359, Bouwen 2002a, 6). In order to gain insight into the process of resource exchange between private and public actors at the EU level, Bouwen focuses on the resources that are exchanged between these two groups and analyses the process of their exchange (see Bouwen 2002a, 7–8, Bouwen 2002b, 365). The resource required by private actors is 'access' to the European institutions. The EU institutions demand certain 'access goods' crucial for their own functioning, which are based on different kinds of information. Private actors can only gain access – and may provide access goods in exchange – if the access goods are also simultaneously demanded by the targeted EU institution (Bouwen 2002a, 13).

The exchange approach is criticised by Michalowitz, who appreciates its value in systematisation but claims that it neglects the intermediary actors, so-called agents of lobbying, and their impact (Michalowitz 2004, 43). She analyses lobbying based on the principal-agent approach in order to explain why the private actors engage in exchange with governmental actors and how this exchange proceeds. Her conclusion is that the lobbying patterns are generalisable and that lobbying activities and lobbying success are determined by the characteristics of the agents (Michalowitz 2004, 271).

A third perspective – however without using the term 'lobbying' – is taken by research on protest mobilisation and social movements. Researchers with a social movement background also tend to focus on resources, but, in this case, in terms of staff and funding of protest groups. The EU's democratic deficit is here seen from the standpoint of mass politics. Researchers try to explain national and transnational protest mobilisation; with regard to the EU, they seek to explain how Europeans mobilise to make claims against policies made in their names. Their hypothesis is 'if Europe is becoming a polity, sooner or later ordinary citizens will turn their claims and their forms of contentious politics beyond their borders and towards this level of governance [...] and European integration might be creating an opportunity structure for the formation of transnational social movements' (Imig and Tarrow 2001, 7–8). On the EU level, there are only few major protest actions attracting the attention of the public and the media. Rucht gives an explanation for this, at least in the environmental field, by stating that lobbying the EU institutions is by far more adequate and effective than the kind of unconventional protest action that is so common at national and subnational levels (Rucht 2001, 136). Recently, this strand of research is becoming more like interest group and lobbying studies.

The phenomenon of 'lobbying' is attracting more and more research attention due to the large number of actors in the Brussels lobbyist community. Indeed, there are different approaches with their advantages and disadvantages as well as empirical studies in different policy fields, but no general theory of interest intermediation at the European level. There is a need for further investigation concerning special groups of actors like non-business actors and the integration of actors from new member states in the interest intermediation process at the European level (Charrad forthcoming). The main task, namely to develop a theoretically established framework of research hypotheses for the analysis of lobbying behaviour, is not yet completed.

2.2.2. Societal Integration

Civil society organisations not only articulate and represent interests, they can also contribute to societal integration in two ways. On an individual level, civil society organisations provide a space in which individual citizens get in touch and interact with each other, concentrating on common objectives. On a collective level, civil society organisations and their free interaction foster the integration of the diverse – and often enough divergent – interests and preferences existing in societal sub-groups and facets. Through this integrating function, civil society organisations can not only work against exclusion on an individual basis, but also counteract the effects of over-individualisation on an aggregate level. As Zimmer puts it, civil society organisations 'are responsible for systemic integration, which translates into the integration of the various societal communities into the political and cultural system of a respective country, a region or most prominently the European Union' (Zimmer 2004, 13).

In the context of European integration, civil society organisations could thus bring European citizens closer together and intermediate across national borders between different sets of interests. They could ultimately even create some sense of belonging to the EU through systemic integration. This perspective seems the more promising against the backdrop of a deplored lack of 'we-ness' among the EU citizenry.

Another promise lies in the values and skills fostered in associational life: Due to the values ideally lived in civil society, such as tolerance, respect and peaceful conflict resolution, associations can contribute to the education and proliferation of civic values. They can also train in organisational and argumentation skills indispensable for an active citizenry in a democratic community (Fung 2003, 519–20). This function was already described by de Tocqueville, who is prominently quoted as dubbing associations 'schools of democracy'. Research on social capital (see above) specifically emphasises one of the aspects fostered by associational life, namely generalized reciprocity or trust. With regard to the EU, civil society associations could thus, 'beyond the system-building hopes that neofunctionalists held for private interest groups', be 'weaving denser strands of mutual understanding and co-operation across member state borders' (Warleigh 2006, 69).

A research perspective in that direction was taken in Warleigh's study on whether NGOs could act as 'agents of political socialization in the context of EU policy-making' (Warleigh 2001, 619), thus Europeanizing civil society. Applying several variables such as collaboration with other NGOs and like-minded actors, independence, democratic internal governance, and cognitive impact on supporters, he came to a conclusion of scepticism regarding the catalyst role of NGOs in Europeanising civil society.

2.2.3. Participation

In addition to their integrative and educative potential, civil society organisations also offer ways in which citizens can actively take part in societal, cultural and social life. In political NGOs, local or supra-regional associations, they can take matters in their own hands beyond mere participation in elections and engage themselves beyond traditional political party routines.

With regard to the EU, which is generally accused of suffering a democratic deficit (cf. Follesdal and Hix 2005, Holland 1980, Andersen and Burns 1996, Raunio 1999), a complementation of the channels of representative democracy through 'participatory democracy' – highly in fashion in recent debates and publications (e.g., Reale 2003, Saurugger 2004, Schmalz-Bruns 2002) – seems especially promising.

> In a system in which the central actor for initiating and pursuing the formulation of policies (i.e., the Commission) lacks democratic accountability, and the Parliament has only a limited influence on the legislative process, functional representation gains in importance. The consent of societal organisations is a welcome substitute for democratic legitimacy. It is quite clear that the Commission is trying to introduce a 'mix' of legitimising elements of representation to make up for the Community's 'democratic deficit' (Eising and Kohler-Koch 1999, 270).

The involvement of civil society organisations in European decision- and policy-making could thus contribute to democratising the EU and increasing its legitimacy: 'All types of dialogues, general and issue-specific, have the potential to bolster EU legitimacy' (Goehring 2002, 134–5). This holds true in two regards: Input legitimacy is strengthened through increased citizen involvement with political processes via civil society organisations. (This assumption, however, again raises the issue how representative the organisations involved are, cf. Greenwood and Halpin 2005.) Output legitimacy is then fostered through a gain in efficiency by involving stakeholders and taking decisions on the base of a sound knowledge of the field – two advantages of civil society involvement. Both strategies have been pursued, for example, by the European Commission through the establishment of various consultation circles.

In spite of the high ranking of 'participatory democracy' in public debates, though, this concept remains somewhat fuzzy. As Schmalz-Bruns rightly states, 'it is obvious that "participation" as such is undetermined in several dimensions that are crucial to the idea of democratic legitimacy' (Schmalz-Bruns 2002, 66). Smismans also points to the problematic usage of the tag 'participatory democracy' for processes of functional representation: '[R]ather than direct citizen participation they provide another form of indirect participation, i.e., another form of participation via representation, namely via representatives of associations instead of via territorial representatives' (Smismans 2003, 494).

And as for the democratic panacea that participation through civil society organisations is often treated as, Hurrelmann states that 'it is not sufficient to evade the problem of societal preconditions of European democracy simply by conjuring up the integration strength of civil society' (Hurrelmann 2003, 687, translated by GE).

To sum up, the options for civic engagement and participation are importantly increased through the involvement of civil society organisations in the political process in the EU, even if this potential has not yet been fully realized.

2.2.4. Public Space as a Counterweight to State Power

In addition to their functions in interest articulation and representation, societal integration and participation, civil society organisations are said to play a crucial role in providing a public space. This assumption picks up the thread of Habermas, who understands civil society as 'the social foundation of autonomous public spaces' differing from 'the economic system of action as well as from public administration'. According to Habermas, the essential element is the communication that can take place in these autonomous public spaces: 'These subject-less communications – inside and outside of political bodies programmed for decision-making – form arenas in which takes place the formation of more or less rational opinion and preferences on topics concerning the whole society and issues requiring regulation' (Habermas 1992, 23, translated by GE).

The autonomous public sphere encompassed by civil society constitutes a counterbalance to state power. This sphere exercises public control over the administration and monitors state action. Civil society here provides a critical forum outside public administration and the electoral system in which the concerns of the citizens at large, but also of minorities and societal sub-groups, can be voiced.

The space opened up for critical discussions and independent points of view in civil society was decisive for the peaceful transformation processes ringing in the end of the Eastern Bloc. This historical development highlighted the particular value of this function.

Civil society organisations exercise the role of an independent watchdog also with regard to the EU. Particularly in the face of the often deplored underdevelopment of a European public, the formation of which is hampered by the national and linguistic fragmentation of public discussions and the mass media, high hopes are attached to civil society's potential to form a common public space (cf. e.g., Closa 2001, Pérez-Díaz 1998, Soysal 2001).

The EU institutions, on their part, attach importance to civil society's communication function. The EU sees great opportunity in civil society's capacity to help communicate European issues to the level of the citizens and assist the EU in reaching the citizens, thus contributing to a more widespread knowledge and potential acceptance of the EU. Especially after the negative referenda on the constitutional treaty in France and the Netherlands in 2005, communication ranks high on the EU agenda. It is therefore no surprise that the 2006 White Paper on a European Communication Policy also lists civil society organisations as partners 'to develop Europe's place in the public sphere' (European Commission 2006, 5).

2.2.5. Governance Partners

Civil society organisations are of interest not only with regard to their qualities in creating a public space, but also as governance partners. In European governance, such organisations have become indispensable actors, whose involvement is evident not only at the early stages of the policy cycle, but stretches out to the concrete implementation of policies: 'A broad variety of involvement strategies has been developed over the years and is employed throughout the policy cycle: from inter-group discussions and round tables in the phase of problem definition and agenda setting, to a variety of instruments of consultation and deliberation during a policy formulation, to effecting partnership arrangements in implementation and providing societal actors with rights of monitoring and legal control' (Kohler-Koch 2005, 8). Schuppert analyses how, in the 'functional privatisation of governance' that is underway, civil society actors are able to act as governance partners in the implementation of sector-comprehensive strategies on different policy levels (Schuppert 2004). And Smismans also states, '[t]he governance dimension allows us to [...] address the role of civil society organisations at multiple stages of policy-making, such as in the implementation and control of EU regulation [...] or in the implementation of EU programmes' (Smismans 2006, 299). Here, because of their social embeddedness, civil society organisations can implement policy measures, for example, in social policy, in a way that is closer to the citizens. This perspective is in tune with the neo-corporatist argument that the delegation of certain tasks to private interests offers more effective implementation of the measures adopted and better resource allocation.

In the context of the EU, which hardly disposes of proper facilities for policy implementation, the potential contribution of civil society organisations to implementing policies 'in the field' seems especially attractive. Moreover, compliance with policies adopted through the consent of civil society, involved at both ends of the policy cycle, is 'a particularly helpful benefit given the EU's weak capacity to enforce policy implementation' (Warleigh 2006, 71–72).

Regarding the described functions of civil society organisations, it can in summary be stated that they are particularly relevant with regard to the European Union. Civil society organisations provide channels for participation. This is of particular importance against the backdrop of claims of a democratic deficit in the political system of the European Union: Civil society organisations can offer means for democratic participation that complement the 'traditional' political process, which is hard to extend to a supranational polity in a satisfyingly democratic way. In the face of a diagnosed lack of a European *demos* considered essential for enhancing democracy within the European Union, societal integration and participation via a European civil society is regarded as a possible alternative or at least as a complement.

The functions ascribed to civil society are therefore very attractive for actors trying to build a stronger and more integrated European political community:

First and foremost, organized civil society offers avenues for civic engagement and active citizenship, thus facilitating integration and participation for the individual citizen, both of which are necessary prerequisites for the deepening and strengthening of democracy. Moreover, organized civil society is in the position to satisfy those needs and demands of citizens that neither the market nor the state is able or willing to serve. And finally organized civil society is able to buffer those societal shocks and upheavals that always accompany processes of political, economic and societal transition and modernization (Zimmer 2004, 12).

It is essential to note the double-sided function of organized civil society: On the one hand, civil society associations are active on the input side of a polity. They are able to give voice to the diverse facets and societal subgroups of European citizens and, as interest and lobby groups, to transfer their issues and claims not only to the national, but also to the European level of policy-making. On the other hand, they are active on the output side of policies, often working together with public administration on regional and local levels. If they favour the EU and European integration – which is often optimistically assumed by its institutions (Smismans 2003, 491, see also Rumford 2003, 38) – , civil society organisations could promote European issues and, more generally, the European cause on the citizens' level. Thus capable of acting as a two-way channel bridging the gap between the EU and its citizens, organised civil society is a very attractive intermediary partner for European governance.

Of course, these hopes need to be seen in the light of the restrictions imposed on them. There needs to be a balance between a genuinely societal impulse on the one hand and institutionalised forms of involvement on the other. In this regard, Greenwood states, '[i]ronically, the Commission's need for [...] [civil society] groups to act as bridges to citizens in the member states is hampered by the institutionalised nature of these relationships' (Greenwood 2004, 146).

From interest representation to social integration and participation to creation of a public space as a counterweight to state power to policy implementation: in this part, we have described the functions that civil society can fulfil. Civil society organisations, though, do not act in a vacuum. The stage on which they play is set by over-arching developments in European governance and Europeanisation. In the next part, we will turn to these developments in order to take fully into account the backdrop against which civil society unfolds its potential.

2.3. The Wider Context: Governance and Europeanisation

The focus of the academic debate on the European Union shifted in recent years from European integration to the effects of being a member of the EU. This put not only single member states, but also civil society more in the research focus. These research trends can be subsumed under the key words 'governance' and 'Europeanisation'. In the following, we present these two concepts in which civil society is attributed an important role.

The notion of governance is neither new in the academic discussion, nor is it a concept reserved uniquely for the EU. It is, however, best suited for consideration of a special polity such as the EU and its decision-making processes (cf. Wind 1997, 1–4). The distinctive feature of the EU is that it is 'governed without a government' (Kohler–Koch 1999, 14), as the institutional framework of the EU corresponds not to the government of any national state and its governance model (cf. Benz and Papadopoulos 2006, 15), thus presenting a particular mode of governance.

First used in economics, the concept of governance emerged in political science in the branch of international relations as a distinction from the notion of government of the national state. It comprised the non-hierarchically organised and permanently changing patterns of cooperation of states and interactions between governments and transnational actors, based on coordination, communication, and negotiations (for more see Benz 2003, 16–17). Later, the notion of governance was most commonly used as 'new modes of governance' in the other branches of political science, especially in EU research, where the increasingly popular term has inspired a multitude of publications. There are different descriptions of governance in the academic literature as 'governance without government' (Rosenau and Czempiel 1992), 'modern' (Kooiman 1993) or just 'new' (Héritier 2002). Contrary to the conventional hierarchical or market governance, '[m]odern governance is characterised by decision systems in which ter-ritorial and functional differentiation disaggregate effective problem-solving capacity into a collection of sub-systems of actors with specialised tasks and limited competence and resources' (Hanf and O'Toole 1992, 166). Meanwhile, on the one hand, efforts toward consolidation and categorisation (Benz 2004, Schuppert 2005) and, on the other hand, further differentiation into the fields of regional governance, local governance, environmental governance etc. can be observed in the academic debate.

The EU has been described as a system of *multi-level governance* (Marks 1993, Hooghe 1996a, Jachtenfuchs and Kohler-Koch 1996) with the peculiarity that it involves in decision-making different 'layers of authority': European or supranational, national and sub-national (Hooghe 1996a, 18). In this system, resources and political power are dispersed 'over various territorial levels and over various functional decision-making arenas' (Grande 2003, 46). Furthermore, this particular type of governance focuses 'on the intermeshing of overlapping networks operating simultaneously in multiple functional arenas and at multiple geographic scales' (Ansell 2000, 322). The principle of competence sharing between various levels is the subsidiarity principle, which forms part of the European Treaties. Unique to the EU is the involvement of the sub-national tier with the same status as the other two tiers, national and supranational (Hooghe 1996a).

Civil society actors can articulate their interests starting from the sub-national level, then on the national level and finally on the European level; they can operate simultaneously at all levels or, after failing at one of the levels, try at another one (cf. Andersen and Eliassen 2001, 51, Benz 2006, 99). They have the choice of how they promote their interests up to the highest, the European level: by utilising member state channels, by setting up their own offices in Brussels and seeking direct access to the European arena, by working together with other like-minded actors, or by joining European-wide associations or networks that are organised around specific issues (Hooghe and Keating 1994, Hooghe 1996a, Hooghe 1996b). The main advantage multi-level governance entails is 'a multitude of points of access' for civil society organisations (Benz 2006, 102). Fairbrass and Warleigh, arguing from a democratic theory perspective, see a valuable opportunity in the multi-level structure for civil society organisations or societal groups disadvantaged at the national level: '[A]ctors excluded from, or marginalized in, policy networks at the national level in theory have an opportunity to make good such peripheralization by engaging with the EU' (Fairbrass and Warleigh 2002, 4). European policy-making thus 'opens up to a plurality of interests' (Benz and Papadopoulos 2006, 16). No actor has exclusive competence over a particular policy; diverse actors on different levels pool competence needed for policy-making (Marks et al. 1996, 42).

Analyses emphasising the relationships between state institutions and civil society organisations have put forward *network governance* as a concept (Kohler-Koch and Eising 1999): The EU – lacking a binding ideology for unifying action, instead being based on a functional *raison d'être* – is governed by 'reaching agreement in a highly interwoven negotiating system' in which a plurality of interests needs to be recognised and '[o]ptimising performance calls for a sympathetic treatment of target groups'. In the EU as a *network system* of governance, the role of the 'state' as mediator and activator is to bring together 'the relevant actors of society' by 'offering institutional frameworks', organising 'the arena for political exchange and agreement' and 'building issue-specific constituencies'. Negotiating in a 'community-friendly' way without losing sight of one's partial interests is the main rule of behaviour for actors involved. 'The core idea of "network governance" is that political actors consider problem-solving the essence of politics and that the setting of policy-making is defined by the existence of highly organised social sub-systems.' In sectoral sub-structures and 'policy communities', private and public actors interact in a way that is only minimally hierarchical. Political action takes place on different and often decentralised and functionally specific levels (all: Kohler-Koch and Eising 1999, 5 and 24–26).

The second research trend, Europeanisation studies, mushroomed with the 2004 Eastern enlargement of the European Union. Europeanisation is commonly understood as a process that changes governance patterns (Kohler-Koch 1996), but there is no consensus in research about the direction and origin of this process as well as about the analytical tools best apt to grasp the dynamics at work.

Europeanisation studies can roughly be classified into four categories. The first, top-down studies analysing the impact of the EU on the domestic politics in the member states, is the most used approach. It considers the EU as the origin or cause of particular developments on the national level. Studies focus on the Europeanisation of single policy fields, of institutions and administrations, or recently also of civil society organisations. A second approach regards Europeanisation as a horizontal process from state to state, as 'sharing best practice models especially in areas where the EU lacks competences to exert top-down pressures' (Lenschow 2006, 57). Third, Europeanisation is considered as a bottom-up process, originating from the member states and influencing the EU level (for the definition see Cowles et al. 2001). This approach has been criticised due to the fact that it is hardly distinguishable from European integration. The fourth characterisation found in research is the circular understanding of Europeanisation, as a round-about process from the national level to the EU level and back to the national level (e.g., Goetz 2002)[7].

Europeanisation research with the first, top-down background paid special attention to the Central and Eastern European (CEE) countries as new member states, asking

---

7   For an overview on existing definitions of Europeanisation see Lenschow (2006: 57–8).

to what extent the European Union has changed their domestic political structures and policy-making patterns (cf. Sedelmeier 2006, 8). These countries present a particularly challenging case as the researcher needs to differentiate between the parallel processes at work: post-communist reform, modernisation and Europeanisation (Grabbe 2003, 311). Empirical research pointed to different aspects in which the EU impacted political structures and policy-making already in candidate countries (see Fink Hafner 1998 on Europeanisation of interest groups, Fink Hafner and Lajh 2003 on administration, Szczerbiak and Taggart 2001 on political parties). These impacts increased after the CEE candidates joined the EU. These countries provide a good terrain for comparing the Europeanisation process and its dynamics in the old member states and the newly joined states.

The studies on the Europeanisation effects on civil society are rare, especially with regard to CEE member states with a disrupted tradition of civil society organisations (Sittermann forthcoming). It is essential to encourage such studies in order to fill this gap in knowledge on Europeanisation as well as to better capture the complex interplay between civil society organisations and various levels of European governance.

2.4. Conclusions

This chapter intended to give an overview of existing research related to civil society and European governance. First, we traced what is understood by the term 'civil society' and in which contexts it has been applied in research. This term surely poses some analytical difficulties due to its versatility, but herein lies also one of the reasons for the attraction it has for academia as well as for policy debates.

Civil society organisations are extremely promising for fostering active citizenship in democratic societies at a general level and mitigating the deplored democratic deficit of the European Union at a more specific level. Societal interests are articulated, aggregated, and intermediated via associations. Citizens are societally integrated both at an individual and at a collective level through vibrant civic activities. Avenues for societal and political participation are opened up by civil society organisations, thus complementing traditional channels of participation. The public space encompassed by civil society interaction and communication provides a counterweight to state power from which decisive impulses of control of public administration as well as important voices of a critical forum outside public administration and the electoral system can emanate. In European governance, civil society organisations are regarded as partners of public authorities, providing them with essential knowledge and field-related resources indispensable for the functioning of European policy-making and its implementation. The relationship between interest groups and EU institutions is thus characterised by mutual dependence.

As European governance modes rely on the interaction of public and private actors in sectoral sub-systems and policy networks, there is a functional need for civil society actors. Through a strengthened dialogue with civil society, the European institutions also hope to bring the Union closer to the citizens.

How Europeanisation processes impact on citizens in their surroundings, including the impacts on governance in the member states and on civil society organisations, can still not be clearly stated. Now that the EU consists of 27 member states after the past two enlargement rounds, an interesting question is how civil society organisations from the new member states are adapting themselves to the EU. The special challenge for civil society actors from CEE countries is their simultaneous establishment on the domestic level as well as on the European level. Academic research on the specifics of the new actors and on their integration into the mechanisms of European governance is still rare.

The discussions about civil society involvement as a panacea to all the EU's problems, such as the democratic deficit and distance from the citizens, became en vogue in recent years in the research community as well as in the broader public. Is the rejuvenating elixir, which civil society participation is often enough in public discourses claimed to be, effective? This question can not be answered with a clear 'yes' or 'no', but it has become clear that civil society involvement holds potential for the improvement of the overall health of a democratic EU.

Bibliography

Alexander, J.C. (ed.) (1998): *Real Civil Societies. Dilemmas of Institutionalization*, Sage, London.

Andersen, S. S. /Burns, T. (1996): *The European Union and the Erosion of Parliamentary Democracy: A Study of Post-parliamentary Governance*, in: Andersen, S. S. /Eliassen, K. A. (eds.), *The European Union: How Democratic Is It?*, Sage, London, pp. 227–251.

Andersen, S. S. /Eliassen, K. A. (2001): *Informal Processes: Lobbying, Actor Strategies, Coalitions and Dependencies*, in: Andersen, S. S. /Eliassen, K. A. (eds.), *Making Policy in Europe*, Sage, London, pp. 44–60.

Anheier, H. (2002): *The third sector in Europe: Five theses*, Civil Society Working Paper no. 12, http://www.lse.ac.uk/collections/CCS/pdf/CSWP12.pdf, accessed 10 April 2007.

Anheier, H. K./Freise, M. (2004): *Der Dritte Sektor im Wandel: zwischen New Public Management und Zivilgesellschaft*, in: Gosewinkel, D., Rucht, D. et al. (eds.), *Zivilgesellschaft – national und transnational*, WZB-Jahrbuch 2003, edition sigma, Berlin, pp. 129–150.

Ansell, C. (2000): *The Networked Polity: Regional Development in Western Europe*, Governance 13:3, pp. 303–333.

Aspinwall, M. /Greenwood, J. (1998b): *Conceptualising Collective Action in the European Union. An Introduction*, in: Aspinwall, M. /Greenwood, J. (eds.), *Collective Action in the European Union*, Routledge, London, pp. 1–30.

Aspinwall, M./Greenwood, J. (eds.) (1998a): *Collective Action in the European Union: Interests and the New Politics of Associability*, Routledge, London.

Balme, R. /Chabanet, D. et al. (2002): *L'action collective en Europe*, Presses de Sciences Po, Paris.

Benz, A. (2003): *Governance – Modebegriff oder nützliches sozialwissenschaftliches Konzept?*, in: Benz, A. (ed.), *Governance – Regieren in komplexen Regelsystemen*, VS Verlag Wiesbaden, pp. 11–28.

Benz, A. (2006): *Policy-making and Accountability in EU Multilevel Governance*, in: Benz, A. / Papadopoulos, Y. (eds.), *Governance and Democracy. Comparing National, European and International Experiences*, Routledge, London, pp. 99–114.

Benz, A. (ed.) (2004): *Governance – Regieren in komplexen Regelsystemen. Eine Einführung*, VS Verlag für Sozialwissenschaften, Wiesbaden..

Benz, A./ Papadopoulos, Y. (2006): *Governance and Democracy: Concepts and Key Issues*, in: Benz, A. / Papadopoulos, Y. (eds.), *Governance and Democracy. Comparing national, European and international experiences*, Routledge, London, pp. 1–26.

Bermeo, N. (2000): *Civil Society After Democracy: Some Conclusions*, in: Bermeo, N./Nord, P. (eds.), *Civil Society Before Democracy. Lessons from Nineteenth-Century Europe*, Rowman & Littlefield, Lanham, pp. 237–260.

Beyme, K. (2000): *Zivilgesellschaft – Karriere und Leistung eines Modebegriffs*, in: Hildermeier, M. / Kocka, J. et al. (eds.), *Europäische Zivilgesellschaft in Ost und West. Begriff, Geschichte, Chancen*, Campus, Frankfurt a. M., pp. 41–55.

Biliouri, D. (1999): *Environmental NGOs in Brussels: How Powerful are Their Lobbying Activities*, Environmental Politics 8:2, pp. 173–182.

Bomberg, E. (1998): *Issue Networks and the Environment: Explaining European Union Environmental Policy*, in: Marsh, David (ed.), *Comparing Policy Networks*, Open University Press, Buckingham, pp.167–185.

Börzel, T. (1997): *What's so Special about Policy Networks? – An Exploration of the Concept and its Usefulness in Studying European Governance*, European Integration online Papers (EIoP) 1:016, http:andandeiop.or.atandeiopandtexteand1997-1016a.htm.

Börzel, T. (1998): *Organizing Babylon – on the Different Conceptions of Policy Networks*, Public Administration, 76, pp. 253–273.

Bouwen, P. (2002a): *A Comparative Study of Business Lobbying in the European Parliament, the European Commission and the Council of Ministers*, Max-Planck-Institut für Gesellschaftsforschung, Köln.

Bouwen, P. (2002b): *Corporate Lobbying in the European Union: the Logic of Access*, Journal of European Public Policy, 9:3, pp. 365–90.

Bouwen, P. (2002c): *Gaining Access to the European Union: a Theoretical Framework and Empirical Study of Corporate Lobbying in the European Union*, European University Institute, Florence.

Bouwen, P. (2004): *Exchanging Access Goods for Access: a Comparative Study of Business Lobbying in the European Union Institutions*, European Journal of Political Research, 43:3, pp. 337–369.

Brumlik, M. (1991): *Was heißt „Zivile Gesellschaft"? Versuch, den Pudding an die Wand zu nageln*, Blätter für deutsche und internationale Politik, 36, pp. 987–993.

Bunce, V. (2000): *The Historical Origins of the East-Wets Divide: Civil Society, Political Society, and Democracy in Europe*, in: Bermeo, N./Nord, P. (eds.), *Civil Society before Democracy. Lessons from Nineteenth-Century Europe*, Rowman & Littlefield, Lanham, pp. 209–236.

Burnell, P. /Calvert, P. (eds.) (2004): *Civil Society in Democratization*, Frank Cass, London.

Charrad, K. (forthcoming): *Participants or Observers in European Governance? Lobbyists from Central and Eastern European countries in Brussels*, Nomos, Baden-Baden.

Claeys, P. /Gobin, C. et al. (eds.) (1998): *Lobbying, Pluralism and European Integration*, European Interuniversity Press, Brussels.

Closa, C. (2001): *Requirements of a European public sphere. Civil society, self, and the institutionalization of citizenship*, in: Eder, K. /Giesen, B. (eds.), *European citizenship between national legacies and postnational projects*, Oxford University Press, Oxford, pp. 180–204.

Cohen, J. L. /Arato, A. (1992): *Civil Society and Political Theory*, MIT Press, Cambridge.

Cowles, M. G./Caporaso, J. et al. (eds.) (2001): *Transforming Europe*, Cornell University Press, New York.

Curtin, D. M. (2003): *Private Interest Representation or Civil Society Deliberation? A Contemporary Dilemma for European Union Governance*, Social and Legal Studies, 12:1, pp. 55–75.

Czada, R. (1994): *Konjunkturen des Korporatismus: Zur Geschichte eines Paradigmenwechsels in der Verbändeforschung*, in: Streeck, W. (ed.), *Staat und Verbände*. Politische Vierteljahresschrift Sonderheft, 25, Westdeutscher Verlag, Opladen.

Dimitrov, P. (2003): *Corruption Rife Among Macedonia's NGOs*, in: *Transitions Online*, http:// www.tol.cz/look/wire/article.tpl?IdLanguage=1&IdPublication=10&NrIssue=740& NrSection=1&NrArticle=10337, accessed 10 March 2004.

Eisele, G. (forthcoming): *The European Union and civil society*, Nomos, Baden-Baden.

Eising, R. (2001): *Interessenvermittlung in der Europäischen Union*, in: Reutter, W./Rütters, P. (eds.): *Verbände und Verbandsysteme in Westeuropa*, Leske+Budrich, Opladen, pp. 453–476.

Eising, R. /Kohler-Koch, B. (1999): *Governance in the European Union. A Comparative Assesment*, in: Eising, R./Kohler-Koch, B., *Transformation of Governance in the European Union*, Routledge, London, pp. 267–285.

European Commission (2001): *White Paper on European Governance*, (COM(2001) 428), Brussels.

European Commission (2006): *White Paper on a European Communication Policy*, (COM(2006) 35 final), Brussels.

Fairbrass, J. /Warleigh, A. (2002): *Introduction. The New Politics of Persuasion, Advocacy and Influence in the European Union*, in: Fairbrass, J. /Warleigh, A. (eds.): *Influence and Interests in the European Union: The New Politics of Persuasion and Advocacy*, Europa Publications, London, pp. 1–15.

Fink Hafner, D. (1998): *Organised Interests in the Policy-making Process in Slovenia*, Journal of European Public Policy, 5:2, 285–302.

Fink Hafner, D./Lajh, D. (2003): *Managing Europe from Home: The Europeanisation of the Slovenian Core Executive*, Faculty of Socil Sciences FDV, Ljubljana.

Follesdal, A./Hix, S. (2005): *Why There is a Democratic Deficit in the EU: A response to Majone and Moravscik*, European Governance Papers (EUROGOV), No. C-05-02, http://www.connex-network.org/eurogov/pdf/egp-connex-C-05-02.pdf, accessed 8 March 2007.

Freise, M. (2004): *Externe Demokratieförderung in postsozialistischen Transformations- staaten*, LIT-Verlag, Münster.

Fung, A. (2003): *Associations and Democracy: Between Theories, Hopes, and Realities*, Annual Review of Sociology, 29:1, pp. 515–539.

Goehring, R. (2002): *Interest representation and civil society formation*, in: Warleigh, A./ Fairbrass, J. (eds.), *Integrating Interests in the European Union: The New Politics of Persuasion, Advocacy and Influence*, Europa Publications, London, pp. 118–137.

Goetz, K. (2002): *Four Worlds of Europeanisation*, Paper presented for the ECPR Joint Session, Turin, Italy, 22–27 March 2002.

Goetz, K./Dimitrov, V. et al. (2006): *Post-Communist Executives and European Governance*, in: Schuppert, G. F. (ed.), *The Europeanisation of Governance*, Nomos, Baden-Baden, pp. 93–131.

Gorges, M. (1996): *Euro-Corporatism? Interest Intermediation in the European Community*, University Press of America, Lanham.

Gosewinkel, D./Rucht, D. et al. (2004): *Einleitung: Zivilgesellschaft – national und transnational*, in: Gosewinkel, D./Rucht, D. et al. (eds.), *Zivilgesellschaft – national und transnational*, edition sigma, Berlin, pp. 11–26.

Grabbe, H. (2003): *Europeanisation Goes East: Power and Uncertainty in the EU Accession Process*, in: Featherstone, K./Radaelli, C. M. (eds.), *The Politics of Europeanization*, Oxford University Press, Oxford, pp. 303–327.

Grande, E. (1996): *The State and Interest Groups in a Framework of Multi-level Decision-making. The Case of the European Union*, Journal of European Public Policy, 3:3, pp. 318–338.

Grande, E. (2003): *How the Architecture of the EU Political System Influences Business Associations*, in: Greenwood, J. (ed.), *The Challenge of Change in EU Business Associations*, Palgrave Macmillan, Houndmills, pp. 45–59.

Greenwood, J. (2002): *EU Public Affairs and the White Paper on Governance*, Journal of Public Affairs, 1:4, pp. 423–435.

Greenwood, J. (2003): *Interest Representation in the European Union*, Palgrave Macmillan, Basingstoke.

Greenwood, J. (2004): *The search for input legitimacy through organised civil society in the EU*, Transnational Associations, 2, pp.145–155.

Greenwood, J. (2007): *Interest Representation in the European Union*, Palgrave Macmillan, Houndmills.

Greenwood, J. (ed.) (1995): *European Casebook on Business Alliances*, Prentice Hall, London.

Greenwood, J./ Grote, J. et al. (eds.) (1992): *Organized Interests and the European Community*, Sage, London.

Greenwood, J./Halpin, D. (2005): *The Public Governance of Interest Groups in the European Union: does regulating groups for 'representativeness' strengthen input legitimacy?*, Paper presented at ECPR conference in Budapest, 8–10 September 2005.

Habermas, J. (1992): *Drei normative Modelle der Demokratie: Zum Begriff deliberativer Politik*, in: Münkler, H., *Die Chancen der Freiheit. Grundprobleme der Demokratie*, Piper, München, pp. 11–24.

Hanf, K./O'Toole, L. J. (1992): *Revisiting Old Friends: Networks, Implementaon Structures and the Management of Inter-organisational Relations*, European Journal of Political Research, 21, (Special Issue 'Policy Networks'), pp.163–80.

Havel, V./Klaus, V. (1996): *Rival Visions. Civil Society After Communism*, Journal of Democracy, 7:1, pp. 12–23.

Henning, C.A. (2000): *Macht und Tausch in der Europäischen Agrarpolitik. Eine positive Theorie kollektiver Entscheidungen*, Campus, Frankfurt a.M..

Héritier, A. (2002): *New Modes of Governance in the European Union: Policy-Making without Legislation?*, in: Héritier, A. (ed.), *Common Goods. Reinventing European and International Governance*, Rowman and Littlefield, Lanham, pp.185–206.

Hix, S. (1999): *The Political System of the European Union*, Macmillan, London.

Holland, S. (1980): *Uncommon Market: Capital, Class and Power in the European Community*, St. Martin's Press, New York.

Hooghe, L. (1996a): *Building a Europe with the Regions: Cohesion Policy and European Integration. Building Multi-level Governance*, in: Hooghe, L. (ed.), *Cohesion Policy and European Integration. Building Multi-level Governance*, Oxford University Press, Oxford, pp. 89–126.

Hooghe, L. (1996b): *Introduction. Reconciling EU-Wide Policy and National Diversity*, in: Hooghe, L. (ed.), *Cohesion Policy and European Integration. Building Multi-level Governance*, Oxford University Press, Oxford, pp. 1–24.

Hooghe, L. /Keating, M. (1994): *The Politics of EU Regional Policy*, Journal of European Public Policy, 1, pp. 53–79.

Hurrelmann, A. (2003): *Europäische Demokratie ohne europäischen Demos? Zivilgesellschaftliche Integration und die Reform der Europäischen Union*, ZPol, 13:2, pp. 661–692.

Imig, D./Tarrow, S. (eds.) (2001): *Contentious Europeans. Protest and Politics in an Emerging Polity*, Rowman&Littlefield, Lanham.

Jachtenfuchs, M. /Kohler-Koch, B. (1996): *Regieren im dynamischen Mehrebenensystem*, in: Jachtenfuchs, M. /Kohler-Koch, B. (eds.), *Europäische Integration*, Leske+Budrich, Opladen:, pp. 15–44.

Jordan, G. (1998): *What Drives Associability at the European level? The Limits of the Utilitarian Explanation*, in: Aspinwall, M./Greenwood, J. (eds.), *Collective Action in the European Union*, Routledge, London, pp. 31–63.

Kassim, H. (1994): *Policy Networks, Networks and European Union Policy Making: A Sceptical View*, West European Politics, 17:4, pp. 15–27.

Kendall, J./Anheier, H. (1999): *The third sector and the European Union policy process: an initial evaluation*, Journal of European Public Policy, 6:6, pp. 283–307.

Klein, A. (2001): *Der Diskurs der Zivilgesellschaft. Politische Hintergründe und demokratie-theoretische Folgerungen*, Leske + Budrich, Opladen.

Kocka, J. (2000): *Zivilgesellschaft als historisches Problem und Versprechen*, in: Hildermeier, M. / Kocka, J. et al. (eds.), *Europäische Zivilgesellschaft in Ost und West. Begriff, Geschichte, Chancen*, Campus, Frankfurt a. M., pp. 13–39.

Koeppl, P. (2001): *The Acceptance, Relevance and Dominance of Lobbying the EU Commission – A First-time Survey of the EU Commission's Civil Servants*, Journal of Public Affairs, 1:1, pp. 69–80.

Kohler-Koch, B. (1994): *Changing Patterns of Interest Intermediation in the European Union*, Government and Opposition, 29: 2, pp. 166–180.

Kohler-Koch, B. (1996): *Catching up with Change. The Transformation of Governance in the European Union*, Journal of European Public Policy, 3:3, pp. 359–380.

Kohler-Koch, B. (1999): *The Evolution and Transformation of European Governance*, in: Eising, R. /Kohler-Koch, B. (eds.), *The Transformation of Governance in the European Union*, Routledge, London, pp. 14–35.

Kohler-Koch, B. (2005): *European governance and system integration*, European Governance Papers (EUROGOV), No. C-05-01, http://www.connex-network.org/eurogov/pdf/egp-connex-C-05-01.pdf, accessed 5 July 2005.

Kohler-Koch, B. /Conzelmann, T. et al. (2004): *Europäische Integration – Europäisches Regieren*, VS Verlag, Wiesbaden.

Kooiman, J. (ed.) (1993): *Modern Governance. New Government-Society Interactions*, Sage, London.

Kopecký, P./Mudde, C. (2003): *Uncivil Society? Contentious Politics in Post-communist Europe*, Routledge, London.

Kubik, J. (2000): *Between the State and Networks of "Cousins": The Role of Civil Society and Noncivil Associations in the Democratization of Poland*, in: Bermeo, N./Nord, P. (eds.), *Civil Society before Democracy. Lessons from Nineteenth-Century Europe*, Rowman & Littlefield, Lanham, pp. 181–207.

Lenschow, A. (2006): *Europeanisation of Public Policy*, in: Richardson, J. (ed.), *European Union. Power and Policy-making*, Routledge, Oxon, pp. 55–69.

Mansfeldová, Z. / Nalecz, S. et al. (2004): *Civil Society in Transition: Civic Engagement and Nonprofit Organizations in Central and Eastern Europe after 1989*, in: Zimmer, A./ Priller, E. (eds.), *Future of Civil Society. Making Central European Nonprofit-Organisations Work*, VS Verlag für Sozialwissenschaften, Wiesbaden, pp. 100–119.

Marks, G. (1993): *Structural Policy and Multilevel Governance in the European Community*, in: Cafruny, A./Rosenthal, G. (eds.), *The State of the European Community* (New York: Lynne Rienner), pp. 391–410.

Marks, G. / Nielsen, F. et al. (1996): *Competencies, Cracks and Conflicts: Regional Mobilization in the European Union*, in: Marks, G. / Scharpf, F. W. et al. (eds.), *Governance in the European Union*, Sage, London, pp. 40–63.

Marsh, D. / Rhodes, R.A.W. (eds.) (1992): *Policy Networks in British Government*, Oxford University Press, Oxford.

Mazey, S. / Richardson, J. (eds.) (1993): *Lobbying in the European Community*, Oxford University Press, Oxford.

Mazowiecki, T. (1998): *Chancen der Civil society in Mitteleuropa*, in: Czechowski, I. (ed.), *Drei Meilen vor dem Anfang. Reden über die Zukunft*, Reclam, Leipzig, pp. 9–20.

Merkel, W. / Lauth, H. J. (1998): *Systemwechsel und Zivilgesellschaft: Welche Zivilgesellschaft braucht die Demokratie?*, Aus Politik und Zeitgeschichte, B 6–7, pp. 3–12.

Michalowitz, I. (2002): *Beyond Corporatism and Pluralism: Towards a New Theoretical Framework*, in: Warleigh, A. / Fairbrass, J. (eds.), *Influence and Interests in the European Union: The New Politics of Persuasion and Advocacy*, Europa Publications, London, pp. 35–53.

Michalowitz, I. (2004): *EU Lobbying. Principals, Agents and Targets: Strategic Interest Inttermediation in EU Policy-Making*, LIT-Verlag, Münster.

Milbrath, L.W. (1960): *Lobbying as a Communication Process*, Public Opinion Quarterly 24:1, pp. 32–53.

Nollert, M. (1997): *Verbändelobbying in der Europäischen Union – Europäische Dachverbände im Vergleich*, in: Alemann, U./Weßels, B. (eds.), *Verbände in vergleichender Perspektive: Beiträge zu einem vernachlässigten Feld*, Sigma, Berlin, pp. 107–136.

Olson, M. (1965): *The Logic of Collective Action. Public Goods and the Theory of Groups*, Harvard University Press, Cambridge.

Pedler, R. (ed.) (2002): *European Union Lobbying: Changes in the Arena*, Palgrave, Basingstoke.

Pedler, R. / Van Schendelen, R. (1994): *Lobbying the European Union: Companies, Trade Associations and Issue Groups*, Dartmouth, Aldershot.

Pérez-Díaz, V. (1998): *The Public Sphere and a European Civil Society*, in: Alexander, J. C. (ed.), *Real Civil Societies. Dilemmas of Institutionalization*, Sage, London, pp. 211–238.

Peterson, J. (1995): *Policy Networks and European Union Policy Making: A Reply to Kassim*, West European Politics, 18:2, pp. 389–407.

Pietrzyk, D. I. (2003): *Democracy or Civil Society?*, Politics, 23:1, pp. 38–45.

Pollack, M. (1997): *Representing Diffuse Interests in the European Union*, Journal of European Public Policy, 4:4, pp. 572–590.

Putnam, R. D. (ed.) (2001): *Gesellschaft und Gemeinsinn*, Bertelsmann Stiftung, Gütersloh.

Raunio, T. (1999): *Always One Step Behind? National Legislatures and the European Union*, Government and Opposition, 34:2, pp. 180–202.

Reale, A. (2003): *Representation of interests, participatory democracy and lawmaking in the European Union: Which role and which rules for the social partners?*, Jean Monnet Working Paper 15/03, http://www.jeanmonnetprogram.org/papers/03/031501.pdf, accessed 1 February 2006.

Rosenau, J. N./Czempiel, E. O. (eds.) (1992): *Governance without Government. Order and Change in World Politics*, Cambridge University Press, Cambridge.

Roth, R (2003): *Die dunklen Seiten der Zivilgesellschaft*, Forschungsjournal Neue Soziale Bewegungen, 16:2, 59–73.

Rucht, D. (2001): *Lobbying or Protest? Strategies to Influence EU Environmental Politics*, in: Imig, D./Tarrow, S. (eds.), *Contentious Europeans*, Rowman&Littlefield, Lanham, pp. 125–143.

Rumford, C. (2003): *European Civil Society or Transnational Social Space? Conceptions of Society in Discourses of EU Citizenship, Governance and the Democratic Deficit: An Emerging Agenda*, European Journal of Social Theory, 6:1, pp. 25–43.

Sachße, C. (2004): *Nonprofit Organizations in Germany: Organizational Types and Forms*, bonus material on the CD of Zimmer, A./Priller, E. (eds.), *Future of Civil Society. Making Central European Nonprofit-Organisations Work*, VS Verlag für Sozialwissenschaften, Wiesbaden.

Salisbury, Robert H. (1969): *Interests and Institutions: Substance and Structure of American Politics*, University Press, Pittsburgh.

Saurugger, S. (2002): *Analyser les modes de représentation des intérêts dans l'Union Européenne: construction d'une problématique*, Questions de Recherche, 6, Centre d'études et de recherches internationales, Sciences Politiques, Paris.

Saurugger, S. (2004): *Representative versus participatory democracy? France, Europe and Civil Society*, ECPR Joint Sessions of Workshops, University of Uppsala, Sweden.

Schade, Jeanette (2002): *„Zivilgesellschaft" – eine vielschichtige Debatte*, INEF Report, Institut für Entwicklung und Frieden der Gerhard-Mercator-Universität Duisburg, 59/2002, pp.1–80.

Scharpf, F. W. (2004): *Legitimationskonzepte jenseits des Nationalstaats*, in: MPfG Working Paper 04:6, http:andandmpi-fg-koeln.mpg.deandpuandworkpapandwp04-6and-wp04-6.htm, November 2004.

Schmalz-Bruns, R. (2002): *The Normative Desirability of Participatory Democracy*, in: Participatory governance in multi-level context. Concepts and experience, Leske+Budrich, Opladen, pp. 59–74.

Schmidt, V. (1999): *National Patterns of Governance under Siege: the Impact of European Integration*, in: Kohler-Koch, B. / Eising, R. (eds.), *The Transformation of Governance in the European Union*, Routledge, London, pp. 155–172.

Schmitter, P. (1979): *Still the Century of Corporatism?*, in: Schmitter, P. / Lehmmbruch, G. (eds.), *Trends Toward Corporatist Intermediation*, Sage, London, pp. 7–53.

Schmitter, P. / Streeck, W. (1991): *From National Corporatism to Trans-national Pluralism: Organised Interests in the Single European Market*, Politics and Society, 19:2, pp. 133–164.

Schneider, V. / Dang-Nguyen, G. et al. (1994): *Corporate Actor Networks in European Policy-Making: Harmonizing Telecommunications Policy*, Journal of common market studies, 32:4, pp. 473–498.

Schuppert, G. F. (2001): *Europäische Zivilgesellschaft – Phantom oder Zukunftsprojekt?*, Forschungsjournal Neue Soziale Bewegungen, 14:4, pp. 5–13.

Schuppert, G. F.(2004): *Governance-Leistungen der Zivilgesellschaft*, in: Gosewinkel, D. / Rucht, D. et al. (eds.), *Zivilgesellschaft – national und transnational*, edition sigma, Berlin, pp. 245–264.

Schuppert, G. F. (ed.) (2005): *Governance-Forschung. Vergewisserung über Stand und Entwicklungslinien*, Nomos, Baden-Baden.

Sedelmeier, U. (2006): *Europeanisation in New Member and Candidate States.* Living Reviews European Governance, 1:3, http://www.livingreviews.org/lreg-2006-3, accessed 26 November 2006.

Sittermann, B. (forthcoming): *The Europeanisation of the Third Sector*, Nomos, Baden-Baden.

Smismans, S. (2003): *European civil society – shaped by discourses and institutional interests*, European law journal, 9:4, pp. 473–495.

Smismans, S. (2006): *Civil society and European governance: the interdisciplinary challenge of reflexive deliberative polyarchy*, in: Smismans, S., *Civil Society and Legitimate European Governance*, Edward Elgar, Cheltenham, pp. 299–317.

Soysal, Y. N. (2001): *Changing boundaries of participation in European public spheres. Reflections on citizenship and civil society*, in: Eder, K./Giesen, B. (eds.), *European citizenship between national legacies and postnational projects*, Oxford University Press, Oxford, pp. 159–179.

Szczerbiak, A. /Taggart, P. (2001): _Parties, Positions and Europe: Euroscepticism in the EU Candidate States of Central and Eastern Europe_, SEI Working Paper No 46, University of Sussex, Brighton.

The Economist (2007): _Europe's mid-life crisis. A successful club celebrates its 50th birthday in sombre mood_, The Economist 382:8520, 11, 17–23 March 2007.

Van Schendelen, R (2005): _Machiavelli in Brussels. The Art of Lobbying the EU_, 2nd fully updated Edition, Amsterdam University Press, Amsterdam.

Van Schendelen, R (1993): _National Public and Private Lobbying_, Dartmouth, Aldershot.

Venables, T. (2004): _The EU's relationship with NGOs and the issue of "participatory democracy"_, Transnational Associations 2, pp.156–159.

Wallace, H./Young, A. R. (eds.) (1997): _Participation and Policy-making in the European Union_, Clarendon Press, Oxford.

Warleigh, A. (2000): _The Hustle: Citizenship Practice, NGOs and 'Policy Coalitions' in the European Union_, Journal of European Public Policy, 7:2, pp. 229–243.

Warleigh, A. (2001): _'Europeanizing' Civil Society: NGOs as Agents of Political Socialization_, Journal of Common Market Studies, 39:4, pp. 619–639.

Warleigh, A. (2006): _Civil society and legitimate governance in a flexible Europe: critical deliberativism as a way forward_, in: Smismans, S., _Civil Society and Legitimate European Governance_, Edward Elgar, Cheltemham, pp. 68–86.

Warleigh, A. and Fairbrass, J. (eds.) (2002): _Influence and Interests in the European Union: The New Politics of Persuasion and Advocacy_, Europa Publications, London.

White, G. (2004): _Civil Society, Democratization and Development: Clearing the Analytical Background_, in: Burnell, P./Calvert, P. (eds.), _Civil Society in Democratization_, Frank Cass, London, pp. 6–21.

Wind, M. (1997): _Rediscovering Institutions: Allmenn Reflectivist Critique of Rational Institutionalism_, in: Joergensen, K.E: (ed.), _Reflective Approaches to European Integration_, St. Martin's Press, New York, pp. 15–35.

Zimmer, A. (2004): _Civil Society Organizations in Central and Eastern European Countries: Introduction and Terminology_, in: Zimmer, A. / Priller, E. (eds.), _Future of Civil Society. Making Central European Nonprofit-Organisations Work_, VS Verlag für Sozialwissenschaften, Wiesbaden, pp. 11–27.

Zimmer, A. / Priller, E. (eds.) (2004): _Future of Civil Society. Making Central European Nonprofit-Organisations Work_, VS Verlag für Sozialwissenschaften, Wiesbaden.

Heiko Pleines

3.   Civil Society Groups from the Central and East European Member States in EU Governance. A Missing Link

3.1.   Post-Socialist Civil Societies

The integration of ten Central and East European countries (CEEC)[1] into the EU as part of the 2004 and 2007 enlargements poses new challenges to EU governance, as the number of countries involved has thereby increased dramatically. However, the actors coming from the new member states also face challenges as they attempt to integrate themselves into EU decision-making processes. Whereas state actors from the new member countries receive formal representation and voting rights that safeguard against their marginalisation in the system of EU governance, civil society organisations from the new member states find it much harder to gain access to decision-making processes at the EU level. At the advent of the 2004 enlargement, civil society organisations from the CEEC accounted for a mere 2% of the Brussels-based lobbying community.

To grasp the dynamics of the status quo, it is important to understand the legacy faced by civil society organisations in the post-socialist member states. To that end, David Lane argues in his contribution to this volume:

> Civil society associations in the new Central and East European members of the European Union have had a different trajectory from those of the old members. All of the latter have had relatively robust (though differently constituted) forms of civil society associations before joining the Union. In the former, most public associations were highly dependent on, and controlled by, the state. A major task of early 'transformation policy' was 'to dismantle the central government control inherited from the communist system' (EU Subcommittee on Civil Society Organisations 1999).

Accordingly, few civil society organisations in the new Central and East European member states are ready to act effectively at the EU level. The civil society organisations in these countries all face the same debilitating problem: they lack financial sustainability, exacerbated by a decreasing number of donors. Thus, they rely most heavily on state funding, with only a small portion of support coming from private sponsors or membership fees. Due to their tight budgets, the organisations remain chronically understaffed; lacking the funds to pay full-time employees, their staffs primarily consist of volunteers or part-timers (only the most established organisations have permanent employees). The civil society sector in the post-socialist member states therefore

---

1   The Czech Republic, Estonia, Hungary, Latvia, Lithuania, Poland, Slovakia and Slovenia joined the EU in May 2004. Bulgaria and Romania joined in January 2007.

accounts for a much smaller percentage of employment than the EU average. Moreover, civil society organisations in the post-socialist EU member states lack internal codes of ethics. Relatively few organisations publish annual reports and only large organisations can afford to perform annual audits. Furthermore, their members' activities are mostly limited to attendance at annual meetings (few of the organisations meet on a more frequent basis). To summarise, the civil society sector in the new EU member states still retains a relatively low profile. Their organisations are poorly financed, lacking in transparency and hampered by ill-qualified as well as too few staff members. (For an overview, see USAID 2005 and Howard 2003.)

As Lane points out, the specific characteristics of post-socialist civil societies set the stage for the role the organisations can play.

> It is important to note that the new institutions – linked to a capitalist and market type of society – were created on the foundations of the cultural and political traditions of specific countries. There were not only state socialist institutions but also cultural forms, which predated the communist regimes. Forms of answerability and accountability then may require different types of institutions and processes than in the old European Union societies. Policy might need to consider how to strengthen civil society as an 'autonomous social sphere', acting in a real intermediary role between the state and the individual, in addition to defining means to increase answerability.

On the other hand, as Lars Hallstrom concludes in his case study of EU environmental policy, the EU Commission is marked by a very specific approach to civil society organisations.

> The view of CEE environmental NGOs as generally weak and of limited use by EU officials is not entirely unfounded, but hinges largely on a very specific set of ideas and preferences about the role(s) for citizen-based groups in the integration and policymaking process. Environmental NGOs that are not consistent with these ideas and preferences, particularly those that do not bring technical expertise or knowledge to the policy process, are typically viewed as recipients, rather than providers, of policy-relevant information (Hallstrom 2004, 182).

This assessment is also confirmed by Mudde (2007) on a broader empirical basis.

Lane's and Hallstrom's observations suggest that an examination of the civil society organisations' capacity for meaningful participation in EU governance is indispensable if an assessment of the impact of enlargement on EU governance as well as of the Europeanisation of the new member states' societies is to be undertaken. In this context, it is important to keep in mind that the capacity to engage in EU governance typically varies between different forms of organisations and between different policy fields. Though civil society in CEECs is unquestionably weak, the individual capacity of post-socialist civil society organisations to act at the EU level nonetheless has to be examined on a case-by-case basis.

3.2. Research So Far

Though there is ample research on civil society in the Central and East European EU member states, its primary focus has been on the national democratisation process. Its studies have examined the capacity of civil society organisations to foster the transformation from authoritarian regimes with centrally planned economies to pluralist democracies with liberal market economies. The results of these studies unequivocally expose the structural weaknesses of civil society organisations in Central and Eastern Europe. Prominent recent examples are: Crowley (2004), Zimmer/Priller (2004), Bauerkämper (2003), Glenn (2003), Howard (2003), Kopecký/Mudde (2003), Drauss (2002), Meier-Dallach/Juchler (2002), Mendelson/Glenn (2002) and Merkel (2000).

A vast number of case studies on specific civil society groups or movements in the CEECs have also been conducted. Recent studies focusing on the countries and policy fields covered in this book[2] are Jehlička/Sarre/Podoba (2005), Pleines (2005), Fehr (2004), Hoecker/Fuchs (2004), Kohl/Platzer (2004), Carmin (2003), Dvorakova (2003), Dzwończyk (2003), Fagan (2003), Fuchs (2003), Hála et al. (2003), Krok-Paszkowska (2003), Magner (2003), Otte (2003), Tatur (2003) and Blažek (2002).

The complexities of the decision-making processes at the EU level have also been analysed in depth. Overviews are provided e.g. by Elgström (2005), Arregui Moreno (2004), Jupille (2004), Selck (2004) and Smith (2004). A thorough summary of the research on the role of civil society organisations in EU governance is given by Greenwood (2007). Broader analyses of different aspects of the role of interest groups at the EU level include Eising/Kohler-Koch (2005), Knodt/Finke (2005), Beyers (2004), Bouwen (2004), Christiansen/Piattoni (2004), Michalowitz (2004a+b), Ruzza (2004), Smismans (2004) and Warntjen/Wonka (2004). There are also policy-field-specific analyses of political decision-making processes and the involvement of interest groups at the EU level. Studies focusing on the policy fields covered in this book are Neal (2004), Wörner (2004), Liebert (2003), Compston/Greenwood (2001), Hartenberger (2001), Falkner (2000), Meester (2000), Pollack/Hafner-Burton (2000) and Schmidt (2000).

In summary, there is an abundance of literature on civil society in the CEECs and there also is a huge amount of analyses of political decision-making at the EU level and the role of interest groups in EU governance. However, there is hardly any substantial empirical study on the integration of civil society groups from the new Central and East European member states into EU governance.

---

2   These are the policy fields of environmental policy, gender policy, agricultural policy and labour relations for civil society organisations from Poland and the Czech Republic.

3.3. A Missing Link

An investigation of the experience of civil society organisations from the Central and East European member states would provide the critical missing link between the research on post-socialist civil societies and EU governance. An analysis of the organisations' activities at the EU level would help to assess EU multi-level governance in a number of ways.

First, the eastern enlargement is the first large-scale test of how open the post-Maastricht governance system is to newcomers. This concerns the openness of civil society umbrella organisations to an influx of new members as well as the ability of EU institutions to engage in consultations in the face of a rapid increase in the number of interested parties.

Second, as most civil society organisations from the new member states are relatively weak, examining their role in EU governance also helps to assess how nominal representation is related to meaningful participation. For example, although the share of smaller groups in umbrella organisations is increasing considerably, are they succeeding in gaining decision-making powers? Do the challenges of collective action hamper the representation of a common interest?

Third, CEECs offer interesting cases for an analysis of the impacts of multi-level governance on the political role of civil society organisations. Because the accession negotiations were long and formalised, the European Commission initiated a number of programmes to prepare civil society organisations from the candidate countries for participation in EU governance. At the same time, these civil society organisations in most cases did not have close links at the national level due to the socialist legacy. Accordingly, they were free to build coalitions between the different levels of EU governance. What has determined the civil society organisations' and political actors' choices of coalition partners?

3.4. The Structure of this Book

This book analyses these three aspects by means of a focused comparison of civil society organisations from the Czech Republic and Poland in four policy fields. The guiding question is whether civil society organisations from the Central and East European member states have (or can gain) the capacity for meaningful participation in EU governance.

In the following second part of this book, the actors and rules of EU governance will be profiled. Daniela Obradovic and Jose M. Alonso Vizcaino give a detailed overview of the regulatory framework developed by the EU to organise the different forms of governance involving civil society organisations. This includes new modes of governance, like the open form of co-ordination, as well as more traditional forms of governance, such as the social dialogue. David Lane then summarises the state of civil society organisations in the post-socialist EU member states and their potential for an active role in EU governance. He offers a quantitative and qualitative assessment of their general capacity and discusses the implications for questions of accountability. Finally, Daniela Obradovic and Redmar Damsma examine the role of post-socialist civil society organisations as a constituency in the European Commission's consultations.

The next two sections of the book present case studies designed to obtain a better understanding of the capacity, impact and accountability of civil society organisations from new Central and East European member states in EU multi-level governance. The case studies address the civil society organisations most actively involved in EU governance, namely typical NGOs, trade unions, employers' organisations and business associations. In order to allow for comparison, all cases centre on the Czech Republic and Poland, two of the most populous new member countries with relatively strong civil societies.

The case study by Kristýna Bušková and Heiko Pleines examines the experiences of Czech environmental NGOs with EU governance, while the contribution by Silvia Payer and Gesine Fuchs focuses on women's NGOs, highlighting the Polish case. The next two case studies by Iglika Yakova and Heiko Pleines examine the role of Czech and Polish agricultural lobbies in EU multi-level governance. In the final pair of case studies, Zdenka Mansfeldová and Joanna Einbock analyse the involvement of Czech and Polish trade unions and employers' associations in the EU social dialogue.

References

Arregui Moreno, Francisco (2004): *Negotiation in Legislative Decision-making in the European Union*, Rijksuniv, Groningen.

Bauerkämper, Arnd (ed.) (2003): *Die Praxis der Zivilgesellschaft. Akteure, Handeln und Strukturen im internationalen Vergleich*, Campus, Frankfurt/ Main.

Beyers, J. (2004): *Voice and Access: Political Practices of European Interest Associations*, in: European Union Politics, 5(2), pp. 211–240.

Blažek, Petr (2002): *Reprezentace zemědělských zájmů v politickém systému České republiky*, in: Politologická revue, 1, pp. 22–38.

Borragán, Nieves Pérez-Solórzano (2003): *The Organisation of Business Interests in Central and East European Countries for EU Representation*, in: Greenwood, J. (ed.), *The Challenge of Change in EU Business Associations*, Palgrave, Basingstoke, pp. 213–225.

Bouwen, Pieter (2004): *The Logic of Access to the European Parliament*, in: Journal of Common Market Studies, 42(3), pp. 473–495.

Carmin, JoAnn (2003): *Non-governmental Organisations and Public Participation in Local Environmental Decision-making in the Czech Republic*, in: Local Environment, 8(5), pp. 541–552.

Christiansen, T./ Piattoni, S. (eds) (2004): *Informal Governance in the European Union*, Edward Elgar, Cheltenham.

Compston, H. / Greenwood, J. (eds) (2001): *Social Partnership in the European Union*, Palgrave Macmillan, Basingstoke.

Crowley, Stephen (2004): *Explaining Labor Weakness in Post-Communist Europe*, in: East European Politics and Society, 18(3), pp. 394–429.

Drauss, Franciszek (2002): *La société civile organisée en Pologne, République Tchèque, Slovaquie et Hongrie*, Office des Publications Officielles des Communautés Européennes, Luxembourg.

Dvorakova, Z. (2003): *Trade Unions, Works Councils and Staff Involvement in the Modernising Czech Republic*, in: International Journal of Public Sector Management, 16(6), pp. 424–433.

Dzwończyk, Joanna (2003): *The Barriers for the Development of Civic Society in Poland After 1989*, in: Polish Political Science Yearbook 2003, pp. 117–125.

Einbock, Joanna (2006): *Polish Trade Unions and the EU*, in: KICES Working Papers No. 7, pp. 15–30.

Eising, Rainer/ Kohler-Koch, Beate (eds) (2005): *Interessenpolitik in Europa*, Nomos, Baden-Baden.

Elgström, Ole (ed.) (2005): *European Union Negotiations: Processes, Networks and Institutions*, Routledge, London.

Fagan, Adam (2004): *Environment and Democracy in the Czech Republic*, Edward Elgar Publishing, Cheltenham.

Falkner, Gerda (2000): *The Council or the social partners? EC social policy between diplomacy and collective bargaining*, in: Journal of European Public Policy, 7(5), pp. 705–724.

Fehr, Helmut (2004): *Eliten und Zivilgesellschaft in Ostmitteleuropa. Polen und die Tschechische Republik (1968–2003)*, in: Aus Politik und Zeitgeschichte, (B) 5–6, pp. 48–54.

Fuchs, Gesine (2003): *Die Zivilgesellschaft mitgestalten. Frauenorganisationen im polnischen Demokratisierungsprozess*, Campus, Frankfurt/M.

Fuchs, Gesine (2006): *Polish Non-Governmental Women's Organisations and the EU*, in: KICES Working Papers No. 7, pp. 31–44.

Glenn, John K. (2003): *Framing Democracy: Civil Society and Civic Movements in Eastern Europe*, Stanford University Press, Stanford.

Grant, Wyn (1997): *The Common Agricultural Policy*, Macmillan, Basingstoke.

Greenwood, Justin (2007): *Interest Representation in the European Union*, 2nd ed., Palgrave, New York.

Hála, J./ Kroupa, A./ Kux, J./ Mansfeldová, Z./ Rakušanová, P. (2003): *Social Dialogue and EMU in the Czech Republic*, in: European Foundation for the Improvement of Living and Working Conditions (ed.), *Social Dialogue and EMU in the Acceding Countries*, European Foundation for the Improvement of Living and Working Conditions, Dublin, pp. 81–106.

Hallstrom, Lars (2004): *Eurocratising enlargement, EU elites and NGO participation in European environmental policy*, in: Environmental Politics, 13(1), pp. 175–193.

Hartenberger, Ute (2001): *Europäischer Sozialer Dialog nach Maastricht. EU-Sozialpartnerverhandlungen auf dem Prüfstand*, Nomos, Baden-Baden.

Hicks, Barbara (2004): *Setting agendas and shaping activism. EU influence on Central and Eastern European environmental movements*, in: Environmental Politics, 13(1), pp. 216–233.

Hoecker, Beate / Fuchs, Gesine (2004): *Handbuch Politische Partizipation von Frauen in Europa*, VS-Verlag, Wiesbaden.

Howard, Marc Morjé (2003): *The Weakness of Civil Society in Post-Communist Europe*, Cambridge University Press, Cambridge.

Jehlička, Petr / Sarre, Philip / Podoba, Juraj (2005): *The Czech Environmental Movement's Knowledge Interests in the 1990s: Compatibility of Western Influences with pre-1989 Perspectives*, in: Environmental Politics, 14(1), pp. 64–82.

Jupille, Joseph (2004): *Procedural Politics: Issues, Influence, and Institutional Choice in the European Union*, Cambridge University Press, New York.

Knodt, Michéle / Finke, Barbara (eds) (2005): *Europäisierung der Zivilgesellschaft. Konzepte, Akteure, Strategien*, Verlag für Sozialwissenschaften, Wiesbaden.

Kohl, Heribert/ Platzer, Hans-Wolfgang (2004): *Arbeitsbeziehungen in Mittelosteuropa. Transformation und Integration. Die acht neuen EU-Mitgliedsländer im Vergleich*, Nomos, Baden-Baden.

Kopecký, Petr/ Mudde, Cas (eds) (2003): *Uncivil Society? Contentious Politics in Post-communist Europe*, Routledge, London.

Krok-Paszkowska, Ania (2003): *Samoobrona. The Polish Self-defence Movement*, in: Kopecký, P. / Mudde, C. (eds), *Uncivil Society? Contentious Politics in Post-communist Europe*, Routledge, London, pp.114–133.

Liebert, U. (ed.) (2003): *Gendering Europeanisation*, Peter Lang, Bruxelles.

Magner, Michael (2003): *Stalemate in Civil Society: Post-communist Transition in Poland and the Legacy of Socialism*, Oficyna Wydawnicza, Warszawa.

Meester, Gerrit (2000): *EU Institutions and the Decision-making Process for Agricultural Policy*, in: Burrell, A./ Oskam, A. (eds) *Agricultural Policy and Enlargement of the European Union*, Wageningen Pers, Wageningen, pp. 37–52.

Meier-Dallach, Hans-Peter/ Juchler, Jakob (eds) (2002): *Postsocialist Transformations and Civil Society in a Globalizing World*, Nova Science Publications, Huntington.

Mendelson, Sarah E./ Glenn, John K. (eds) (2002): *The Power and Limits of NGOs: A Critical Look at Building Democracy in Eastern Europe and Eurasia*, Columbia University Press, New York.

Merkel, Wolfgang (ed.) (2000): *Systemwechsel 5. Zivilgesellschaft und Transformation*, Leske + Budrich, Opladen.

Michalowitz, Irina (2004a): *EU Lobbying: Principals, Agents and Targets. Strategic Interest Intermediation in EU Policy-making*, Lit, Münster.

Michalowitz, Irina (2004b): *Analysing Structured Paths of Lobbying Behaviour: Why Discussing the Involvement of 'Civil Society' Does not Solve the EU's Democratic Deficit*, European Integration, 26(2), pp. 145–173.

Mudde, Cas (2007): *Civil society*, in: White, Stephen / Batt, Judy / Lewis, Paul G. eds., *Developments in Central and East European Politics 4*, Palgrave (forthcoming).

Neal, A. (ed.) (2004): *The Changing Face of European Labour Law and Social Policy*, Kluwer, The Hague.

Otte, Thomas (2003): *Die Vertretung der polnischen Unternehmen innerhalb des Sozialen Dialogs durch die nationalen Arbeitgeberkonföderationen*, in: Osteuropa Wirtschaft, 1. pp. 41–63.

Pleines, Heiko (2005): *Der politische Einfluss der polnischen Agrarlobby*, in: Osteuropa Wirtschaft, 50(2), pp. 151–164.

Pleines, Heiko / Bušková, Kristýna (2007): *Czech Environmental NGOs. Actors or agents in EU multi-level governance?*, in: Contemporary European Studies, 2(1), pp. 20–31.

Pollack, Mark A. / Hafner-Burton, E. (2000): *Mainstreaming gender in the European Union*, in: Journal of European Public Policy 7(3), pp. 432–456.

Ruzza, Carlo (2004): *Europe and Civil Society: Movement Coalitions and European Governance*, Manchester University Press, Manchester.

Schmidt, V. (2000): *Zum Wechselverhältnis zwischen europäischer Frauenpolitik und europäischen Frauenorganisationen*, in: Lenz, Ilse et al. (eds): *Frauenbewegungen weltweit. Aufbrüche, Kontinuität, Veränderungen*, Leske + Budrich, Opladen, pp. 199–230.

Selck, Torsten J. (2004): *The Impact of Procedure: Analyzing European Union Legislative Decision-making*, Cuvillier, Göttingen.

Smismans, S. (2004): *Civil Society and Legitimate European Governance*, Edward Elgar, Cheltenham.

Smith, Andy (ed.) (2004): *Politics and the European Commission: Actors, Interdependence, Legitimacy*, Routledge, London.

Tatur, Melanie (2003): *Das Erbe der Solidarnosc als Ressource und Problem der Transformation in Polen*, in: Höhmann, H.-H./ Pleines, H. (eds), *Wirtschaftspolitik in Osteuropa zwischen ökonomischer Kultur, Institutionenbildung und Akteursverhalten. Russland, Polen und Tschechische Republik im Vergleich*, Edition Temmen, Bremen, pp. 147–179.

US Agency for International Development (2005): *The 2004 NGO Sustainability Index for Central and Eastern Europe and Eurasia*, USAID, Washington, D.C.

Warntjen, Andreas/ Wonka, Arndt (eds) (2004): *Governance in Europe. The Role of Interest Groups*, Nomos, Baden-Baden.

Wasner, Barbara (2005): *Europäische Institutionenpolitik und die Vernetzung sozialpolitischer Verbände*, in: Knodt, M./ Finke, B. (eds), *Europäische Zivilgesellschaft. Konzepte, Akteure, Strategien*, Verlag für Sozialwissenschaften, Wiesbaden, pp. 129–152.

Wörner, Tilmann (2004): *Einflussmöglichkeiten von NGOs auf die Umweltpolitik der Europäischen Union*, Tectum, Marburg.

Zimmer, Annette/ Priller, Eckhard (eds) (2004): *Future of Civil Society. Making Central European Nonprofit-Organizations Work*, Verlag für Sozialwissenschaften, Wiesbaden.

Part II. Rules and Actors

Daniela Obradovic and Jose M. Alonso Vizcaino[1]

4. Good Governance Requirements Concerning the Participation of Interest Groups in EU Consultations

4.1. Introduction

Although civil interest groups have been involved in the governance of the European Union (EU) since its creation, their structured incorporation into the European policy formation process is relatively recent. The Commission has formalised the dialogue with civic groups by adopting general principles and minimum standards that govern the process of consultation with interested parties (hereafter referred to as 'minimum standards') (Commission of the European Communities, 12/2002a). The Commission defines consultations as those processes through which it wishes to solicit input from interested parties in the shaping of policy prior to its final decisions (Commission of the European Communities, 1/2006, p. 11). The term 'interested parties' encompasses any individual or group wishing to participate in consultations run by the Commission, including profit or non-profit organisations and private citizens (ibid.). In order to participate in EU stakeholder consultations, the in-depth impact assessments conducted by the Commission prior to the drafting of legislative proposals or the open method of co-ordination (OMC), interest groups must fulfil the following criteria: representativeness, accountability and transparency. The Commission has identified these qualities as requisite for good governance (Commission of the European Communities, 7/2001, p. 8).

With respect to the civil interest groups' relatively recent entry into EU governance, a number of issues remain unclear, such as the scope of application of the standards adopted by the Commission or the legal status of the entitlements of interest groups vis-à-vis participation. The relationship between the standards and principles drawn up in different contexts, including the proposed, but not adopted, Statute for a European Association, also requires greater scrutiny. The article examines these issues, starting from the application of the Commission's criteria and their impact upon civil dialogue in the EU. In particular, it assesses whether the implementation of the criteria, given their vagueness and imprecision, is even feasible.

---

1   This article is prepared as a part of the research programme 'Constitutional Order and Economic Integration' of the Amsterdam Center for International Law, University of Amsterdam and the Sixth Framework Project 'New Modes of Governance' sponsored by the European Commission.

4.2. Role of EU Consultations with Civil Groups in European Governance

Before examining in more detail how the participation of civil groups is regulated, it is useful to recall the context in which such participation is to be assessed. The formalisation of civil groups' involvement in EU policy conception and implementation is part of the new forms of governance introduced by the European Union to improve its efficiency and legitimacy (Commission of the European Communities, 7/2001, p. 11 and Harlow, 2005, pp. 59–60 and 63–65). In this new mode of governance, sketched in the Commission's White Paper on Governance, the border between the public and private spheres has been softened (Harlow, 2005, p. 59). Private activity does not merely seek to influence government decision-making, but is actually involved in the process (Schapiro, 2001, p. 369). In this new mode of EU governance, the government's tasks are to enable socio-political interactions, to encourage different arrangements for coping with problems and to distribute services among the various actors. Negotiation and mediation play the same central role in these systems of governance as authority and sovereignty did in the classical system (Harlow, 2005, pp. 59–60).

Under this approach, the Commission's task is not simply to act as a policy entrepreneur that collects views, recommends policies for action and then enforces the resulting policies as the 'watchdog' of EU interests (ibid., p. 63); its role is to facilitate or regulate a public-private network and to create, foster and maintain the relationships in this network (ibid., p. 65). Obviously, in this mode of governance, interaction between civil interest groups and public institutions operating at different levels is crucial for the functioning of the system. The importance of this interplay was recognised in the White Paper on Governance, which promises 'wide participation through the policy chain – from conception to implementation' (Commission of European Communities, 7/2001, p. 10). The Commission also pledges to 'reach out to citizens and involve civil society, construct and consult better networks, and establish procedures and timetables for consultation' in the Paper (ibid., p. 14). It asserts that the active participation of civil society in EU governance in the form of early consultations will not only make the European integration process more inclusive and ensure that EU issues are debated by a wide range of interested parties, but will also contribute to more effective policy-shaping in the Union (ibid., p. 15). The Commission's advocacy of civil society involvement in the debate on the future of Europe (Commission of the European Communities, 10/2005, p. 6), illustrates how important this issue has become. The promotion of civil participation in EU governance is also one of the main objectives of the Action Plan to improve communication in the Union (Commission of the European Communities, 7/2005, p. 3) and the European Transparency Initiative (Commission of the European Communities (1/2006, p. 2).

The interaction between civil interest groups and public institutions operating at different levels is critical to the functioning of the European Union as a system. This was acknowledged in the White Paper on Governance, which promises 'wide participation through the policy chain – from conception to implementation' (Commission 7/2001, 10; see also Makinen 2007). It also pledges to 'reach out to citizens and involve civil society, construct and consult better networks, and establish procedures and timetables for consultation' (ibid, 14).

The commitment to provide wider opportunities for stakeholders to actively participate in EU policy-shaping is one of the 'Strategic Objectives 2005–2009' with which the European Commission launched its 'Partnership for European Renewal.' In a communiqué, the Commission emphasised that "consultation and participation" are inherent to the idea of partnership (Commission of the European Communities, 1/2005, p. 5).

4.3. Civil Dialogue in the European Union

The greater involvement of civil society in EU governance is to be achieved through the civil dialogue,[2] which refers to a range of consultation forums. These include the Dialogue with Business,[3] the Dialogue with Citizens,[4] the European Round Table on Democracy, (Commission of the European Communities, 10/2005, p. 8), Green and

---

2   In the future, the obligation of the Commission to consult civil society prior to drafting EU policy proposals will be codified as a Treaty category. The new EU Treaty will contain the provisions agreed to at the 2004 Intergovernmental Conference on participatory democracy (Brussels European Council 21/22 June 2007, Presidency Conclusions (http://www.eu2007.de/en/News/download_docs/Juni/0621-ER/010conclusions.pdf, at p.17). Those provisions are as follows:
'Article I-47
The principle of participatory democracy
1. The institutions shall, by appropriate means, give citizens and representative associations the opportunity to make known and publicly exchange their views in all areas of Union action.
2. The institutions shall maintain an open, transparent and regular dialogue with representative associations and civil society.
3. The Commission shall carry out broad consultations with parties concerned in order to ensure that the Union's actions are coherent and transparent.
4. Not less than one million citizens who are nationals of a significant number of Member States may take the initiative of inviting the Commission, within the framework of its powers, to submit any appropriate proposal on matters where citizens consider that a legal act of the Union is required for the purpose of implementing the Constitution. European laws shall determine the provisions for the procedures and conditions required for such a citizens' initiative, including the minimum number of Member States from which such citizens must come.'
(Conference of the Representatives of the Governments of the Member States (2004): Treaty establishing a Constitution for Europe, 29 October 2004, Brussels, http://www.consilium.europa.eu/igcpdf/en/04/cg00/cg00087-RE02.en04.pdf).
3   http://europa.eu.int/business/en/index.html
4   http://europa.eu.int/citizens/en/index.html

White Papers,[5] workshops, permanent consultative groups,[6] the dialogue with national associations of regional and local authorities (Commission of the European Communities, 12/2003), around 25 Multi-Stakeholder Forums (e.g. the EU Health Policy Forum, the Corporate Social Responsibility European Multi-stakeholder Forum[7] and the Trade Dialogue with Civil Society[8]) and Internet consultations that take place on the Your Voice in Europe web portal.[9] These are conducted between the Commission and interest groups in the pre-drafting phase of European legislation or the open method of co-ordination (OMC)[10] guidelines preparation process. The Commission views Your Voice in Europe as a single access point offering citizens, consumers and businesses an opportunity to play an active role in the process of shaping Commission policy (Commission of the European Communities, 2004, p. 12). This Internet site is to be replaced in the near future by a more encompassing contact centre, Europe Direct, which will promote 'one-stop-shopping' access for citizens (Commission of the European Communities, 7/2005, p. 30).

The Commission has contact with around 1500 interest groups, representing 2600 special interest groups, whose activities generate an estimated annual turnover of 60 to 90 million euros (Commission of the European Communities, 12/2005, p. 4). Two-thirds of these groups represent business interests while one-fifth is concerned with civil interests. The remainder represent professions, trade unions, and public sector organisations at the national and regional levels (Greenwood, 2007, p. 12). In addi-

---

5   For an overview of Green and White Papers and communications, see Commission of the European Communities (2/2007, 35).
6   For the list of formal or structured consultative bodies in which civil society organisations participate, see database for Consultation, the European Commission and Civil Society (CONECCS) http://europa.eu.int/comm/civil_society/coneccs/index_en.htm
7   http://forum.europa.eu.int/irc/empl/csr_eu_multi_stakeholder_forum/info/data/en/CSR%20 Forum%20Rules.htm
8   http://trade.ec.europa.eu/doclib/docs/2005/june/tradoc_113527.pdf
9   http://europa.eu.int/yourvoice
10   The OMC is not designed to produce law at the European level; it aims to co-ordinate the actions of the member states in a given policy domain and to create conditions for mutual learning that hopefully will introduce some degree of voluntary policy convergence. It also helps member states to develop their own policies through the discussion and dissemination of best practices, with the aim of reaching commonly agreed goals. The OMC is concretised through the production of guidelines drafted by the Commission and issued by the Council of Ministers, to be translated into national policy through national action plans (NAPs), combined with periodic monitoring by the Commission, evaluation and peer review organised as mutual learning processes and accompanied by indicators and benchmarking as means of comparing best practices. The OMC is applied as an instrument for the development of budgetary, economic, employment and social inclusion policy, and also as a strategy in pension reform, information society, research and innovation, education and training and youth policy; see Obradovic (2006, pp. 261–327). On the significance of the involvement of civil society groups in the OMC, see the Lisbon European Council of 23 and 24 March 2000 Presidency conclusions, http://www.consilium.europa.eu/ueDocs/cms_Data/docs/pressData/en/ec/00100-r1.en0. htm, point 38 and the Brussels European Council of 22 and 23 March 2005, http://www.consil ium.europa.eu/ueDocs/cms_Data/docs/pressData/en/ec/84335.pdf, point 6.

tion to these interest groups, an estimated 350 large firms, 200 regions and about 350 organisations supplying commercial public affairs services are actively engaged in EU politics (Coen, 2007, p. 334 and European Parliament (2003)). The groups include both specialised interest groups that advocate particular societal causes and the so-called 'diffuse' interest groups, which promote broader causes (e.g. non-governmental environmental protection organisations) in the civil dialogue.[11] Furthermore, not only European-level interest groups are consulted, but also regional and national ones (Commission of the European Communities, 7/2005, p. 25), such as those taking part in the European Citizens' Panels established in some member states to discuss specific policy areas (the Panels will supposedly be organised at the inter-regional level in the future) (Commission of the European Communities, 10/2005, pp. 9, 18).

The Commission consults interest groups when formulating policies; it also seeks their opinions when it starts to draw up legislative initiatives or OMC guidelines. These consultations enable the Commission to solicit input from interested parties before anything is set in stone. They also allow the Commission to assess the potential impact of any legislation or policy co-ordination objective (Christiansen et al., 2003, p. 9). The consultation process is supposed to help the Commission and the other EU-level institutions to arbitrate between competing claims and priorities and to aid in the development of a longer-term policy perspective. The consultations provide the Commission with the information, data, statistics, knowledge and expertise necessary for discharging its responsibility to initiate law in the European Union. Since its in-house expertise is limited, information provided by private actors helps the Commission to offset the informational advantage of national officials (Christiansen et al., 2003, p. 9).

The Commission considers the consultations beneficial for the legislative drafting process because they help to ensure that its proposals are sound. At the same time, it regards itself as legally bound to conduct them (Commission of the European Communities, 12/2002a, p. 3). The Commission's duty to consult widely flows from Protocol No. 7 on the application of the principles of subsidiarity and proportionality. The Protocol was appended to the Amsterdam Treaty, which stipulates that 'the Commission should [...] consult widely before proposing legislation and, wherever appropriate, publish consultation documents.'

---

11   In the Commission's view, civil society includes the following groups: trade unions and employers' organisations (social partners); organisations representing social and economic players that are not social partners in the strict sense of the term (for instance, consumer organisations); non-governmental organisations that bring people together in a common cause, such as environmental organisations, human rights organisations, charities; professional associations; grass roots organisations and organisations that involve citizens in local and municipal life with a particular contribution from churches and religious communities (Commission of European Communities, 7/2001, 14). The Commission has adopted the Economic and Social Committee's definition of civil society (Economic and Social Committee (11/1999).

4.4. Eligibility Requirements for the Participation of Interest Groups in EU Consultations

The civil dialogue was only recently formalised,[12] although informal consultations with interest groups have figured regularly in the Commission's pre-drafting phase of the legislative preparation process from the very beginning of European integration (Sargenet, 1985, p. 236). The Commission endorsed a policy of unrestricted access to its officials by interest groups and declined to introduce any system of licensing or particular criteria for these groups (Commission of the European Communities, 12/1992). This 'relaxed' approach changed after the publication of the Commission's White Paper on governance in 2001, in which it called for the establishment of a stable framework to facilitate a more co-ordinated and structured dialogue with civic associations (Commission of the European Communities, 7/2001, p. 17; European Commission, 2002, p. 74). The Commission's open access policy towards interest groups was later modified on the grounds that 'with better involvement comes greater responsibility' (Commission of European Communities, 7/2001, pp. 15, 17, 18).

The Commission formalised the civil dialogue process by introducing minimum standards for potential consultees and general principles for the consultation process; these were set out in its communiqué entitled 'Towards a reinforced culture of consultation and dialogue: General principles and minimum standards for consultation of interested parties by the Commission' (Commission of the European Communities, 12/2002a). They have been in force since January 2003.[13]

The Commission enumerates the following general principles for the consultation process: participation, openness, accountability, effectiveness and coherence (ibid., pp. 16–18). It provides a very brief indication of the content of these principles. The following five minimum standards slightly concretise the requirements vis-à-vis the Commission's conduct in the consultation process: A) *Clear content of the consultation process*: all communications relating to consultation should be clear and concise, and should include all necessary information to facilitate responses; B) *Consultation target groups*: when defining the target group(s) in a consultation process, the Commission should ensure that the relevant parties have an opportunity to express their opinions; C) *Publications*: the Commission should ensure adequate awareness-raising publicity and adapt its communication channels to meet the needs of all target audiences. Without excluding other communication tools, open public consultations should be

---

12 For an extensive account of the civil dialogue prior to its codification, see Obradovic (2006, 261–327)

13 From the beginning of 2003, when the minimum standards entered into force, until 1 May 2007, the Commission had completed approximately 455 major proposals to which the minimum standards applied: 60 in 2003, 95 in 2004, 106 in 2005, 129 in 2006 and 65 in the first 4 months of 2007 (see the contribution of Obradovic and Damsma in this volume).

published on the Internet and announced at the 'single access point';[14] D) *Time limits for participation*: the Commission should provide sufficient time for participants to plan and respond to invitations and written contributions. The Commission should allow at least 8 weeks for responses to written public consultations and 20 working days' notice for meetings; and E) *Acknowledgement and feedback*: the receipt of contributions should be acknowledged. The results of open public consultations are supposed to be displayed on websites linked to the single access point (ibid., pp. 19–22). In the following, we will refer to the whole set of requirements as 'the principles and standards' or the 'minimum standards'. As a result of the application of these minimum standards, civil society participation in EU governance is contingent upon the interest groups' compliance with principles of good governance[15]: representativeness, accountability and transparency.

The Commission claims that the principles and standards should ensure that all parties affected by a given proposal can become more involved, and on a more equal footing, in the process of consultations preceding EU legislation formulation. They are also meant to enhance the transparency of the parties' involvement and to encourage all of the Commission's departments to adopt a consistent approach to the consultation process (Commission of the European Communities, 2004, p. 15; Commission of the European Communities, 6/2002a, p. 6).

The principles and standards should provide the parties concerned with an opportunity to express their opinions. According to the Commission, the purpose of introducing the five minimum standards is to provide the legislator with some degree of 'quality assurance' and to ensure the equitable treatment of the various parties engaging in the consultations leading up to major political proposals. The implementation of the minimum standards is also geared to systematise and rationalise the wide range of consultation practices and procedures, and to guarantee the feasibility and effectiveness of the operational process. It is further meant to ensure the transparency of the consultation from both the interest groups' and legislator's points of view. A third objective of the implementation is to demonstrate accountability vis-à-vis the bodies or players consulted, by making public, as far as possible, the results of the consultations (Commission of the European Communities, 6/2002b, p. 3). The Commission wants to assure that all parties involved in the consultation are properly addressed and that an adequate balance is struck between them, depending on their social or economic character, size, specific target groups and country of origin (Commission of

---

14   See http://europa.eu.int/yourvoice/consultations/index_en.htm
15   The concept of good governance entails understanding that public decision-making and implementation thereof should be conducted in accordance with particular standards comprising an efficient, open, accountable and audited public service (Harlow, 2005, 59). See also the Commission's definition of the concept of good governance in Commission of European Communities, 7/2001, 8.

the European Communities, 12/2002a, pp. 19–20). However, this has not in fact been achieved. Business groups still remain the prime interlocutor of the most influential directorate generals of the Commission (Fazi and Smith, 2006, p. 7) and the participation levels of civil associations from East and Central European countries in the Commission's consultations is very low.[16]

The minimum standards are systematically applied to all major policy initiatives.[17] They should be considered a tool created by the Commission for the purpose of operationalising its new commitment to introduce an impact assessment analysis for its initiatives in all major EU policy areas. The economic, social and environmental impacts of the proposals are all taken into consideration in the analysis (Commission of the European Communities, 6/2002c and 6/2002a). The Commission has had considerable experience in single-sector type impact assessments, including the business, trade, environment, health and employment sectors. These impact assessments were, however, often partial in that they only examined certain sets of effects. This incomplete approach has made it difficult for policymakers to assess trade-offs and compare different scenarios when deciding on a specific course of action. The newly adopted Extensive Impact Assessment (ExIA) is intended to integrate, reinforce, streamline and gradually replace all of the previously adopted separate impact assessment mechanisms for the Commission's proposals.[18] This strategy provides for all of the major policy proposals listed in its Annual Work Programme[19] to be assessed in terms of their impact upon the widest possible group of potential stakeholders. Addressing the scope of impact will in turn ensure that the assessments do not merely focus on the measures' potential impact on elites or those who are active in the process of consultation. The impact assessments should therefore increase the opportunities for associations to learn about new initiatives and influence the outcome of new EU policies and proposals early on in the process.

The first stage of the impact assessment process consists of applying the minimum standards to consultations preceding major Commission or OMC initiatives. The application of the standards should help to identify trade-offs in achieving competing objectives, but it is not a substitute for the political judgement of the EU decision-makers.

The Commission claims that it wishes to maintain an inclusive approach and not erect hurdles or restrict access to the consultation process. In other words, it does not

---

16   See the contribution by Obradovic and Damsma in this volume.
17   The largest number of consultations related up to now have included agriculture and fisheries; employment and social policy; external relations; industry; justice and home affairs; transport and energy; environment; economic policy; information society and health; and consumer protection (Commission of the European Communities, 2004, 3)
18   Impact assessment website http://ec.europa.eu/governance/impact/index_en.htm. See also the latest impact assessment guidelines in Commission of the European Communities 4/2005.
19   Work programme website http://ec.europa.eu/atwork/programmes/index_en.htm

intend to create new bureaucratic obstacles that would limit the number of partici-pants in the consultation process. Indeed, it provides assurances that 'every individual citizen, enterprise or association will continue to be able to provide the Commission with input (Commission of the European Communities, 12/2002a, p. 11). Its objective is to achieve a balance between open and focused, targeted consultation of those with a pertinent interest.

In the Commission's view, the minimum standards should improve the repre-sentativeness of civil society organisations and structure their debate with EU insti-tutions. The standards are intended to reduce the risk of policy-makers listening to only one side of an argument or granting particular groups privileged access (Com-mission of the European Communities, 7/2001). However, these standards do not con-tain the accreditation system requested by some NGOs (Platform of European Social NGOs, 1999). The Commission has always rejected an official consultative status for NGOs along the lines of the existing accreditation systems in the United Nations, the Council of Europe or the European Parliament. The proposals are therefore put on the Internet for comments.[20] Although this approach has widened the scope of groups consulted, it has eroded traditional bi-lateral discussions between the Commission and certain interest groups.

The idea of drawing up more extensive partnership agreements with certain organised civil society sectors was considered but eventually rejected by the Com-mission (Commission of the European Communities, 12/2002b, p. 11; Commission of the European Communities, 2004, p. 5). These partnership agreements would have involved more stringent criteria than the minimum standards and would have encour-aged civil society organisations to rationalise their internal structure, give guarantees of openness and representativeness, and to demonstrate their ability to relay infor-mation or to conduct debates within the member states (Commission of the Euro-pean Communities, 7/2001, p. 17). On the Commission's part, partnership arrange-ments would have entailed a commitment to additional consultations. In the end, the concept failed to gain momentum, partly because the European Parliament opposed the partnerships and due to the concern that a *de facto* regime of privileged associ-ations would have emerged. The Commission does, however, make an exception to its policy of refraining from entering into special partnership agreements with inter-est groups: The relations between the Humanitarian Aid Office of the Commission (ECHO) and around 200 non-governmental organisations with which it co-operates are governed by the Framework Partnership Agreements (FPAs). The purpose of the FPAs is to define the roles, responsibilities, and legally binding rights and obligations

---

20   Open web consultations can be viewed at http://europa.eu.int/yourvoice/consultations/in dex/
en.htm

of the ECHO and the relevant NGOs in the implementation of humanitarian operations financed by the European Union.[21]

The codification of standards for conducting the civil dialogue was accompanied
by the establishment of the CONECCS database (Consultation, European Commission and Civil Society), which offers the general public information on European-level
civil society organisations as well as on the committees and other consultative bodies the Commission uses when consulting organised civil society in an either informal
or structured manner.[22] The database helps the Commission's Directorate Generals to
find the relevant discussion partners for policy proposals. At present, it lists more than
800 organisations. The Commission constructed this database as a follow-up to the
directory on European non-profit associations published in 1996 (European Commission, 1996). However, in addition to NGOs, it also lists private interest organisations,
including the World Federation of Advertisers, the European Demolition Associations
and the Banking Federation of the European Union. CONECCS became fully operational in June 2002. The index, which is compiled on a voluntary basis, is intended to
serve as an information source and not as an instrument for securing exclusive access
to the Commission's consultative process. Although it forms a part of the organised
consultative process based on the minimum standards, it does not represent a system for accrediting certain organisations by the Commission. It merely aims to provide an overview of the advisory committees set up by the Commission and a non-ex-
haustive list of organisations active at the European level. There is thus no substantive
incentive for a civil society organisation to register with the database despite the relative ease (i.e. lack of eligibility requirements) of doing so. By the same token, there
is no penalty for failing to do so. The lack of an enforcement mechanism means that
the information provided is frequently out of date.

4.5. Legal Status of the Interest Groups' Entitlements in EU
     Consultation

The introduction of minimum standards does not confer any legally enforceable participatory rights upon civil dialogue protagonists. The objective of the civil dialogue
is not to establish procedural rights that are subject to judicial control and review
(European Commission, 2002, p. 73). The Commission insists that 'a legally-binding
approach to consultation is to be avoided, for two reasons: First, a clear dividing line
must be drawn between consultations launched on the Commission's own initiative prior to the adoption of a proposal, and the subsequent formalised and compulsory decision-making process according to the Treaties. Second, a situation must be

---

21   http://europa.eu.int/comm/echo/partners/fpa_ngos_en.htm
22   http://europe.eu.int/comm/civil_society/coneccs

avoided in which a Commission proposal could be challenged in the courts on the grounds of alleged lack of consultation of interested parties. Such an over-legalistic approach would be incompatible with the need for timely delivery of policy, and with the expectations of the citizens that the European institutions should deliver on substance rather than concentrate on procedures' (Commission of the European Communities, 12/2002a, p. 10). Consequently, an association that feels it has received unsatisfactory feedback regarding its contribution to an EU consultation is not entitled to a judicial review. Some scholars argue that the lack of an appeal mechanism vis-à-vis the quality of feedback strips the consultation process of its credibility; it ends up being a rubber stamp for decisions that actually depend on other parameters (Schutter, 2002, p. 214). The fact that the minimum standards have been adopted in the form of a communication – an atypical instrument that is not provided for in the Treaty – does not mean they are immune to judicial review. The case law of the Court of Justice demonstrates that communications producing legal effects can be challenged in legal proceedings.[23] Whether the minimum standards have legal effects is another matter.

Although interested parties are not entitled to challenge the Commission in court for non-compliance with the minimum standards, they can complain to the European Ombudsman. Empowered by Article 195 EC to investigate complaints from EU citizens concerning instances of maladministration in EU institutions, this officer is nevertheless not authorised to pass legally binding judgements. The Ombudsman regards any failure of the Commission to comply with the minimum standards for consultations as maladministration (European Ombudsman, 2005, Paragraph 3.8). It notes that the standards are intended to ensure equitable treatment for all participants in EU consultations. To this end, the Commission is required to give each party's input due weight in the decision it takes. The European Code of Good Administrative Behaviour, whose infringement constitutes the practice of maladministration, upholds those principles.[24]

The consultation process provides interested parties with an opportunity to be heard; the Commission thus views the consultations as 'the listening process' (Commission of the European Communities, 10/2005, p. 9; 7/2005, p. 4). The minimum standards do not, however, require the Commission to issue individual invitations to all interested civil society organisations to participate in EU consultations, nor do they obligate the Commission to provide the groups with feedback on how their contributions and

---

23   Case C-366/88, *France v Commission* [1990] ECR-I-3571,, Case C-303/90 *France v Commission* [1991] ECR I-5315, Case C-325/91 *France v Commission* [1993] ECR I-3283, Case C-57/95 *France v Commission* [1997] ECR I-1627. See also Lefevre 2004.

24   Articles 5 (Absence of discrimination) and 9 (Objectivity) of the European Code of Good Administrative Behaviour (2005), Luxembourg: Office for Official Publications of the European Communities. See also Cases T-70/99, *Alpharma Inc. v Council*, 2002 ECR II-03495, paragraph 140.

opinions affected the eventual policy decision.[25] This is confirmed by the Ombudsman, who finds that the publication of the results of EU consultations with civil groups on the web portal 'Your Voice in Europe' adequately fulfils the minimum standard C on publications (European Ombudsman, 2005, Paragraphs 3.12, 3.13).

A real dialogue would imply an organisation's right to receive a reasoned response to the suggestions it puts forward, the sheer number of participants renders the provision of individual feedback impossible (Schutter, 2002, p. 211). The participants in the civil dialogue are thus not entitled to receive feedback, and the minimum standards do not provide for an effective follow-up procedure. Paradoxically, the standards oblige the Commission to react appropriately to comments received, but do not confer any rights upon the parties that contributed those comments. The commission is simply not required to disclose the extent to which the comments shaped the relevant EU policy. The Commission finds the idea of providing feedback on an individual basis ('feedback statements') incompatible with the efficiency requirement in the decision-making process (Commission of the European Communities, 12/2002a, p. 12). In its more recent documents, however, the Commission acknowledges the necessity 'to draw more systematically on feedback from citizens' (Commission of the European Communities, 7/2005, p. 8). Regarding the provision of feedback, the minimum standards merely obligate the Commission to issue an explanatory memorandum outlining the results of the consultation and the consideration taken of the stakeholders' contributions as a whole in its final legislative proposal . However, in an analysis of two-thirds of the cases reviewed up to 2004, it was found that precious little was said on why comments were either taken into account or disregarded (Commission of the European Communities, 13/2005, p. 4). Consultation participants therefore had no idea if their comments had had any impact whatsoever on the final policy proposal (Commission of the European Communities, 1/2006, p. 12). For example, the majority of contributions submitted by NGOs in the course of the consultation on the Fundamental Rights Agency were apparently disregarded by the Commission (Fazi and Smith, 2006, p. 48). Recently, the Commission pledged to provide better feedback, including explaining how and to what extent the comments are taken into account. It also acknowledged the need to ensure that a plurality of views and interests are expressed in the consultations (Commission of the European Communities, 1/2007, p. 6). In spite all of this the Commission is of the opinion that the standards for the Commission consultations have been properly and successfully applied by its departments.[26]

---

25   Prior to the publication of the minimum standards, the Commission gave some indication that such feedback should be guaranteed (Commission of the European Communities, 1/2000, 10)

26   The Better Lawmaking reports report on application of the minimum standards for consultation: Better Lawmaking 2006: http://eur-lex.europa.eu/LexUriServ/site/en/com/2007/com 2007_0286en01.pdf; Better Lawmaking 2005: http://eur-lex.europa.eu/LexUriServ/site/en/com/

Further, the minimum standards do not introduce the minimum standards also do not confer any accreditation rights upon civic groups taking part in the civil dialogue. The Commission may seek information and solicit consultations from any source it wishes. It has the authority to determine the eligibility of associations to participate in the civil dialogue and selects them accordingly. These organisations, however, are granted neither a representational monopoly nor accreditation, and in practice, the Commission consults numerous organisations. Interest groups are not officially recognised or licensed by the Commission. In essence, the Commission therefore has a carte blanche to choose which organisations to consult. On account of its virtually unlimited discretion, the Commission has formulated a set of conditions for participation in the civil dialogue consultations.

It must be emphasised that the determination of the groups' eligibility to take part in consultations rests firmly with the Commission. However, because it does not wish to reduce the number of potential participants in the civil dialogue, the Commission does not subject them to a prior eligibility check. Instead, it examines whether the groups meet its requirements at a later stage, i.e. when assessing the relevance or quality of the comments made during the consultation.

4.6. The Scope of Application of the EU Consultation Standards

The scope of application of the criteria for taking part in the civil dialogue is not very well delimited; the exact area of applicability is equally unclear. The minimum standards requirements are applicable exclusively to consultations conducted by the Commission;[27] although some civil groups have asked for the civil dialogue standards to be applied to consultations carried out with other EU institutions (Venables, 2004, p. 158). There is currently no common institutional framework for consultation with interested parties, despite various steps taken in that direction. The Governance White Paper called on the Commission, the European Parliament and the Council to review their

---

2006/com2006_0289en01.pdf; Better Lawmaking 2004: http://europa.eu.int/eur-lex/lex/Lex UriServ/site/en/com/2005/com2005_0098en01.pdf; Better Lawmaking 2003: http://europa. eu.int/eur-lex/en/com/rpt/2003/com2003_0770en01.pdf

27 The European Parliament (EP) has a system of accreditation for those needing frequent access to the institution – defined as five days or more per year (European Parliament, 2005). This system grants physical access to the Parliament. Special passes are issued by the Quaestors and are valid for one year. These passes state the person's name, the name of the firm they work for and the organisation they represent. A lobbyist register is published on the EP website. It is simply an alphabetical list and only provides the name of the badge holder and the organisation he or she represents. No indication is given of the interests being promoted. The European Economic and Social Committee (EESC) recently established a Liaison Group that aims to bring representatives of EU-wide NGOs into the EESC's structure. This group is composed of twenty EESC members and fourteen representatives of civil society organised at the European level, which meet the conditions stipulated by the EESC (European Economic and Social Committee, 2/2004).

practices and contribute to the general reference framework for consultation by 2004 (Commission of the European Communities,7/2001, p. 17). The June 2003 better law-making initiative urges the three institutions to improve the co-ordination of their pre-paratory work and to adopt a common methodology for carrying out impact assess-ments.[28] All three institutions have endorsed the concept of a common approach to impact assessment (Commission of the European Communities, 2/2007, p. 16). None-theless, a standard protocol for consultations has failed to crystallise. One possible hin-drance may be the European Union's institutional structure: it is based upon the prin-ciple of inter-institutional balance, which means that each institution has a degree of autonomy in the regulation of its operational rules (Jacqué, J.P., 2007).

The minimum standards are applicable to the Internet-based consultations under-taken during the first stage of a Commission impact assessment. The Commission con-ducts the assessments whenever it intends to launch a policy initiative or legislative or OMC guideline proposal. The second area of application of the minimum standards concerns the work of the Commission's informal advisory committees for organising an exchange of views with civic associations listed in the CONECCS database. While the Commission clearly states that consultations taking place in the committees estab-lished by the Treaty or EU legislation fall outside the scope of the minimum standards, it indicates that the standards should be applied to the activities of its ad hoc com-mittees (Commission of European Communities, 7/2001, p. 17). At present, the Com-mission runs nearly 700 such committees, which cover a wide range of policies (Euro-pean Commission, 2002, p. 75). Although set up by the Commission, the grounds for their establishment cannot be found in the Treaty or EU legislation. Their composition, activities and impact remain rather opaque. By their very nature, these forums provide privileged access to the Commission policy-shaping process for a limited number of stakeholder organisations. Cars 21, an expert group that consists of Commission offi-cials, chief executive officers and lobbyists from the automobile industry, enjoys priv-ileged access through this channel ((Fazi and Smith, 2006, p. 44).

However, the scope of the application of the eligibility criteria stipulated in the minimum standards is very vague. The reasons for the lack of clarity surrounding their use are the following: (a) the existence of several types of concurrent consultations conducted by the Commission prior to the formulation or adoption of legislative pro-posals; (b) the engagement of the same groups in different types of consultations in the pre-drafting stage of the EC legislative process; (c) the fact that some groups par-ticipate in a different capacity in a variety of the pre-legislation consultations; (d) the fragmentation of consultations throughout policy areas; and (e) the Commission Sec-retariat Generals do not apply the same template for conducting consultations nor do

---

28   Inter-institutional agreement on better law-making, OJ C 321, 31.12.2003, pp. 1-5, points 4 and 30.

they report the consultation outcomes in a uniform manner. For example, the Directorate General of SANCO (Health and Consumer Protection) carries out consultations in accordance with its Scoping Paper, which aims to provide all the necessary information to discuss and launch an initiative in a single document, while the other Directorates General issue no such document in the course of their consultations.

The Commission has established that the minimum standards criteria are not to be deployed in the specific consultation frameworks provided in the Treaty (e.g. consultations within the European Economic and Social Committee, the Committee of Regions, the Article 138 EC social dialogue consultation, the Article 79 EC transport committee, or the Article 113 EC committee) or in other consultative bodies based upon EU legislation.[29] The criteria also do not apply to any consultation required under international conventions,[30] the comitology process,[31] the consultation of experts,[32] the dialogue

---

29 E.g. the Social Protection Committee established by the Council decision of 29 June 2000, setting up a Social Protection Committee, 2000/436/EC, OJ L 172/26, 12.7.2000; or the Article 147 EC Advisory Committee for the European Social Fund operating in accordance with Article 49 of the Council Regulation EC no 1083/2006 of 11 July 2006 laying down general provisions on the European Regional Development Fund, the European Social Fund and the Cohesion Fund and repealing Regulation EC No 1260/1999, Official Journal of the European Union, L 210/25 of 31.7.2006.; or scientific committees in the field of consumer health and food safety set up by the Commission Decision 97/579/EC of 23 July 1997, OJ 1997 L 237, p. 18.

30 For example, the conditions for participation of interested parties, including NGOs, required under Article 8 of the Aarhus Convention (Convention on Access to Information, Public Participation in Decision-Making and Access to Justice in Environmental Matters, http://europa.eu.int/comm/environment/aarhus/index.htm), to which the EU is party, is referred to in Article 9 (2) of the Regulation (EC) No. 1367/2006 of the European Parliament and of the Council of 6 September 2006 on the application of the provisions of the Aarhus Convention on Access to Information, Public Participation in Decision-making and Access to Justice in Environmental Matters to Community institutions and bodies OJ 2006 L 246/13 (EC Environmental Consultations Regulation). On the relationship between the EC Environmental Consultations Regulation and the minimum standards, see Obradovic, 2007, pp. 59-63.

31 The notion of comitology concerns the system of committees composed of member states' representatives that assist the Commission in the execution of its implementing powers under Article 202 EC. See Council Decision 1999/468/EC of 28 June 1999 laying down the procedures for the exercise of implementing powers conferred on the Commission, OJ 1999, L 184/23.

32 This consultation is to be conducted in accordance with the standards laid down in the (Commission of the European Communities, 12/2002c). The register of expert groups to which those guidelines are applicable can be found at http://europa.eu.int/comm/secretariat_gen eral/regexp/index.cfm?lang=EN. It contains details of over 1200 expert groups. The register covers formal bodies established by Commission decisions and informal advisory bodies set up by the Commission services. It provides key information on those groups, such as the lead service in the Commission and the group's tasks as well as the category of participants. The register also contains direct links to the Commission department's website, where more detailed information is available. In addition, since 2005, a web application called the SINAPSE e-Network (Scientific Information for Policy Support in Europe) http://europa.eu.int/sinapse offers Commission services the following communication and information tools for the ad hoc collection of expertise: (1) a library of scientific advice and opinion; (2) a consultation module that allows services to conduct informal scientific consultations, complementing formal advisory processes; (3) an early warning system that the scientific community and other stakeholders can use as a channel for raising awareness on scientific issues that require or could benefit from the attention of

with European and national associations of regional and local governments in the EU (Commission of the European Communities, 12/2003) or the consultations required to be carried out by the member states per European secondary legislation for the purpose of the implementation of the European cohesion policy.[33] The implications of the limitations imposed by the Commission upon the scope of application are quite significant for the further development of the civil dialogue in the Union. The most important consequence concerns the fragmentation and proliferation of the rules governing the consultation of civic groups by Union institutions. The balkanisation of those rules as well as the Commission's lack of a holistic and coherent approach to the selection of collaborators among interested organisations obscures the already Byzantine matrix of the civil dialogue. The codification of the participation of civic groups in EU governance is simply not regulated in an encompassing way.

This proliferation and segmentation of standards guiding the civil dialogue reflects the complexity of the concept itself. The notion of civil dialogue in the EU embraces a wide range of actors (various non-profit interest groups and social partners); it relates to diverse forms of consultative processes (pre-drafting of legislative proposals, such as the consultation held in different policy forums; consultation in committees on Commission proposals that have already been formulated, such as the consultation in the European Economic and Social Committee);[34] and proliferates throughout the different modes of EU governance (e.g. lawmaking and policy co-ordination based upon the OMC). The deployment of the civil dialogue concept in such an extensive and diffuse way leads to compartmentalisation of the EU norms enacted for the purpose of regulating that dialogue. The lack of an operational definition of the notion of the European civil dialogue and its frequent use in dissimilar contexts of EU governance contribute to the mushrooming of participation regulations. There is no coherent set of eligibility criteria for the participation of organisations in the civil dialogue as a whole. Each and every segment of this process is subject to a distinct regime. Not only different types of actors taking part in different forms of consultation (for example, social partners consulted under Article 138 EC and non-profit groups participating in the Social Pol-

---

public authorities; and (4) a 'Yellow Pages' section to quickly identify and contact scientists or scientific organisations with specific expertise. By December 2006, more than 800 European and international scientific organisations were registered, along with 2400 members. Several e-communities have been created, including the European Science Advice Network for Health (EuSANH) (Commission of the European Communities, 2/2007, p. 6).

33   Article 10 of the Council Regulation EC no 1083/2006 of 11 July 2006 laying down general provisions on the European Regional Development Fund, the European Social Fund and the Cohesion Fund and repealing Regulation EC No 1260/1999, Official Journal of the European Union, L 210/25 of 31.7.2006.

34   The European Economic and Social Committee believes that it should play a crucial role in defining and structuring the civil dialogue and become a 'meeting place for organized civil society', an 'essential link' between the European Union and organised civil society and a forum for civil dialogue (European Economic and Social Committee, 2/2004, 8).

icy Forum) but also the same types of actors delivering opinions in the same phase of the same mode of governance are subject to different eligibility criteria. For example, the Commission consultations with environmental interest groups taking part in the Environmental Policy Forum should be governed by the minimum standards. However, the Commission will gather exploratory opinions from the same groups, when required under the international Aarhus Convention on lawmaking requirements in environmental matters, but in accordance with entirely different criteria laid down in the EU documents implementing this convention.[35] The Aarhus Convention requires interest group consultation only in certain areas of environmental decision-making, such as the granting of permits, plans, programmes and policies relating to the environment and the preparation of executive regulations and/or generally applicable legally binding normative instruments (Articles 6, 7 and 8, respectively). The minimum standards are thus applicable to all other environmental matters.

The situation is even more complicated as a result of the entry of the European Economic and Social Committee (EESC) into the pre-drafting stage of the EU legislative process. The EC Treaty provides for the EESC to give its opinion after, rather than before, proposals have been transmitted to the legislature.[36] It does not officially participate in the pre-drafting phase of the EU legislative process, but delivers its opinion on the Commission's proposals ex post facto. Having found that the impact of the Committee's opinion on EU decision-making is thereby minimised (Commission of the European Communities, 7/2001, p. 15) yet convinced that the Committee should become 'an indispensable intermediary between the EU institutions and organised civil society,' the Commission signed a Protocol with the EESC entailing that the Commission would invite the EESC to issue exploratory opinions and rely on the EESC to deepen its relations with organised civil society.[37] The rationale behind this Protocol is to reinforce the EESC's function as an intermediary between the EU institutions and organised civil society. The Protocol provides for the Commission to consult the Committee on certain issues on an exploratory basis prior to drawing up its own proposals, allowing the Committee to play a useful consultative role at an earlier stage in the decision-making process. This means that civil associations organised at the national level and participating in EESC work are consulted prior to the drafting of EU law twice, once in their capacity as EESC members, and again when they take part in the Internet consultations. On the first occasion, their representativeness should be judged against EU rules governing the EESC's activities, and in the second situation, the minimum standards are applicable.

---

35   See above.
36   Article 257 EC.
37   Protocol governing arrangements for co-operation between the European Commission and the Economic and Social Committee, 24 September 2001, CES 1253/2001.

Additional confusion regarding the application of the minimum standards stems from the fact that certain groups take part in both civil and social dialogues in different capacities. For instance, when the Commission consults social partners on the social policy issues within the Article 138 EC consultations, it applies its social dialogue requirements, and when it seeks their opinion on identical issues within the framework of the European Social Forum, the minimum standards apply. However, when the social partners are addressed by the Commission in their capacity as members of a variety of committees set up by EC law operating parallel to the civil dialogue process described above and social dialogue consultations, they are subject to a set of eligibility criteria that differs both from the minimum standards and the social dialogue requirements.[38]

We can therefore conclude that the application of the minimum standards is strictly confined to the pre-drafting stage of legislative proposal formulation and that they are not intended to govern the participation of interest groups in the civil dialogue as a whole. More precisely, those standards are deployed by the Commission in three situations that arise in the pre-legislative consultative process: (1) in the first stage of the Commission's impact assessment analyses of its draft legislative proposals or any initiative it intends to launch (Commission of the European Communities, 12/2002a, p. 15); (2) when the Commission evaluates contributions delivered in response to an Internet-based consultation; and (3) when the Commission seeks advice from its numerous informally set up committees.

The criteria apply only to consultations taking place outside the forums institutionalised by virtue of the Treaty or EU legislation. The organisations to which those requirements should apply are mainly those listed in the CONECCS database, although the criteria that must be met by organisations seeking inclusion in this database differ substantially from those stipulated in the minimum standards as a whole. The CONECCS eligibility criteria are as follows: (1) an organisation must be a non-profit representative body organised at the European level, i.e. with members in three or more EU countries; (2) be active and have expertise in one or more of the policy areas of the Commission's activity; (3) have some degree of formal or institutional existence and a document that sets out its objectives and the way it is to be managed; (4) have authority to speak for its members; (5) operate in an open and accountable manner; and (6) be prepared to provide any reasonable information about itself required by the Commis-

---

38   In principle, the participants of those committees are co-opted from national government committees and national organisations of employers and employees. Three representatives are sent from each member state. Only representatives of trade unions and management serving on the Advisory Committee on Equal Opportunities for Women and Men are not chosen from the national level social partners' organisations, but instead originate from the respective European confederations. For more details, see Smismans (2004, 189–192).

sion, either for publication on the database or in support of its request for inclusion.[39] The main difference between the minimum standards and CONECCS criteria is that whilst only European umbrella organisations can be registered in the database, both national and EU-level associations are allowed to participate in consultations governed by the minimum standards. Similarly, as in the case of the minimum standards, the Commission has reinforced its requirements regarding the accountability and openness of potential consulting partners as well as their capacity to provide input to the Commission. The Commission reserves the right to exclude an organisation from the database if it does not satisfy the stated requirements or to remove any organisation that does not or has ceased to satisfy those requirements. The Commission will not include an organisation that has, as its stated or actually pursued purpose, any activity that is contrary to the purpose or principles of the European Union.

Until recently, it was unclear whether the minimum standards apply to lobbying activities. Originally, it was maintained that the standards should not preclude lobbying (Commission of the European Communities, 12/2002a, p. 13).[40] The Commission has not managed a system of accreditation nor has it run a compulsory register of the organisations it consults. Lobbying with the Commission has been conducted in accordance with the 1992 voluntary and self-regulatory code of conduct, whose standards are not terribly stringent.[41] This code covers the same type of consultations between the Commission and civil society organisations as do the minimum standards. Lobbyists are invited by the Commission to adopt their own codes on the basis of those minimum requirements. Up till now, only two umbrella organisations of European lobbyists have adhered to those minimum requirements and adopted voluntary codes of conduct: the Society of European Affairs Professionals (SEAP)[42] and the European Public Affairs Consultancies Association (EPACA).[43] Those codes are based upon the common core principles selected by those two associations in 2007.[44] The organisations targeted by those codes do not cover the majority of active lobbyists at the

---

39   http://europa.eu.int/comm/civil_society/coneccs/inscription.cfm?CL_en
40   For information on associations involved in lobbying EU institutions, see 'Lobbying in the European Union', (2005), 4th ed., London: Routledge, The Directory of Trade and Professional Associations in the European Union (2004), 6th ed., London: Routledge and Goergen, P. (2006).
41   Commission of the European Communities (1992) 'Communication on an open and structured dialogue between the Commission and special interest groups', OJ C 63, 5.3.1993 and its Annex II: 'Minimum requirements for a code of conduct between the commission and special interest groups'. The main features of these criteria are as follows: (1) lobbyists should act in an honest manner and always declare the interest they represent; (2) they should not disseminate misleading information; (3) they should not offer any form of inducement in order to obtain information or receive referential treatment.
42   http://www.seap.eu.org
43   http://www.epaca.org/code_of_conduct.php
44   Society of European Affairs Professionals (2007) 'SEAP response to the European Commission communication: Follow up to the Green Paper "European Transparency Initiative"', 8 May 2007 (http://www.seap.eu.org/linkdocs/ETI_position_paper.pdf), p. 5 .

EU level, nor have the codes so far addressed the issue of facilitating greater transparency vis-à-vis the general public.

The Commission recently decided to introduce more formal regulation of lobbying and to link it to the aforementioned consultation process with stakeholders governed by the minimum standards. The new Union register of lobby groups is combined with the standard template for Internet consultations. It invites lobbyist and interest groups working to influence decisions taken in European Union institutions to subscribe to the public register. Groups that decline the invitation will not fulfil the criterion of representativeness when the Commission assesses their contributions to its Internet-based consultations (Commission of the European Communities (1/2007).

The CONECCS database will be replaced by the new register of interest representatives in 2008. This change will pose various problems. First of all, the motivation for registration is based upon the criteria for the assessment of interest groups' contributions submitted in the Commission's consultation process. This implies that the eligibility criteria for access to the register must be compatible with the minimum standards. On the other hand, if the CONECCS database is going to be replaced by a new register, the new eligibility criteria must be similar to the existing CONECCS enrolment requirements. This is hardly possible, however, because as we have already explained, the minimum standards criteria differ from those governing inclusion in CONECCS. For example, an association is required to be organised at the European level with members in at least three member states in order to be included in CONECCS. This requirement is not imposed by the minimum standards. Secondly, whilst the CONECCS database is open to non-profit civil society organisations, the minimum standards stipulate that the opinions of both non-profit and for-profit groups should be taken into consideration (depending on the policy area) during the Commission's consultations. For instance, in the consultations carried out by the Commission Directorate General on Competition, the majority of participants are profit-making companies and their associations. Moreover, organisations listed in CONECCS are required to be active and possess expertise in the Commission's policy area(s) as well as capable of providing meaningful input. According to the minimum standards, however, the participants' degree of expertise does not factor into the assessment of their comments. Consequently, it remains unclear how the Commission will replace CONECCS with a new register for lobbyists that is based upon an incentive policy incompatible with the existing criteria for inclusion.

4.7.   The Requirement of Representativeness

The Commission imposes the criterion of representativeness on organisations intending to participate in the civil dialogue, just as it does for social dialogue consultations (Commission of the European Communities, 12/2002a, p. 11). However, it does not elaborate on what representativeness actually means as a criterion for assessing the eligibility of groups taking part in the civil dialogue.[45] The Commission claims that the requirements regarding representativeness vary according to the nature of the responsibilities conferred on the participants. They are limited in the event of a simple consultation, but more binding in instances in which the social partners lay down rules with the potential to become law (Commission of the European Communities, 12/2002a, p. 9). Consequently, the criterion of representativeness as applied in the context of the social dialogue may be inappropriate in the area of the civil dialogue.

In its document on the minimum standards, the Commission never explicitly states that the concept of representativeness should be understood as an organisation's ability to contribute expertise or information to the EU consultation process. This interpretation was put forward by the European Economic and Social Committee (2/2006, points 8.1–8.4) and is one of the conditions that must be fulfilled by European-level groups wishing to gain entry into CONECCS.[46] It is worth mentioning here that in its earlier papers on co-operation with NGOs, the Commission indeed cited an organisation's capacity to advise in a specific field and to work as a catalyst for the exchange of information and opinions between the Commission and the citizens of the country of origin as criteria for the selection of NGOs with which it intended to develop a closer partnership (Commission of the European Communities, 1/2000, p. 11). The Commission also does not base the concept of representativeness of civil society groups on geographic coverage as advocated by the European Economic and Social Committee (2/2006, point 7.2) for some European associations, e.g. the Confederation of European Business UNICE (Greenwood, 2007, 193), or as required of organisations wishing to be included in CONECCS.[47]

Representativeness in the social dialogue is predominantly determined in terms of membership,[48] but this is hardly adequate grounds for assessing the representative-

---

45 The recommendations for defining the criterion of representativeness put forward by the Economic and Social Committee are interesting. The Committee states that 'In order to be eligible, a European organisation must: exist permanently at Community level; provide direct access to its members' expertise and hence rapid and constructive consultation; represent general concerns that tally with the interests of European society; comprise bodies that are recognised at the Member State level as representatives of particular interests; have member organisations in most of the EU Member States; provide for accountability to its members; have authority to represent and act at the European level; be independent and not bound by instructions from outside bodies; and be transparent, especially financially and in its decision-making structures' (European Economic and Social Committee,1/2002, point 4.2.5; European Economic and Social Committee, 2/2006, point 3.1.2).
46 See below.
47 See below
48 Commission of the European Communities (12/1993); Case T-135/96, Union Europeenne de l'Artisanat et des Petites et Moyennes Entreprises (UEAPME) vs. Council, [1998] ECR II-2334, consideration 85. The representativeness of the social partners measures membership density, both of the candidate organisations themselves and of each of their members.

ness of civil dialogue participants. NGOs are almost never representative in terms of membership. There are some highly organised groups, such as the Young European Federalists, that can claim impressive European-wide membership (Goehring, 2002, 123). Meanwhile, the most highly confederated civil interest group, the EU Civil Society Contact Group, comprises the seven biggest European umbrella organisations and encompasses more than 200 organisations (Greenwood, 2007, pp. 120–121). However, these two examples are exceptions to the rule. For the vast majority of NGOs, membership is confined to particular states; for example, Eurofora, which has around 200 citizen members, is largely based on national (in this case Italian) membership.[49] Furthermore, valuable input is often provided by single-issue NGOs that are not necessarily organised at the EU level or by advocacy groups and think tanks that do not have members or representative structures.

An NGO's representativeness cannot be established exclusively in terms of the members for whom it purports to speak. Representativeness must also take stock of these organisations' ability to put forward constructive proposals and to bring specialist knowledge to the process of democratic opinion-forming and decision-making. After all, the objective of the civil dialogue consultation is to provide a range of views on a particular issue as well as information. Therefore, in the case of civil dialogue, representativeness should be gauged more in terms of the range of interests that an actor champions than in terms of membership profile.

Since the social partners are expected to play an important role in the implementation of the EU decisions preceded by the social dialogue consultation, their capacity to do so effectively is a significant measure of their representativeness. The social partners' capacity to implement agreements or legislation is dependent upon their membership; that is why the Commission takes the extensiveness of an association's membership into consideration when it assesses its representativeness. In contrast, the civil dialogue protagonists are not significantly involved in the implementation of EU rules resulting from the decision-making processes. From this perspective, membership cannot be regarded as a decisive attribute of the civil dialogue actors' representativeness either. At the same time, it is very difficult to identify the groups' constituencies with any precision due to the great variety of organisations in any given field.

The organisational structures of many associations are highly unstable, fluid and changeable. For instance, the regulation of the postal service in the 1990s created competition in the sector, resulting in myriad interest groups (Greenwood, 2002, p. 235). Furthermore, almost one-fifth of European-level groups include other European-level organisations within their membership, suggesting some degree of overlapping networks (ibid., p. 243). Recent years have witnessed the growth of collective structures in Europe that are not formal groups, but rather platforms, coalitions and alli-

---

49   See www.sspa.it/sitocde/gruppinteresse

ances (such as the Civil Society Contact Group[50]) linking different and diverse types of interests. These could be groups that comprise other member groups (but not necessarily) and exhibit varying degrees of permanence (Greenwood, 2002, p. 249). Such alliances normally operate with minimal structure; they often consist of ad hoc meetings or phone contacts.

The NGOs' claim that they represent civil society is not easy to validate because there are no established rules concerning their operation. Each sets up its own modus operandi. How independent are NGOs from their donors or funding sources? By which mechanisms do NGOs receive input from the constituencies they are supposed to represent? These questions cannot be answered with a high degree of certainty. Civic groups usually revolve around particular causes, whereas the social partners strive to further the economic interests of their members.

In addition, an NGO may derive its legitimacy not so much from assembling a great number of people, but from picking up an issue that is important to citizens but insufficiently addressed by public institutions. NGOs are groups for, not of, a particular cause, and cannot demonstrate representativeness in the same way that a business association can claim to represent a proportion of the total potential membership constituency (Halpin, 2001, p. 28). A good example is the group SOS VIOL, which supports rape victims: women who have been raped do not necessarily register with associations (Grote, 2003, p. 92). In fact, some interest groups do not purport to represent a constituency from which members are recruited, but show solidarity with the interests of a 'third party' constituency or 'client' group, as in the political prisoners championed by Amnesty International or the Roma supported by the European Roma Rights Centre. The constituencies of these interest groups demonstrate solidarity that simply cannot be organised. Claims to speak for such constituencies are legitimated not by the accountability of leaders to their affiliates, but by epistemic claims – to knowledge, experience or expertise (Greenwood/Darren, 2005, p. 25).

NGOs and Social Movement Organisations (SMOs) point out that civil society increasingly expresses fluidity in the type of formations that represent its values and opinions. New organisations often emerge quickly with strong popular support and then dissolve or change into different organisations just as rapidly. Therefore, an insistence on calculating membership would lead to the exclusion of more transient groups, which are an important part of civil society (Ruzza, 2004, p. 46).

---

50 The Civil Society Contact Group encompasses seven large platforms from the main European civil sectors: The European Social Platform, the Human Rights and Democracy Network (HRDN), the European Women's Lobby (EWL), the Green 10, the European NGO Confederation for Relief and Development (CONCORD), the European Public Health Alliance (EPHA) and the European Forum for the Arts and Heritage (EFAH), plus the European Trade Union Confederation (ETUC), which acts as an observer http://www.act4europe.org.

A question that has not even been broached by the minimum standards is whether only the opinions of the stakeholders, that is, those affected by a specific Commission initiative, should be considered by the Commission, or whether contributions from a wide range of citizens ought to be examined. This is particularly important if we bear in mind examples of draft legislation in which massive public input was solicited, e.g. the chemicals package, Registration, Evaluation and Authorisation of Chemicals (REACH) and Genetically Modified Organisms (GMO) proposals (Venables, 2004, p. 157). However, in other cases, only the stakeholders have been consulted and not civil society at large. For example, the European Citizen Action Service (ECAS) has taken the Commission to task vis-à-vis the consultation on the future of EU structural funds after 2006; extensive debates with regional authorities were undertaken, but NGOs and civil society more generally were barely consulted at all (ibid., p. 158).

It seems that the Commission prefers to listen to the stakeholders rather than to civic interest groups in general. In the minimum standards, the Commission stresses the need to define the target group, i.e. all the relevant parties that must be included in the process, and to be selective in cases 'where access to consultation is limited for practical reasons' (Commission of the European Communities, 12/2002a, p. 11). Regarding the first premise, Standard B stipulates that the consultation process must include those affected by the policy, the parties that will be involved in its implementation and those bodies whose objectives make them an interested party (ibid., p. 19), but not civic groups in general. However, although the Commission mainly tends to consult stakeholders on a particular matter, it nevertheless adopts a wide definition of the term, encompassing not only directly affected groups, but also those indirectly concerned by the issue. It also acknowledges the convenience of including parties possessing expertise, technical knowledge or experience in previous consultations and, where appropriate, non-organised interests (ibid., pp. 19–20).

The difficulties in applying the criterion of representativeness to the civil dialogue organisations have been recognised by the Commission. It emphasises that the issue of representativeness at the European level should not be the sole criterion used in the assessment of the relevance or quality of the organisations' comments. Other factors, such as a group's track record and ability to contribute substantial policy input to the discussion, are equally important. The Commission concedes that not only the opinions from European-level organisations should be taken into consideration, but also those of groups operating at the national, regional and local levels (ibid. pp. 11–12). In other words, the Commission recognises that minority views form an essential dimension of the open discourse on policies. On the other hand, it underscores the importance of gauging how representative views are when taking a political decision following a consultation process (ibid.). Some NGOs, such as the European Citizen Action Service (ECAS), disagree with this approach; they believe that the Commission should assign greater weight to the positions and arguments of civic associations that have members in all or most of the EU countries. So far the Commission has not clarified what constitutes evidence of representativeness or whether the opinions of representative organisations are the only ones that should be taken into account.

4.8. The Requirements of Openness and Accountability

The Commission supplements representativeness with two additional requirements: accountability and transparency. As described above, associations are expected to be able to participate effectively and constructively in the opinion-forming and decision-making processes. The introduction of these two additional criteria reflects the Commission's position that greater involvement brings greater responsibility, as stated in the Governance White Paper. Interest groups' contributions solicited in the consultations should, in the Commission's view, be accessible to the general public. To this end, the Commission plans to refine the rule on how to publish policy submissions received from external stakeholders, as required by the minimum standards (SEC, 12/2005, p. 6). It also intends to step up its monitoring of the interest groups' compliance with the minimum standards requirement of providing information about their structure and functioning. The Commission is keen to improve public scrutiny of the consultation participants (Commission of the European Communities, 1/2007, p. 9).

Consequently, civil society must follow the same principles of good governance (including accountability and openness) that govern the conduct of Union institutions (Commission of European Communities, 7/2001, pp. 15, 17). It is not at all obvious, however, as to why all civil society organisations should be held to the same accountability standards as political organisations, when, as we explained above, they do not perform any policy-forming tasks within the EU (Follesdal, 2003, p. 78).

The Commission maintains that openness and accountability are important guiding principles for organisations seeking to participate in EU policy development. The organisations are required to disclose: (1) which interests they represent and (2) how inclusive that representation is. Interested parties wishing to submit comments on a policy proposal must therefore be ready to furnish the Commission and the public at large with this information (Commission of the European Communities, 12/2002a, p. 17).

To better organise and monitor this information, the Commission decided to establish a register of interest representatives. It is to be launched in spring 2008 and will replace the CONECCS database. Registration will be voluntary. After one year of operation, the Commission will evaluate the system, particularly in terms of participation. The number of registrations will be used to measure the success of the voluntary system.[51] Should too few organisations come on board, compulsory registration and reporting will be considered (ibid). Registrants would then be required to supply the following information: (1) whom they represent; (2) their objectives and goals; (3) how they are funded and by whom. Financial disclosure is one of the register's most important elements. Interest groups will be obligated to declare their funding sources and major clients. This is supposed to ensure that the Commission as well as the public can identify and assess the driving forces behind the organisations' positions and interests. In practice, financial disclosure entails declaring the turnover linked to groups lobbying EU institutions as well as the relative weight per client (for professional consultancies and law firms), the relative share of funding from various sources in relation to total funding (for NGOs, think tanks, etc.) or the cost associated with lobbying (for companies, trade associations, etc.).[52] The purpose of the disclosure per se is not to demonstrate the fiscal independence of particular interest groups from public authorities as a prerequisite for membership (as advocated by the Confederation of European Business UNICE); a great number of EU-level civil interest organisations receive funding from European institutions (Greenwood, 2007, p. 193). The operationalisation of the financial disclosure requirement should be compatible with Union legislation on data protection applicable to its institutions. For the performance of its tasks in the public interest, the Commission may find it necessary to make more data publicly available, as stated in Article 5(a) of Regulation 45/2001.[53] These data could include the information that organisations are supposed to disclose in the proposed register for lobbyists. Publication of this data is in line with the Regulation, provided that lobbyists are duly informed when their data are collected.[54] This requirement is not meant to single out interest groups and NGOs active at the EU level as especially susceptible to fraudulent practice;[55] the requirement is merely a part of the broader

---

51   European Commission Press release MEMO/07/110 The European Transparency Initiative: Frequently asked questions, 21 March 2007, http://europa.eu/rapid/pressReleasesAction.do?reference=MEMO/07/110&format=HTML&aged=0&language=EN&guiLanguage=en

52   The European Commission press release, IP/07/367, 21 March 2007, http://europa.eu/rapid/pressReleasesAction.do?reference=IP/07/367&format=HTML&a...

53   Regulation (EC) No 45/2001 of the European Parliament and of the Council of 18 December 2000 on the protection of individuals with regard to the processing of personal data by the Community institutions and bodies and on the free movement of such data, OJ L8, 12.1.2001, pp. 1-22.

54   See Article 11 of the Regulation. See in particular European Data Protection Supervisor, (EDPS) Case 2006-95, Transparency and data protection: conclusions on releasing further information about lobbyists, 31 August 2006, http://www.edps.europa.eu/EDPSWEB/webdav/site/mySite/shared/Documents/EDPS/Publications/Papers/BackgroundP/06-08-31_transparency_lobbyists_EN.pdf

55   Statistics do not reflect a disproportionate number of fraud cases involving NGOs as compared to other types of organisations. Indeed, out of 3000 enquiries into different sectors benefiting from European funding investigated by OLAF (European Anti-Fraud Office) since 2001 and passed on to the competent authorities for legal prosecution, only 10 concerned NGOs (see Report written by F.M. Partners Limited on behalf of Open Society Institute-Brussels, Concord,

EU initiative to improve the transparency of Union finances.[56] The applicants for the register have to subscribe to a code of conduct per the Commission of the European Communities, 1/2007, p. 5). Observation of the code will be become mandatory for lobbyists wishing to be included in the new register. The Commission will introduce such a code after consulting stakeholders. It plans to review and update the existing 1992 code for lobbyists.

The application of the criteria of openness and accountability is intended to allay concerns about the credibility of the internal governance procedures of interest groups, which are commonly regarded to be insufficiently democratic. The main problem seems to be that the decision-making of interest organisations is left in the hands of key officers, with very little – if any – input from supporters (Sudbery, 2003, p. 94; Warleigh, 2001, p. 623). None of those associations functions as a supporter-run organisation. Decision-making about lobbying or campaigning is heavily centralised and shaped entirely by the relevant officers, not by supporters. The organisations' internal governance is apparently too elitist to allow the grass roots to have a role in shaping policies, campaigns and strategies (Peters, 2004, p. 61); NGOs supposedly cannot be held accountable to their own membership (ibid). Supporters play no formal role in the decision-making process and their input vis-à-vis the organisations' governance is usually minimal (Warleigh, 2001, p. 631). This imbalance leads to clientelism, with the NGOs often undertaking activities about which their supporters know or understand very little, and with which they might disagree. Recently conducted fieldwork studies show that most NGO supporters do not seek to play an active role in the governance of the organisation (ibid., p. 634). Major groups and platforms that regularly submit contributions within the Commission's consultation process have not taken any measures to promote member or supporter participation in the preparation of those submissions (Alonso Vizcaino, 2005, p. 64).[57]

The Platform of European Social NGOs, SOLIDAR, The European Women's Lobby, Striking a Balance. Efficiency, Effectiveness and Accountability. The Impact of the EU Financial Regulation on the Relationship between the European Commission and NGOs, April 2005, http://www.solidar.org/english/pdf/Striking%20a%20Balance%20Final1.pdf

56 Various regulations provide for the annual ex-post publication of beneficiaries of monies received from the Structural Funds (as of 2008) and the Common Agricultural Policy (as of 2009). In the field of structural funds, the responsibility for collecting and publishing data of beneficiaries clearly rests on the member states and the Commission. Regulations governing fisheries stipulate the same requirement. In the area of agriculture, member states are under obligation to publish the list of beneficiaries. The Commission has itself already started publishing information on beneficiaries under the programmes it manages directly at http://ec.europa.eu/grants/beneficiaries_en.htm and beneficiaries of public contracts at http://ec.europa.eu/public_contracts/beneficiaries_en.htm.

57 The study assesses the practices of the following European level NGOs: the Platform of European Social NGOs (Social Platform), the European Environmental Bureau (EEB), the European Youth Forum (EYF), the European Women's Lobby (EWL) and the European Public Health Alliance (EPHA).

The internal governance of European-level interest organisations is even more detached from supporters. Around three-fifths of all European associations are organised as confederations, i.e. associations of national associations, and do not admit individuals as members (Greenwood, 2007, p. 51). This denotes a structural remoteness from the grass roots interests they represent. Again, the accountability of participants in the civil dialogue cannot be defined in terms of a categorical or functional value within the defined competence of an office or institution. It might therefore be more appropriate to think in terms of a 'culture of responsibility' rather than a line of accountability. This approach to accountability implies a willingness to regard others as sharing in a wider group responsibility, as opposed to the traditional definition of accountability, which simply asks to whom one is answerable (see Considine, 2002, pp. 21–40).

The Commission's intention to assess the quality of interest groups' consultation contributions in terms of the compliance of their internal structure with the principles of good governance may well be appropriate when a great number of interest organisations are operating in an undemocratic manner. Nevertheless, many scholars find that this approach encroaches upon the associations' autonomy (Warleight, 2001, pp. 619–639; Schutter, 2002, p. 216; Geyer, 2001, p. 479). The danger is that civil society groups will become subject to the colonising forces of the EU political and economic systems, both in terms of their organisational forms and their rationalities, which would undermine the structures and values associated with civil society. The European civil sector would thus become governmentalised by means of altering its organisational forms and its rationalities in order to increase its chances of influencing EU governance (Armstrong, 2002, p. 109). The acuteness of this issue is evident if we bear in mind that all participants in the social dialogue have undergone internal organisational reforms (ETUC, 1991; UNICE, 1992; CEEP, 1994; Obradovic, 1995, p. 269), including the introduction of the mandate for negotiation[58] and the removal of requirements for unanimity. They have done so in order to adjust their structures to the social dialogue requirements and improve their abilities to conclude Europe-wide agreements. Similarly, the eligibility and suitability criteria deployed for the selection of NGOs intending to enter into the Framework Partnership Agreements with the Commission's Humanitarian Aid Office (ECHO) that are applicable to the humanitarian operations sponsored by the EU also impose very strict rules with respect to internal organisations.[59] The criteria

---

58 Nevertheless, none of those organisations enjoys a general bargaining mandate; rather, all must seek the agreement of their members afresh each time in order to enter negotiations, i.e. on an issue-by-issue basis. In addition, any agreement concluded through the social dialogue procedure has to be rubber-stamped by all national affiliates.

59 The selection criteria that ECHO applies in order to determine the eligibility of the organisations intending to enter into this partnership are guided by three EC regulations on humanitarian aid; see http://europa.eu.int/comm/echo/partners/selection_en.htm.

include two years of obligatory external audits and specific requirements with respect to the applicants' administrative, financial and operational capacity.

The Commission might try to interfere in the internal structure of interest organisations at some point. It claims to fully respect the autonomy of outside organisations. On the other hand, for the consultation process to be meaningful and credible, it is essential to spell out who participates. By frequently emphasising accountability and autonomy, the Commission seems to assume that the two concepts can be combined (Communication of the European Commission, 1/2000, p. 5), but they in fact differ in many ways and are not easily reconcilable. The paradox has prompted some scholars to conclude that the Commission's approach essentially results in the selection of a limited number of Brussels-based associations with sufficient capacity but forgoes a golden opportunity to harness the energy of a wider range of interest organisations. Many of these civic groups are not necessarily demanding strict participation rights as such but merely wish to engage in an open and lively public debate in which different points of view can be heard (Curtin/Dekker, 2005, p. 17).

4.9. Suggestions for the Operationalisation of the EU Consultation Standards: Statute for a European Association (EA)

The main problem concerning the application of the criteria discussed above lies in the fact that they remain abstract, vague and unintelligible; consequently, it is nearly impossible to determine which organisations actually fulfil them. The Commission has not yet issued any instructions as to how those criteria should be operationalised for the purpose of their application. However, some indications can be found in its proposal for the Statute for a European Association, which, although withdrawn, nevertheless provides helpful clues for interpreting the EU consultation standards developed by the Commission.

The Statute for a European Association (EA) is a part of the general initiative to regulate the establishment of interest associations at the European level. The initiative was launched in 1993, at the same time as proposals for the creation of a European company statute and the statute for a European co-operative society (Commission of the European Communities, 8/1993). Council working groups have amended the Commission's proposal for the EA statute on several occasions.[60] The Regulation on the European Company (SE) and European Co-operative Society Regulation were adopted in 2001 and 2003, respectively.[61] Recognising the need for parallel instru-

---

60 For the latest version, see Council of the European Union, Amended proposal for a Council Regulation (EEC) on the statute for a European Association, 17 March 2003, Council document 6873/03.
61 The Council Regulation (EC) 2157/2001, establishing the legal form of the European Company (SE) according to the legal principles of the public limited liability company, OJ L 294/1, 10.11.2001

ments, the Commission tried to promote the discussion on the draft proposal for an EA in the Council working groups on Company Law, but without success. The lack of interest in adopting an instrument of this sort for associations seems to be rooted in the fact that contrary to shareholder companies and co-operatives, non-profit entities have relatively few cross-border activities and their economic role is rather limited in certain countries. The Commission finally decided in 2005 to withdraw the proposal for a Statute for a European Association.[62]

4.10. The Concept of Representativeness in the EA Statute

The EA statute embodied a concept of representativeness relating to the requirements that an EA be formed by natural and legal persons operating in two or more member states (Article 3) for non-profit-making purposes and that it pursue activities either in the general interest or in order to promote the trade, professional or other interests of its members in the most diverse areas (provided that these activities are compatible with the EU's objectives and the public interest (Article 1)). Non-profit status requires that surpluses and assets be devoted exclusively to the pursuit of the organisation's objectives and may not be divided amongst the members. An almost identical interpretation of these criteria is reproduced in the proposal for the Statute for a European Foundation drawn up by the European Foundation Centre on the recommendation of the High Level Group of Company Law Experts. The proposal was set up by the Commission in 2003 in order to adapt the rule for the establishment of an EA to the particular circumstances, features and characteristics of foundations (European Foundation Centre, 1/2005). The conditions concerning compatibility with the EU/public interest objectives can also be found in other EU documents that prescribe the standards to be met by other social groups taking part in European governance, such as transnational parties.[63]

4.11. Accountability and Transparency in the EA Statute

The good governance standards concerning internal organisation and the capacity to enter into commitments with third parties emanated from the principles of accountability and transparency and occupy prominent roles in the EA statute. The statute pre-

---

and The Council Regulation (EC) 14357/2003 establishing the legal form of the European Cooperative, OJ L 207/1, 18.8.2003.

62   Commission of the European Communities (9/2005) - The proposal for the EA statute has been withdrawn in spite of the fact that the Commission foresaw its adoption in its 2003 Action Plan for Company Law and Corporate Governance (European Commission, 5/2003, 22).

63   Regulation 2004/2003 of the European Parliament and the Council on the regulations governing political parties at European level and the rules regarding their funding, OJ L 297/1, 15.11.2003, Article 3(c).

scribes the internal organisation principles (internal accountability) of the EA in detail, including statute format (Article 4); the structure of organs; rules for guiding, conveying and conducting the meetings; voting procedures; etc. (Articles 28–38). Those rules are tailored to the principles of democratic structure and control, and require the allocation of any surpluses and assets to the objectives of the associations. The association's specific legal form is not requested, however. The internal organisational standards include the principle of the primacy of the individual – reflected in the specific rules on membership, resignation and expulsion, where the 'one man, one vote' rule is laid down and the right to vote is vested in the individual (legal or natural). Members thus do not exercise any rights over the assets of the association. In addition, the involvement of the employees in the work of the EA bodies and organs is clearly prescribed (Commission of the Economic Communities, 8/1993b). Very strict rules on internal organisations developed in the EA statute later came to be applied to NGOs intending to enter into Framework Partnership Agreements with the Commission's Humanitarian Aid Office (ECHO) (ibid.).

The external accountability principles concerning relations with third parties are also set down in Articles 9–12 and Chapter IV. These principles regulate the financial rules of conduct, the auditing of accounts,[64] the production of annual financial statements and reports, and the disclosure of information and documents. They somewhat resemble the financial requirements for obtaining EU funding,[65] the accountability and transparency provisions in the Statute for a European Foundation (European Foundation Centre, 1/2005, Articles 13–14) and the Commission's recommendations to member states regarding a code of conduct for non-profit organisations (Commission of the European Communities, 11/2005, pp. 15–16).

4.12. The Relevance of the EA Statute for the Interpretation of the EU Consultation Requirements

Are the requirements of representativeness, accountability and transparency as set down in the EA statute relevant eligibility criteria for interest groups seeking to participate in EU consultations? The following reasons may initially cast some doubts:

- the proposal for the EA statute was ultimately withdrawn;

---

64 This is to be done in conformity with the Directive 2003/51 EC of the European Parliament and of the Council of 18 June 2003 amending Directives 78/660/EEC, 83/349/EEC, 86/635/EEC and 91/674/EEC on the annual and consolidated accounts of certain types of companies, banks and other financial institutions and insurance undertakings, OJ L 178/16, 17.7.2003, where appropriate.

65 Council Regulation Commission Regulation (EC, Euratom) No 478/2007 of 23 April 2007 amending Regulation (EC, Euratom) No 2342/2002 laying down detailed rules for the implementation of Council Regulation (EC, Euratom) No 1605/2002 on the Financial Regulation applicable to the general budget of the European Communities, OJ L 111, 28.4.2007, pp. 13–45).

- even if it had been adopted, it would have been an optional and supplemental legal form that interest groups active in more than one EU member state might have wanted to use, rather than incorporation under the national law of particular member state; and
- the EA statute's revelations on those principles remain insufficiently clear and precise.

Those arguments do carry some weight, but they cannot be unreservedly accepted. Although the EU institutions failed to adopt the EA statute, its principles of good governance did not become obsolete for regulating interest representation in Europe. Most of them resurfaced in the Commission's recommendations to member states on establishing a code of conduct for non-profit organisations, which is intended to establish 'common general minimum transparency standards for non-profit organisations (NPOs) in the European Union' (ibid., p. 15). Although those recommendations were adopted within the framework of the EU's fight against the misuse of NPOs for terrorist financing and other criminal purposes, they in fact introduce a comprehensive system for the regulation of non-profit sector activities in general.

Since all European or national level interest associations eligible to participate in EU consultations and subject to the criteria for evaluating their contributions to that process are established in accordance with the national rules for the incorporation of non-profit associations,[66] they will be bound by the code of conduct recommended by the Commission to be used by the member states. Given that the Commission established the code in response to requests from the EU member state governments and international bodies,[67] we can safely assume that the code will be enforced in all member states. In its recommendations, the Commission expressly obliges the member states to not only effectively ensure the compliance of non-profit organisations with this code, but to also actively and effectively co-operate with each other for the purpose of promoting the acceptance of those standards by non-profit organisations across Europe (Commission of the European Communities, 11/2005, pp. 12–13). In addition, while the EA statute would have applied to a limited number of non-profit associations involved in cross-border activities in the EU, the recommendations concern a much wider range of non-profit organisations. For the purpose of this recommended code of conduct, 'NPOs are deemed to be organisations, legal persons, or legal arrange-

---

66 Currently, European business associations are established the under national laws of member states for the incorporation of non-profit associations, most commonly under the Belgium law of 2 May 2002 (Lonting, 2003).

67 Declaration on combating terrorism of 25 March 2004 of the European Council, p. 14, http://ue.eu.int/uedocs/cms_data/docs/pressdata/en/ec/79637.pdf; The Council declaration on the EU response to the London bombing of 13 July 2005 as cited in (Commission of the European communities, 11/2005, 9); The EU Financial Action Task Force in its Special Recommendation VIII; G8 Finance Ministers, Finance Ministers' Statement of Deauville, 17 May 2003; G8 Justice and Home Affairs Ministers (7/2005, 1).

ments whose principal purpose is to engage in the raising and/or disbursing of funds for charitable, religious, cultural, educational, social or fraternal purposes, or for the carrying out of other types of good works' (ibid., p. 12).

The Commission's recommendations for introducing the code of conduct for non-profit organisations almost replicate the EA requirements stipulating that organisations must declare their mission/purpose, objectives, policies and priorities and use their resources for those purposes only (ibid., p. 15). The recommendations also contain the EA requirement for registration of non-profit associations at the national or regional level. The Commission's registration system obliges NGOs to declare their name, acronym, address of the registered office, telephone/fax number, website address and record of previous addresses and changes thereof. A particular public body (or possibly a self-regulatory) should have oversight of the non-profit sector in the member states, similar to the entity described in the EA statute (ibid., p. 12). In provisions identical to those of the EA, non-profit organisations operating in the member states should include in their registration documents a description of the NGO's organisational and decision-making structure, reflecting the size of the organisation and indicating the internal financial control system. The recommendations also prescribe particular rules for financial operations, audit and disclosure in financial matters; these rules are identical to those in the EA statute (ibid.). The disclosure rule in financial reporting also features very prominently in the Commission's recent initiative to introduce the register of interest representatives. Moreover, the recommendations also foresee the possibility of introducing of 'labels' or 'seals of approval' to be granted by public or private monitoring bodies or non-profit umbrella organisations to associations adopting the enhanced transparency and accountability measures (Commission of the European communities, 11/2005, p. 13). The promotion of the award of a 'label' for associations complying with transparency and accountability standards stipulated in the Commission's recommended code of conduct has the effect of actually extending the EA statute requirements to all non-profit organisations operating in the member states of the European Union.

In addition, the conditions for the incorporation and registration of associations stipulated in the EA statute are practically replicated in the Regulation Commission's proposal for criteria for the recognition of entities entitled to challenge European environmental law on the EU or national level for the purpose of protecting their consultation rights,[68] in the list of eligibility requirements for submitting a request for funding under the Community programme promoting environmental NGOs,[69] in the list

---

68 Article 12 of (Commission of the European Communities, 10/2003) and Articles 7 and 10 of (European Parliament and the Council, 5/2003)
69 Decision No 466/2002/EC of the European Parliament and the Council of 1 March 2002 laying down a Community action programme promoting non-governmental organisations primarily active in the field of environmental protection, OJ 2002 L 75/1, 16.3.2002, Article 6.

of requirements to be met by NGOs for the Framework Partnership Agreement with ECHO and most importantly, in the list of requirements to be fulfilled by civil groups wishing to enter the newly established register of interest representatives in the European Union that we discussed earlier.

4.13. Conclusions

The era of the open access policy for interest associations intending to take part in the EU consultations launched by the Commission seems to be coming to an end. In recent years, the Commission has adopted various standards and requirements that organisations wishing to participate in EU consultations should meet, based on certain principles of good governance: representativeness, accountability and transparency.[70]

However, in its documents on EU consultation standards, the Commission does not provide sufficient operational instructions for their application. The proposed, but not adopted, Statute for a European Association prescribes rules for the establishment of European-level associations that more or less replicate, in certain details, the good governance standards for participation in EU consultations. Consequently, the EA statute proposal may provide an additional and valuable source for the operationalisation of EU consultation requirements. Although the EA rules were ultimately not adopted, nearly all of them have been included in the Commission's recommendations to member states for introducing a code of conduct for non-profit associations (intended to promote transparency and accountability). To some extent, the rules have also resurfaced in the newly introduced register of interest representatives, which calls for stricter control of the financial operations of NPOs. Irrespective of the fact that these documents cannot be classified as legally binding rules, they nevertheless strongly encourage member states to ensure the application of the principles of good governance. In all of these documents, the Commission has announced its intention to foster and facilitate the compliance of non-profit associations with those principles by, for example, introducing the award of a special label to groups that comply with the good governance requirements. An NPO receiving the label would probably be regarded by the Commission as fulfilling the EU consultation requirements, and their contributions to consultations would thus bear more weight than submissions from organisations lacking the label or that have not joined the register of interest representatives. This is even more probable if we consider the impracticality of carrying out

---

70   Vice President of the European Commission, Siim Kallas, states that 'organisations, groups or persons in the ambit of European institutions which offer advice, represent clients, provide data or defend public causes should also be accountable. People [should be] allowed to know who they are, what they do and what they stand for' – Speech of Vice President of the European Commission (Kallas, 3/2005).

eligibility tests for each and every association contributing to each and every consultation launched by the Commission.

The stipulation of minimum standards for participation in EU consultations, the introduction of the register of interest representatives and the adoption of the recommendations for member states to introduce a code of conduct for the non-profit sector undoubtedly push the relationship between the Commission and NPOs towards greater formalisation and regulation (Commission of the European Communities, 1/2007, p. 2; Commission of the European communities, 11/2005, p. 10). The Commission clearly tries to strike an appropriate balance between statutory regulation and self-regulation for the non-profit sector in all of its documents, respect the principle of freedom of association and not hinder access to the EU policy process, (Commission of the European Communities, 12/2002a, p. 13; Commission of the European Communities, 1/2007, pp. 4, 6; Commission of the European communities, 11/2005, pp. 10, 13). However, our analysis clearly shows that in the future, NPOs will be expected to restructure themselves in order to meet the good governance requirements; they must in fact do so if they want their views to be taken into account in the drafting of European legislation or other co-ordinative acts.

The consequences of the adoption of such a corporatist approach for the ongoing development of the consultation process between EU organs and interest associations have yet to be examined. At present, we can merely conclude that on the one hand, subjecting the organisations to the good governance principles will undoubtedly contribute to the credibility of their submissions to the consultations. On the other hand, the policy will simultaneously create additional burdens for associations and possibly discourage them from engaging in debate with EU institutions.

References

Alonso Vizcaino, J. M. (Sept. 2005): *European civil society organisations and the principles of participatory democracy: 'Hit-and-miss-policy?'*, Master thesis defended at the International School for Humanities and Social Sciences of the University of Amsterdam.

Armstrong, K. A. (2002): *Rediscovering civil society: the European Union and the White Paper on Governance*, European Law Journal, 8(1), pp. 102–132.

Christiansen, T. et al. (2003): *Informal governance in the European Union: an introduction*, in: Christiansen, T / Piattoni, S. (eds.), Informal Governance in the European Union, Edward Elgar, Cheltenham, pp. 1–22.

Coen, D. (2007): *Empirical and theoretical studies in EU lobbying*, Journal of European Public Policy, 14(3), pp. 333–345.

Commission of the European Communities (12/1992): *Communication from the Commission: 'An open and structured dialogue between the Commission and special interest groups'*, SEC (92) 2272.

Commission of the European Communities (12/1993): *Communication on the application of the Agreement on social policy*, COM(93) 600.

Commission of the European Communities (8/1993a): *Amended proposal for a Council Regulation (EEC) on the statute for a European Association*, OJ C 236/01.

Commission (8/1993b): *Amended proposal for a Council Directive supplementing the statute for a European association with regard to the involvement of employees*, OJ C 236/2.

Commission of the European Communities (1/2000): *Commission discussion paper 'The Commission and non-governmental organisations: Building a stronger partnership'*, COM (2000) 11.

Commission of the European Communities (7/2001): *European governance: White paper*, COM (2001) 428.

Commission of the European Communities (6/2002a): *Communication from the Commission: 'Action plan simplifying and improving the regulatory environment'*, COM (2002) 278.

Commission of the European Communities (6/2002b): *Communication from the Commission: 'European Governance: better lawmaking'*, COM (2002) 275.

Commission of the European Communities (6/2002c): *Communication from the Commission on impact assessment*, COM (2002) 276.

Commission of the European Communities (12/2002a): *Communication from the Commission: 'Towards a reinforced culture of consultation and dialogue – General principles and minimum standards for consultation of interested parties by the Commission'*, COM (2002) 704.

Commission of the European Communities (12/2002b): *Report from the Commission on European Governance*, COM (2002) 705.

Commission of the European Communities (12/2002c): *Communication from the Commission on the collection and use of expertise by the Commission: principles and guidelines: improving the knowledge base for better policies*, COM (2002) 713.

Commission of the European Communities (12/2003): *Communication from the Commission 'Dialogue with associations of regional and local authorities on the formulation of European Union policy'*, COM (2003) 811.

Commission of the European Communities (2004): *Report on European governance (2003–2004)*, SEC (2004) 1153.

Commission of the European Communities (1/2005): *Strategic objectives 2005–2009, Europe 2010: A partnership for European renewal prosperity, solidarity and security: Communication from the President in agreement with Vice-President Wallström*, COM (2005) 12.

Commission of the European Communities (4/2005): *Impact Assessment Guidelines*, 15 June 2005, SEC (2005) 791.

Commission of the European Communities (7/2005): *Communication to the Commission: 'Action plan to improve communicating Europe by the Commission'*, SEC (2005) 985.

Commission of the European Communities (9/2005): *Communication from the Commission to the Council and the European Parliament: 'Outcome of the screening of legislative proposals pending before the Legislator'*, COM (2005) 462.

Commission of the European Communities (10/2005): *Communication from the Commission to the Council, the European Parliament, the European Economic and Social Committee and the Committee of the Regions: 'The Commission's contribution to the period of the reflection and beyond: Plan-D for democracy, dialogue and debate'*, COM (2005) 494.

Commission of the European Communities (11/2005): *Commission Communication to the Council, the European Parliament and the European Economic and Social Committee: The Prevention of a fight against terrorist financing through enhanced national level coordination and greater transparency of the non-profit sector: Recommendations for member states and a framework for a code of conduct for NPOs to enhance transparency and accountability in the non-profit sector to prevent terrorist financing and other types of criminal abuse*, COM (2005) 620.

Commission of the European Communities (12/2005): *Communication to the Commission from the President, Ms Wallstrom, Mr Kallas, Ms Fisher Boel proposing the launch of a European Transparency Initiative*, SEC 1300, http://ec.europa.eu/comm/eti/form6_en.htm.

Commission of the European Communities (13/2005): *Commission staff working document*, Annex to the Report from the Commission 'Better lawmaking 2004' pursuant to Article 9 of the Protocol on the application of the principles of subsidiarity and proportionality (12th report), SEC(2005) 98.

Commission of the European Communities (1/2006): *Green paper European Transparency Initiative*, COM (2006) 194.

Commission of the European Communities (1/2007): *Communication from the Commission: Follow-up to the Green Paper European Transparency Initiative*, COM (2007) 127.

Commission of the European Communities (2/2007): *Commission staff working document*, Annex to the Report from the Commission 'Better lawmaking 2006' pursuant to Article 9 of the Protocol on the application of the principles of subsidiarity and proportionality (14th report), SEC (2007) 737.

Considine, M. (2002): *The end of the line? Accountable Governance in the age of networks, partnerships and joined-up services*, Governance, 15(1): 21–40.

Curtin, D. / Dekker, I. (2005): *Good governance: The concept and its application by the European Union*, in: Deirdre M. Curtin / Ramses A. Wessel, (eds.), *Good Governance and European Union: Reflections on Concepts, Institutions and Substance*, Intersentia, Antwerp, pp. 3–21.

European Commission (1996): *Directory of Interest Groups, Office of Official Publications of the European Communities, Luxembourg.*

European Commission (2002): *European Governance: Preparatory Work for the White Paper*, Office for Official Publications of the European Communities, Luxembourg.

European Commission (5/2003): *Communication to the Council and the European Parliament 'Modernising company law and enforcing corporate governance in the European Union – A plan to move forward'*, COM (2003) 284.

European Economic and Social Committee (11/1999): *Opinion on the role and contribution of civil society organisations in the building the Europe*, OJ C 329/30.

European Economic and Social Committee (1/2002): *Opinion on European Governance – White Paper*, CES 357/2002, cited in: The Commission of the European Communities (2002): *Communication from the Commission: 'Towards a reinforced culture of consultation and dialogue – General principles and minimum standards for consultation of interested parties by the Commission'*, COM (2002) 704, p. 11.

European Economic and Social Committee (2/2004): *Final report of the ad hoc group on structured co-operation with civil society organisations and networks*, Rapporteur: Mr Bloch-Laine, CESE 1498/2003, 17 February 2004, http://www.esc.eu.int/sco/group/documents/index_en.asp.

European Economic and Social Committee (6/2005): *Revised preliminary draft opinion of the subcommittee on the representativeness of European civil society organisations in civil dialogue*, Rapporteur Mr Olsson, SC/023.

European Economic and Social Committee (2/2006): *Opinion on the representativeness of European civil society organisations in civil dialogue*, SC/023, 14 February 2006.

European Foundation Centre (1/2005): *Proposal for a Regulation on a European statute for foundations*, Brussels, Version 16, http://www.efc.be/ftp/public/EU/LegalTF/european_statute.pdf.

European Ombudsman (2005): *Decision 948/2004/OV of 4 May 2005,* http//www.euro-ombudsman.eu.int/decision/en/040948.htm.

European Parliament (2003): *Lobbying in the European Union: current rules and practices,* Working paper AFCO 104, April 2003.

European Parliament and Council (5/2003): *Directive 2003/35/EC providing for public participation with regard to the drawing up of certain plans and programmes relating to the environment, and amending with regard to public participation and access to justice,* Council Directive 85/337/EEC and 96/61/EC, OJ 2003 L 156/17.

European Parliament (2005): *Rules of procedure of the European Parliament,* 16th edition, Article 3 of Annex IX, http://www.europarl.eu.int/omk/sipade3?prog=rules-ep&l=en&ref-toc.

Fazi, Elodie / Smith, Jeremy (2006): *Civil Dialogue: making it work better, Study commissioned by the Civil Society Contact Group,* http://act4europe.horus.be/module/FileLib/Civil%20dialogue,%20making%20it%20work%20better.pdf.

Follesdal, A. (2003): *The political theory of the white paper on governance: Hidden and fascinating,* European Public Law, 9(1): 73–86.

G8 Justice and Home Affairs Ministers (7/2005): *Recommendations for enhancing the legal framework to prevent terrorist attacks,* Washington, 11 May 2004 as cited in: European Commission (2005): *Draft recommendations to member states regarding a code of conduct for non-profit organisations to promote transparency and accountability best practices,* JLS/DB/NSK D(2005) 8208.

Geyer, R. (2001): *Can European Union (EU) social NGOs co-operate to promote EU social policy?,* Journal of Social Policy, 30(3), pp. 477–493.

Goehring (2002): *Interest representation and legitimacy in the European Union: The new quest for civil society formation,* in: Warleigh / Fairbrass (eds), *Influence and Interests in the European Union: The New Politics of Persuasion and Advocacy,* Europa Publications, London pp. 118–137.

Goergen, P. (2006): *Lobbying in Brussels: A Practical Guide to the European Union for Cities, Regions, Networks and Enterprises,* www.goergen.be.

Greenwood, J. (2002): *EU interest groups and their members: When is membership a 'collective action problem?',* in: Richard Balme et al., (eds.), *Collective Action in Europe,* Presses de Sciences Po, Paris, pp. 227–253.

Greenwood, J. (2007): *Interest Representation in the European Union,* sec.ed., Palgrave, Houndmills.

Greenwood, J. / Halpin, D. (Sept. 2005): *The public governance of interest groups in the European Union: does regulating groups for "representativeness" strengthen input legitimacy?,* Paper presented at the 3rd ECPR conference, Budapest.

Grote, J. de (2003): *NGOs and Standards of Governance in NGOs, Democratisation and the Regulatory State*, A collection of Papers Presented at the Conferences in London and Brussels, European Policy Forum, London, pp. 91–94.

Halpin, D. (2001): *Integrating conceptions of interest groups: Towards a conceptual framework of sectional interest group imperatives'*, *paper prepared for ECPR (European Consortium for Political Research) General Conference*, University of Kent, 6–8 September 2001, quoted in: Greenwood, J. (2002): *Advocacy, Influence and Persuasion: Has It All Been Overdone?*, in: Warleigh, A. / Fairbrass, J. (eds.), *Influence and Interests in the European Union: The New Politics of Persuasion and Advocacy*, Europa publications, London, pp. 19–34.

Harlow, C. (2005): *Deconstructing government*, Yearbook of European Law, 23 (2004), pp. 57–89.

Jacqué, J.P.(2007): *The principle of institutional balance*, Common Market Law Review, 41(2), pp. 383–391.

Kallas, S. (3/2005): *Speech 'The need for a European transparency initiative' at the European Foundation for Management*, Nottingham Business School, Nottingham, 3 March 2005, http://europa.eu.int/rapid/pressreleasesaction.do?reference=speech/05/1 30&format.

Lefevre, S. (2004): *Interpretative communications and the implementation of Community law at national level*, European Law Review, 29, pp. 808–822.

Lonting, D. (2003): Establishing an EU Business Association under Belgian Law, in: Greenwood, J. (ed.), *The Challenge of Change in EU Business Associations*, Palgrave, Houndmills, pp. 171–191.

Makinen, Katja (2007): Participation and rights in the documents of the European Commission, paper presented at the CINEFOGO Network of Excellence Mid-term Conference "European Citizenship – Challenges and Possibilities", Roskilde, 1–3 June 2007.

Obradovic, D. (1995): *Prospects for corporatist decision-making in the European Union; The social policy agreement*, Journal of European Public Policy, 2(2), pp. 159–183.

Obradovic, D. (2006): *Civil and social dialogue in European governance*, Yearbook of European Law 2005, pp. 261–327.

Obradovic, D. (2007): *The interface between EC rules on public participation in environmental decision-making*, in: Obradovic, D. / Lavranos, N., eds., *Interface between EU Law and National Law*, Europa Law Publishing, Groningen, pp. 53–78.

Obradovic, D. / Hinrichsen, M.C. (2/2007): *Regulation of lobbying in the European Union*, paper to be presented at the ECREA Symposium 2007 'Equal Opportunities and Communication Rights: Representation, Participation & the European Democratic Deficit', 11 and 12 October 2007, Brussels.

Peters, G. (2004): *Interest groups and European governance: A normative perspective*, in: Warntjen, A. / Wonka, A. (eds.), *Governance in Europe: The Role of Interest Groups*, Nomos, Baden-Baden, pp. 57–65.

Platform of European Social NGOs (1999): *Political recommendations on civil dialogue with NGOs at European Level*, 14 October 1999.

Ruzza, C. (2004): *Europe and Civil Society: Movement Coalitions and European Governance*, Manchester University Press, Manchester, p. 46.

Sargenet, J. A. (1985): *Corporatism and the European Community*, in: Wyn G. (ed.), *The Political Economy of Corporatism*, Macmillan, London, pp. 229–253.

Schapiro, M. (2001): *Administrative law unbounded*, Indian Journal of Global Legal Studies, 8.

Schutter, O. de (2002): *Europe in search of its civil society*, European Law Journal, 8(2), pp. 198–217.

Smismans, S. (2004): *Law, Legitimacy, and European Governance: Functional Participation in Social Regulation*, Oxford University Press, Oxford, pp. 189–192.

Sudbery, I. (2003): *Bringing the legitimacy gap in the EU: Can civil society help to bring the Union closer to its citizens?*, Collegium, 26, pp. 75–95.

Venables, T. (2004): *The EU's relationship with NGOs and the issue of 'participatory democracy'*, The Review of the Union of International Associations, Transnational Associations, 2, pp. 156–158.

Warleigh, A. (2001): *'Europeanizing' civil society: NGOs as agents of political socialisation*, Journal of Common Market Studies, 39(4), pp. 619–639.

David Lane

5.   Civil Society Formation in the Post-Socialist EU Member States

5.1.   Introduction

Civil society, understood in its most general form, is that social space between individuals and primary groups (the family) and the political authority (the state); autonomous associations and institutions as well as more amorphous networks of people fill this space[1].

One may distinguish between two approaches to civil society: a normative one – which defines theoretically how civil society ought to be constituted as part of a democratic society; and an empirical one – which describes the constitution in 'actually existing societies'. In the normative approach, civil society is constituted from an autonomous sphere, in which institutions interact with, but are independent from the state. In many existing societies, however, state (or supra-state) bodies finance, regulate and participate in this space and shape the character of civil society. Civil society institutions as forms of governance can be analysed as non-state bodies influencing and having an impact on the legitimate forms of government – as inputs to the political process; they may also be seen as groups, which may take on public duties – as political outputs. Forms of accountability will vary between these two types of activity. In the evolving European Union, civil society institutions are considered to be agents which may perform governmental functions as well as playing a part in the policy making process. The European Union's definition is:

> Civil society includes the following groups: trade unions and employers' organizations (social partners); organizations representing social and economic players which are not social partners in the strict sense of the term… non-governmental organizations which bring people together in common cause, such as environmental organizations, human rights organizations, charities, professional associations, grass roots organizations; organizations that involve citizens in local and municipal life with a particular contribution from churches and religious communities (Commission of European Communities 2001, 14).

Civil society associations in the new East European members of the European Union have had a different trajectory from those of the old members. All of the latter have had relatively robust (though differently constituted) forms of civil society associations before joining the Union. In the former, most public associations were highly dependent on, and controlled by, the state. A major task of early 'transformation policy' was

---

[1]   There is a large literature on civil society which is not detailed here, see the overview provided in chapter 3 and especially Keane 1988a and 1988b, Seligman 1992, Kopecky/Mudde 2003, Mudde 2001.

'to dismantle the central government control inherited from the communist system.' (EU Subcommittee Civil Society Organisations 1999) In a normative sense, social movements extolling the virtues of civil society sought to replace ubiquitous state control, not by participation in the state, but through the 'self-administration' of groups clearly demarcated from the state: '... civil society represents a sphere other than and even distinct from the state' (Cohen/Arato 1992, 74). Whereas in the West European societies, civil society associations were outcomes of developments of the formation of capitalist society (which provided autonomous forms of power derived from private property in its different forms), in the post state socialist societies, civil society organisations were encouraged and took the form advocated 'from the top'. Unlike the normative concept, advocated by writers quoted above such as Arato, civil society took a different form: one increasingly shaped by state and foreign institutions. Foreign institutions – extolling the virtues of democratic societies – became crucial as sponsors of civil society in the formation of the new civil societies. The prevailing Western ideology during the formative period of transformation was that of neo-liberalism which had important effects on the type of civil society which was legitimated. The market was distinguished as a coordinating principle and the state disparaged. Non-government organisations (NGOs) in this context became not just institutions between the state and primary groups, but substitutes for the supposed incapacity of government. This policy has been criticised as promoting a new type of hegemony. Civil society formed in this way, it is contended, is

> ... a kind of political *laissez-faire*, the political equivalent of neo-liberalism. Civil society is seen as a way of minimising the role of the state in society, both [as] a mechanism for restraining state power and as a substitute for many of the functions of the state' (Anheier/ Glasius/Kaldor 2001, 11).

From this viewpoint, it is a social and political counterpart of the economic process of transition to capitalism; it provides not only a safety net but also Western financial support to establish the 'rule of law and respect for human rights without taking account of the primary responsibility of the state in these areas' (Anheier et al. ibid.). Another form of sponsored civil society development is the fostering of partnerships between NGOs, the private and public sector[2]. NGOs then have an 'enabling' role – promoting small business and democratic procedures.

However, it is important to note that these new institutions – linked to a capitalist and market type of society – were created on the foundations of the cultural and political traditions of specific countries. There were not only state socialist institutions but also cultural forms, which predated the communist regimes. Forms of answerability and accountability then may require different types of institutions and processes than in the old European Union societies. Policy might need to consider how to

---

2   In schemes, for example, as the Prince of Wales's Business Leaders Forum.

strengthen civil society as an 'autonomous social sphere', acting in a real intermediary role between state and the individual[3], in addition to defining means to increase answerability.

5.2.   Real Existing Civil Societies

Detailed comparative data on the constitution of civil society in central and eastern European member states of the European Union have been collected by the European Society Survey, the European Values Survey and the World Values Survey[4], and the U.S. Agency for International Development (USAID)[5]. While somewhat ethnocentric concerning the nature of civil society, these sources in combination present a picture of its strengths and weaknesses in the emerging post-communist societies.

The 1995–97 World Values Survey points to a much lower level of participation in thirteen post-communist countries than in eight 'older democracies' (USA, Australia, Sweden, Finland, Japan, Norway, Switzerland, Japan and Federal Republic of Germany). Rates of organisational membership for the former were 2.39 memberships per person compared to only 0.91 memberships in the post-communist countries – Macedonia and the German Democratic Republic were the highest with scores of 1.5 and Hungary had 1.0. All countries of the former Soviet Union were below 1.[6]

A later European Values Survey conducted in 1999/2000 can be used as a basis for comparison between the new and older members of the European Union. Table 1 (on the following page) illustrates the percentage of the respondents in different countries who participated in various types of civil society associations in 1999/2000. To simplify the comparisons with the new member states only three old members of the EU and in addition four non EU members have been selected to illustrate differences. As there were considerable differences between the countries in each group, an average is expressed in terms of the median rather than the arithmetic mean.

In terms of the types of civil society associations, the survey shows important differences between the older democracies and post communist countries and it might be noted that there is a considerable range between different post-communist societies. Hence, something other than the 'legacy' of state socialism needs to be invoked to explain the transformation outcomes. Rather surprisingly perhaps, the new members[7] had some constituencies in which they had higher participation rates than the old members. Trade union participation both in membership and in voluntary activity

3   EU Subcommittee Civil Society Organisations, paragraph 3.7.
4   See: http://www.worldvaluessurvey.org/
5   Data taken from usaid-2003, see: www.usaid.gov/locations/europe_eurasia/dem_gov/ngoin
      dex.htm
6   Data have been conveniently collected by M.M. Howard (2003)
7   New members in this article exclude the 2007 entry of Bulgaria and Romania, unless stated
      otherwise.

is considerably higher than the median for the three West European countries shown; and for the post-communist non-members it is nearly three times as high. Membership of religious associations is also higher (this is probably due to people seeking to distance themselves from association with the discredited ideology of communism) but voluntary work in them is lower – the median for the new members being at the level of Spain.

Table 5-1:   Membership and Active Participation

	Trade Unions		Political Parties		Religious Church		Voluntary Health Orgs		Sports Recreation	
	A	B	A	B	A	B	A	B	A	B
Great Britain	8.2	2.2	2.5	1.4	4.9	6.3	3.0	10.0	3.0	3.9
Germany	7.2	0.4	2.8	0.9	13.5	5.6	2.5	1.3	28.0	6.7
Spain	3.5	1.0	2.0	1.3	5.8	3.7	2.7	1.4	8.5	3.5
Median	*7.2*	*1.0*	*2.5*	*1.3*	*5.8*	*5.6*	*2.7*	*1.4*	*8.5*	*3.9*
New EU members										
Estonia	4.7	0.5	0.1	0.2	7.3	2.8	0.7	0.7	8.8	3.4
Latvia	11.3	2.3	0.6	0.3	5.3	3.8	0.9	0.5	6.6	6.2
Lithuania	1.9	1.3	0.2	0.1	5.4	4.2	2.0	0.5	3.3	2.3
Poland	10.3	2.3	0.4	0.1	5.7	3.7	1.5	0.6	3.1	2.2
Czech Republic	10.5	2.9	0.7	0.4	6.6	2.8	5.9	3.1	22.8	10.5
Slovakia	15.9	5.7	0.2	0.2	16.7	13.1	4.4	3.7	17.6	13.4
Hungary	7.0	1.3	0.3	0.2	12.1	5.4	2.0	1.2	3.8	2.6
Romania	9.2	5.8	0.6	0.4	4.4	3.6	1.0	0.6	2.1	1.2
Slovenia	16.9	3.3	0.8	0.4	6.7	4.5	2.9	2.1	16.9	8.4
Median	*10.3*	*2.3*	*0.4*	*0.2*	*6.6*	*3.8*	*2.0*	*0.7*	*6.6*	*3.4*
Post-Communist: Non-EU Members										
Croatia	11.8	4.2	0.5	0.4	12.2	5.8	3.3	2.3	14.1	7.0
Belarus	39.0	5.3	0.5	0.7	2.1	4.1	0.7	1.7	1.8	1.2
Ukraine	20.6	3.8	0.7	0.2	4.3	2.2	1.7	0.6	1.9	0.7
Russia	23.6	3.6	0.1	0.0	2.3	0.5	0.7	0.3	4.0	1.3
Median	*22.1*	*4.0*	*0.5*	*0.3*	*3.3*	*3.15*	*1.2*	*1.15*	*2.95*	*1.25*
All above former state socialist societies										
Median	*11.3*	*3.3*	*0.5*	*0.2*	*5.7*	*3.8*	*1.7*	*0.7*	*4.0*	*2.6*

A: Which, if any, do you belong to?

B: Which, if any, are you currently doing unpaid voluntary work for?

Data show percent of respondents responding positively

Source: Derived from The European Values Study: A Third Wave. Source book of the 1999/2000 European Values Study Surveys. Loek Halman. Tilburg University. Nd. Accessed on Internet website. Calculations added.

Former communist countries outside the EU still have membership and participation much below the old and new EU members. Sports and recreational associations had on average a lower participation than in the older EU countries: though there are very great differences – with Czech Republic having 23 per cent compared to Romania's 2.1 per cent. Voluntary work in health associations was also at a lower level (except for the Czech Republic and Slovakia). The data for these aspects of civil society associations show a lower level of participation for the new member states, but not excessively so. It is when one considers political associations that a greater gulf is observed. In all the new EU states, membership of political parties is less than one percent, with extremely low participation in Estonia, Lithuania and Slovakia (0.2 per cent and less of the respondents). Comparatively, in the three old EU states, membership is higher than two per cent and in the non-EU post communist societies membership is about the same, even slightly higher. A conclusion we might draw from this analysis is that participation is much lower but comparable to the older democracies in its output form, rather than as inputs to the political system. This is a serious deficiency, as 'input' participation in civil society is important in strengthening the process of a democratic system.

The autonomy of associations is to a considerable extent dependent on the extent of their assets and financial means. The European Social Survey asked people about their financial contributions to various types of voluntary organizations. This survey has the advantage that it enables comparisons to be made with Western European countries with different types of civil society organizations and support structures. Table 5-2 shows the percentage of respondents who contributed financially to the associations and may be used as an index. Here only six countries have been selected to illustrate differences. It shows that in all aspects of financial support, the new member states have a significantly lower level of contributions than in Britain and Germany; there is still a difference from Spain, though this is less marked.

Subscriptions to voluntary associations are derived from a much lower percentage of the population than in the three existing EU states. Four times as many citizens subscribe to voluntary associations in the UK than in the Czech Republic and Poland; even in Spain subscriptions are 1.5 times higher. There are significant differences between the former state socialist societies. Subscriptions to humanitarian associations in Czech Republic, and those to political parties and religious associations in Poland, are made by many more people than in the other former state socialist societies and are at levels similar to the three old EU member states. Contributions to trade unions in Poland are made by more people than in Germany or Spain. The number of subscribers to humanitarian and environmental/peace associations is greater in the Czech Republic than in Spain. One important conclusion to note here is the divergence between different new member states – related no doubt to the cultural and historical heritage of these societies.

Table 5-2:   Personal Financial Contributions to Voluntary Associations

Financial donation	Czech Republic	Poland	Hungary	Germany	UK	Spain
Sports/outdoor activity clubs	0.8	1.4	1	6	6.5	2.7
Cultural/hobby activity associations	0.9	1.5	0.7	5.7	6	2.7
Trade unions	0.4	2	0.3	0.7	3.2	2
Business/profession/ farmer organisation	0.3	0.5	0.4	0.7	2.5	0.8
Consumer/automobile organisation	0.3	0.04	0.3	0.4	1.3	1
Humanitarian associations	7.9	3	1.2	15	12	5.6
Environmental/peace/ animal associations	2.5	1.3	0.4	9	12.7	1.7
Religious/church associations	2.3	4	2.6	9	14.3	3
Political party	0.3	1	0.1	1	1.5	0.5
Science/education/ teacher associations	0.7	1.5	0.2	2.5	4	2
Social clubs etc.	0.2	0.5	0.4	2.2	4.2	1.5
Other voluntary associations	1.2	1	0.7	1.8	5.6	1.7
Average	*1.48*	*1.48*	*0.69*	*4.5*	*6.15*	*2.1*

Source: based on the European Social Survey (responses of a sample of the population of the relevant countries in 2002/2003). The figures refer to the percentage of respondents who donated money to the given organisation within the last 12 month, divided by the number of respondents in the given country, multiplied by 100. Thus the figures represent an index of the role of financial donors (private citizens) in the six countries.[8]

Differences may also be linked to the stage of economic development of various societies. Table 5-3 shows the extent of participation in unpaid voluntary work, and Third World development or human rights activity, and GDP per head (at purchasing power parity) in all European countries. Examination of the table shows the unmistakable downward gradient of GDP as one moves from the old members of the EU to the new members and those currently not in the EU.

---

8   My thanks to Aleksandra Lis for help with this table.

Table 5-3:   Participation in Voluntary Unpaid Work and in Human Rights Associations, GDP per capita.

Country	Unpaid Voluntary Work	Human Rights activity	GDP (PPP) Per capita 2002
Denmark	4.1	1.2	29.4
Austria	3.4	0.8	28.24
Ireland	2.4	1.8	28.04
Netherlands	24.6	3.9	27.47
Belgium	9.8	5	27.35
Germany	0.6	0.2	26.22
France	1.4	0.7	26.12
Great Britain*	2.6	4.3	25.83
Finland	5.9	3.2	25.44
Italy	2.9	1.9	25.32
Sweden	15	4.4	25.08
Spain	2.4	1.3	20.46
Greece	1.8	3.2	18.24
Slovenia	0.8	0.4	17.96
Portugal	0.8	0.6	17.35
Czech	0.7	0.4	14.5
Hungary	0.3	0.2	12.81
Slovakia	0.2	0.2	12.19
Estonia	0.1	0.2	11.12
Poland	0.4	0.1	10.13
Lithuania	0.2	0.1	9.88
Croatia	0.5	0.4	9.76
Latvia	0.6	0.3	8.94
Russia	0.1	0	7.82
Bulgaria	0.4	0.2	6.84
Romania	0.6	0.4	6.29
Belarus	0.5	0.7	5.33
Ukraine	0.7	0.2	4.56
Median	*0.75*	*0.5*	*17.655*
Correlation with levels of GDP Pearson R =	*0.519*	*0.634*	
Medians for Old EU members	*2.9*	*1.9*	*26.12*
Medians for New EU members	*0.4*	*0.2*	*10.625*

Key: *GDP for United Kingdom. GDP measured in 000s US $

Voluntary work, participation in Third World and human rights organizations, percent of respondents answering positively.

Source: own calculations based on European Social Survey and World Development Report 2004. New members here exclude the 2007 additions.

With the exception of Slovenia, all the post socialist countries are below the median GDP, and the same may be said about participation in voluntary work; with the exception of Belarus, all the post socialist countries are again below the median for participation in Third World and Human Rights associations. The medians of the two sets of countries (old and new EU members) bring out that the GDP is 2.44 times greater in the old EU countries; in terms of civil society participation it is 9.5 times greater and for participation in voluntary unpaid work, it is 7.25 times greater. This is evidence of a 'civil society deficit'. Not surprisingly then we see very high correlations between GDP and participation in civil society associations (0.52 and 0.63).

Typically, societies with active civil societies are prosperous and citizens have considerable spare time and disposable income. Overall, however, the new EU members from Central and Eastern Europe had a participation gap far in excess of the differences in GDP.

5.3. Organisational Development

The other side to levels of participation is the structure of civil society associations. The US Agency for International Development (USAID) uses a seven-point scale (1 – high development, 7 – poor) to measure the 'sustainability' of various non-profit organisations. USAID and similar international groups possess a different ideological view of civil society to that of the civil society reformers who legitimated opposition to state socialism. They refer to NGOs (non governmental organisations), which (as noted above) promote certain types of values as well as support for new associations. The vitality of NGOs, nevertheless, is an important indicator of the effects of transformation policies. Moreover, one should address the extent to which such organisations could be made accountable to their members, clients and beneficiaries, as well as to society as a whole.

USAID has measured the 'sustainability' of NGOs in the post communist countries. A score of between 1 and 3 indicates consolidation of the society into a western type democracy; 3 to 5 mid-transition stage and early transition 5 to 7. These scores are aggregated from seven components of civil society associations: legal environment, organisational capacity, financial viability, advocacy, service provision, infrastructure and public image. The top scores giving a 'consolidated civil society' show what Western policy makers consider to be a vibrant civil society.

In a 'consolidated' (as defined here and below by USAID[9]) civil society, the *legislative and regulatory framework* makes special provisions for the needs of NGOs or non-profit organisations, such as tax exemptions and the ability to compete freely for gov-

---

9   US Agency for International Development 2003, NGO Sustainability, Statistical Appendix, http://
     www.usaid.gov/locations/europe_eurasia/dem_gov/ngoindex/2003/index.htm

ernment contracts; the NGOs have sufficient expertise, and a legal framework exists. When *organisational capacity* is consolidated, 'transparently governed and capably managed non-governmental organisations exist across a variety of sectors'; they have boards of directors and clearly defined responsibilities; they have permanent and well-trained staff and a base of volunteers and strong local constituencies. Developed *financial viability* involves a network of organisations having sound management, independent audits, multiple sources of viable funding from local sources (government and corporate) and earned income. *Advocacy* is the term used to describe the ability of the non-governmental sector to 'respond to changing needs, issues and interests of the community and country.' In a consolidated system, NGOs have an institutional base to pursue issues of common interest and they promote legislation. They participate actively in politics by lobbying political parties and they lobby executive bodies. They have a mobilisation capacity both for citizens and for themselves. *Service provision* involves the delivery of products and services in the sphere of 'economic development, environmental protection and democratic government'. Here NGOs contract with government as well as private foundations. *Developed infrastructure* describes organisations and centres that provide training, information, legal support, and units to organise and coordinate fundraising as well as accounting and communication. Finally a consolidated civil society possesses a positive *public image* of non-government organisations. This involves trust in NGOs and voluntary participation in public work. Such an image is furthered by 'increased accountability, transparency and self-regulation within the non-profit sector'.

These criteria are useful indicators of how different is the conception of civil society from that of the more normative accounts attributed to theorists of civil society and civic associations which arose during the fall of state socialism. USAID also takes a much narrower definition of 'non-government organisations': the emphasis in their reports is not on self-sustaining groups but on the development of organisations which may take on activities in place of, or in addition to, presently state sponsored ones, also the organisation is strongly steeped in values of marketisation and destatisation. How one defines 'civil society' is dependent on one's ideological predispositions. However, the definition of the structure and framework of NGOs provides important information about the current development and sustainability of such associations.

Table 5-4 is a summary of the scores achieved by eight new EU members between 1997 and 2003 (for comparison, Romania, Ukraine and Russia are added). The new member states are all in the 'consolidation' phase, with Poland and Estonia having the most sustainable non-government sector – at least in terms of the USAID measurements. The non-EU members, Romania, Russia and Ukraine by 2003 were still at the mid-transition stage. The societies with the strongest NGO sectors were Poland (2.1), Estonia (2.2), Slovakia (2.2); the weakest was Slovenia (3.4). A considerable gap had arisen between the new EU members and Russia (4.4) and Ukraine (3.9). The scores for the components of sustainability are shown in Table 5. Five out of eight new members had relatively poor financial viability with scores of more than three. Hungary (1.3), Lithuania (1.6) and Estonia (1.8) on the basis of this reckoning had more effective legal frameworks in place.

Table 5-4: NGO Sustainability Scores: Former State Socialist Countries 1997 – 2003

	1997	1998	1999	2000	2001	2002	2003
Czech Rep.	na	na	na	2.4	2.3	2.5	2.4
Estonia	na	na	na	2.4	2.1	2.2	2.2
Hungary	2.3	1.6	2.1	2.3	2.6	2.6	2.7
Latvia	3.6	4.2		2.8	2.9	2.8	2.7
Lithuania	4.0	3.0	2.9	3.1	2.9	2.7	2.5
Poland	1.8	2.0	2.1	2.1	2.1	2.2	2.1
Slovakia	2.8	2.8	2.2	1.9	1.9	2.1	2.2
Slovenia	na	na	na	na	na	na	3.4
Romania	3.6	3.8	4.0	4.1	4.0	3.7	3.8
Russia	3.4	3.4	4.1	4.3	4.2	4.0	4.4
Ukraine	4.0	4.2	4.1	4.4	4.3	4.0	3.9

Source: US Agency for International Development 2003, NGO Sustainability, Statistical Appendix. http://www.usaid.gov/locations/europe_eurasia/dem_gov/ngoindex/2003/index.htm

Table 5-5: Dimension Scores of Civil Society 2003

	Legal Environment	Organizational Capacity	Financial Viability	Public Image	Advocacy	Service Provision	Infrastructure	Final Scores
New EU members								
Czech Rep.	3.0	2.9	1.9	2.1	2.0	2.2	3.0	2.4
Estonia	1.8	2.6	2.6	2.2	2.0	2.5	2.0	2.2
Hungary	1.3	2.9	3.3	3.2	3.3	2.3	2.4	2.7
Latvia	2.6	2.9	3.3	2.8	2.0	2.5	2.8	2.7
Lithuania	1.6	2.6	3.0	3.3	1.6	3.4	2.2	2.5
Poland	2.0	2.2	2.8	2.2	1.9	2.0	1.9	2.1
Slovakia	2.5	2.0	3.2	1.8	1.6	2.2	1.9	2.2
Slovenia	3.7	3.5	3.3	3.6	3.0	3.0	3.8	3.4
Average new EU members	2.3	2.8	2.9	2.5	2.1	2.6	2.6	2.5
Romania	4.0	3.8	4.3	4.0	3.8	3.1	3.6	3.8
Russia	4.3	4.3	4.9	4.6	4.5	4.1	4.0	4.4

Source: US Agency for International Development 2003, NGO Sustainability, Statistical Appendix. http://www.usaid.gov/locations/europe_eurasia/dem_gov/ngoindex/2003/index.htm

These quantitative measures, however useful in demarcating differences between different countries, have some drawbacks. In order to justify their own activity and secure further support there may be a tendency for NGOs and their sponsors to paint a rosier picture than is the case. Indeed, as we shall note below, individual country studies conducted by USAID NGOs often show the lack of capacity of civil society organizations in these countries. Governments, too, in seeking to fulfil conditionality requirements of the European Union and other aid giving bodies, have an interest in showing progress towards civil society creation. The rankings, however, bring out the significance of differences between the new states.

5.4. NGO Sustainability: Poland, Hungary, Czech Republic and Ukraine

These measures leave unstated the more qualitative aspects of civil society associations, such as their role in the provision of services and their accountability. Several of these topics are considered in detail by the following contributions in this publication. Here I review Poland, Hungary, Czech Republic and Ukraine. (The last is taken as an example of a country on the periphery of the EU and a possible future member).

Poland has a comparatively large NGO sector in the post-communist societies: there are 41.000 registered organizations, of which 36.000 are associations and the remainder foundations (US Agency for International Development 2003, 145). The most numerous type of NGOs is that of the trade union branches, of which there were over 17,000 in 2003, followed by over 15,000 units of the Roman Catholic Church (Klon/Jawor Association 2004). The activities of NGOs include the provision of basic services – education, health care, social assistance, promotion of culture and environmental protection and the promotion of human rights (USAID NGO Sustainability Index 1999, 79). Many civil society organizations were founded and financed by foreigners, especially American public and private donors (USAID NGO Sustainability Index 2003, 145). While difficult to quantify, it is widely recognized that 'The main problem of NGO infrastructure improvement is [the] dependency [of organizations] on sponsors, most of which are foreign donors'. (USAID NGO Sustainability Index 2003, 152) The Polish-American Freedom Foundation has taken over some of the funding left after the departure of American actors (which led to a fall in Poland's sustainability score in 1999 and in 2002). Other forms of income, particularly government support is gaining ground: 'many local NGOs are vitally dependent on local government decisions to grant subsidies or provide public work space' (USAID NGO Sustainability Index 2003, 147). Financial viability has become weaker since 1998: the viability score has moved from 2.0 in that year to 2.8 in 2003. Government support for NGOs is limited; organizations with the status of Boards of Public Benefit Activity can receive contributions from donors, which are tax free for up to 1 per cent of their income. This in turn involves a government audit. Polish NGOs lack internal ethical codes and many do not publish annual reports. The decline of foreign funding and the parsimony of Polish public funds turn the NGO sector to seek support from the EU, particularly from its structural funds. The Law on Public Benefit Organizations and Volunteer Work requires annual reports though it may not apply to those who get funding from outside bodies.

In 2003, in the Czech Republic were 58.000 registered NGOs. In 2004, NGOs were regulated by legislation covering different associations; there was a law on volunteerism, and one on Civic law was being drafted. NGOs are not required to draft annual reports or to make public their finances. Tax legislation is in place which enables gifts and endowments from foundations to be tax exempt, other donors also have some exemptions. Foreign donors were significant in the early days of transition but their support has declined by 2003 when some 85 per cent of income was domestically sourced. (USAID NGO Sustainability Index 2003, 66) A third of total income originates from public budgets, Czech foundations provided 10 per cent, corporate financing 11 per cent, individual contributions 7 per cent and income generation 20 per cent. There is some public distrust of NGOs and public authorities seek to limit the sector's participation. (USAID NGO Sustainability Index 2003, 67) Political lobbying is poorly developed. As in other new member countries, 'The biggest problem service organisations face is their lack of financial sustainability, exacerbated by the low purchasing power of other NGOs and the decreasing number of donors…' (USAID NGO Sustainability Index 2003, 68) In the Czech Republic, the non-profit sector has a relatively low profile, organisations are poorly financed, lack transparency; have poorly qualified staff and haphazard provision of services.

In Hungary, the sustainability of NGOs has fallen consistently since 1998. In 2003, the non-profit sector was particularly hit by falls in budgets. Overall, the sector lacks financial viability. Staff is low paid and poorly trained. The government is the most active supporter of the sector and foundations established by political parties may receive finance. In 2003 the National Civil Fund Program provided support to the sector. Government matches private contributions to NGOs, and taxpayers may donate one per cent of designated tax liability. By far the preponderance of finance comes from the government making the sector dependent on it. In 2001, 83 per cent of NGOs with a budget under $700 were short of resources. Mid-sized organisations are dependent on state grants and 84 per cent of the income of human rights organisations is derived from international private donors which led to their collapse when international support was withdrawn. (USAID NGO Sustainability Index 2003, 90–91) As in other post-communist societies, the decline in foreign help has been replaced by greater state financing, though this is insufficient. In future EU matching funds are seen as a possible source of support. State maintenance and the bailing out of failing or bankrupt civil society organisations seem to be a developing condition of the NGO sector in Hungary.

Ukraine is not a member of the EU though it is a potential candidate country and is cited here for comparison. According to USAID, it is not at the consolidated stage but in 2003 was still at a transition stage with an overall score of 3.9: this gives a rating suggesting that practices and policies only minimally sustain NGOs: 'progress may be hampered by a stagnant economy, a passive government, a disinterested media or a community of good-willed but inexperienced activists' (USAID NGO Sustainability Index 2003, 5 – criteria for level 4). The NGO sector is highly dependent on foreign sponsors, with little (though growing) support from government and business. Dependence on external donors 'negatively affects the NGO sector's ability to provide goods and services that truly reflect the needs and priorities of their communities'. (USAID NGO Sustainability Index 2003, 206) Such sponsors influence the priorities and activity of associations. The financial basis of most NGOs is unstable; the financial viability index is 4.8. NGOs, as in all continental European societies, are registered with the authorities: in 2003, 30.000 units were registered of which 4.000 were active. (USAID NGO Sustainability Index 2003, 201) Laws regulate the sector and grants, donations and loans are tax-free. A law on Social Services allows government procurement of NGOs to provide services. The legal sphere, however, contains ambiguous and contradictory laws often restricting the activity of NGOs. The sector is not very effective as a lobbying group on government though the government decree 'On Citizens' Engagement in the Decision-Making Process' envisages advisory boards with NGO participation. Most of NGO activity is addressed to the provision of social services – humanitarian assistance, youth initiatives and environmental concerns. The intervention of NGOs in the Presidential elections of 2004/05 highlights the contentious role of foreign sponsored organizations in the electoral process, often to secure the election of their own favoured candidates. The American National Endowment for Democracy had available over fifteen million dollars for the Ukraine alone, in 2004 it spend over two million dollars.'[10]

5.5. The Sustainability of Civil Society Associations

On the basis of this overview, the sustainability of NGOs is confounded by considerable problems. Membership of voluntary organizations is lower than in the old mem-

---

10   The following is one example: $50.000 was given to the Institute for Euro-Atlantic Cooperation 'to build support for greater integration of Ukraine into Western political and economic structures. The Institute will organize four roundtable meetings on 'Ukraine in the Euro-Atlantic Space: Experience and Perspectives' and two training sessions for NGO leaders on management and public relations techniques and the workings of Western institutions such as NATO and the EU. *National Endowment for Democracy Report* made available to current author.

ber states, though there are some exceptions, particularly in the trade unions. Since the collapse of the state socialist system, a legal framework is being set up, though by 2004 it was incomplete and ambiguity remained. Many organizations have been formed on the basis of sponsors' purses; they lack transparency, self-regulation, and independent forms of finance. Since the departure of foreign funding they look to public financial support including that of the EU. The withdrawal of 'long-term supporters such as USAID and British DFID... caus[ed] a substantial reduction in the annual amount of support available to the ... NGO sector.' (Report on Slovakia, 177) NGOs are lacking in resources, the professional qualifications of employees are low and the infrastructure of support is weak. Active membership of civil society organisations is low and puts in question their effectiveness as interest groups articulating public interests. The sector is lacking in organizational capacity and regularized forms of accountability and transparency. In the public image, NGOs are compromised due to their lack of competence and lack of transparency. It might be questioned whether they are bodies which can effectively take over responsibilities currently assigned to local and central government.

Since the disintegration of state socialism, USAID reports have shown considerable progress with respect to the legal framework, citizen participation, organisational capacity, financial support and general public awareness of the civil society groups in the new member states. Social surveys, which have been conducted in European societies, show a lower level in the new EU member states than in the older ones in terms of level of membership, participation and public finance of civil society organizations. As inputs to the political process, the infrastructure of interest groups and political parties needs further development. With respect to civil society associations as political outputs, those in the post-communist countries lack transparency, adequate monitoring and responsibility. Financially, organizations are not viable; there is a dependence on sponsors and reliance on foreign backers, which has left the sector financially vulnerable. The relatively low level of economic productivity in the post-communist societies, and the small amount of personal disposable income precludes the development of financially self-sustaining organizations. NGO activities are often 'donor driven' and lack a local constituency and membership base. While answerable to their sponsors, there is an absence of accountability to users of services. The sector is unable to respond to potential service users' needs. There is a general tendency for these groups to be separate from society; consequently, they are often viewed by the public with suspicion. One might question whether the conditions in the post-communist societies are appropriate for the development of a non-profit sector in ways intended by USAID policy. Attempts to provide alternative social services may weaken even further state provision which itself suffers under stringent budgetary cuts. The influence of foreign donors has even more distorted the provision of services.

From a policy point of view, the further development of civil society groups in the new member states within the context of the European Union should first take account of the unique culture and history of these societies. Civil society organizations in the old states of the European Union have different forms, profiles and priorities: Germany, the United Kingdom and Spain have different kinds of civil societies. However, trade unions in the new EU member states have a very high level of participation and might be considered a base for the exercise of accountability reforms – especially in countering economic corruption. Policy priorities assumed by organizations such as DFID, USAID, the National Endowment For Democracy, the Open Society Foundation, Freedom House do not always coincide with those of people living in the areas concerned. There is therefore a need for greater answerability of the growing number of NGOs and civil society organisations, many of which are founded and funded by foreign bodies.

5.6. Accountability

The development of 'new forms of social and economic governance in the EU', involving the participation of civic society groups from the new member states, is unlikely to be effective until the preconditions of building effective civil society associations have been fulfilled. The EU Subcommittee on Civil Society Organisations, has opined that the 'difficulties besetting both western and eastern European countries are not purely economic, social and financial. They are mostly related to internal changes in the way civil society is organised...' ('The Role and Contribution of Civil Society Organisations in the Building of Europe', Economic and Social Committee 22 September 1999. CES 851/99 D/GW. Paragraph 4.3). But for the post-communist countries, the economic and financial aspects are crucial conditions for the development of civil society in the first place.

Answerability and accountability are clearly important issues. But in addressing the question of how the EU can enhance them, one must not be lose sight of the fact that the normative concept of civil society associations is that they should be autonomous self-sustaining bodies and this entails independence from the state and corporate economy. Had the early Western trade union movement been 'responsible and answerable' for their actions to the state and employers, there would never have been free independent trade unions. Indeed, it may well be that the focus in defining new forms of governance and answerability, should not be on making civil society associations 'answerable', but on encouraging such groups to secure accountability of government and corporate capital. Civil society associations in Western societies promote such accountability through direct action (boycotts, strikes), indirectly through media activity and lobbying and also through cooperation with the state and corporations –

cooptation onto government bodies and worker codetermination on workers councils and governing bodies.

Civil society associations need their own forms of governance: an unambiguous legal framework, particularly with respect to taxation law, defined internal procedures, transparent forms of responsibility are desirable. It is when civil society associations become entangled with public bodies, are dependent on them for assets, income and general finance that accountability becomes more important and requires a regulatory role by the state – and particularly by the EU, should such associations receive financial support. In this context, conditionality of donors might include the provision of annual reports, the audit of accounts and the election of office holders. Answerability may take different forms depending on the type of association. The relevance of different types of stakeholders – sponsors, employees, and clients – has to be addressed in establishing lines of accountability.

For purposes of accountability, civil society organizations may be classified into different types depending on their major form of finance (state, corporate economy, participants/beneficiaries) and type of regulation (direct, indirect and self-regulation). A provisional categorization is suggested in Figure 5-1. The source of finance defines the type of regulation which different associations require. If churches or political parties, for example, receive state finance then they are regulated by four different types of control: general laws (giving rights/ or constraints on association and speech), specific laws (defining the uses to which state provision can be put), taxation law (when appropriate, defining the type of activity which associations may benefit) and self-regulation (statutes binding the association's members and rules of association). Where the corporate economy sources associations, state laws also apply in different ways to regulate the financial provisions, through tax laws for example. Where participants and beneficiaries are self-financing, associations are usually only constrained by general laws and self-regulation (unless they afford themselves of taxation benefits). The table shows various combinations of regulation, depending on choices made by civil society organisations or choices made for them. Only legal regulation is shown here, as a consequence of state finance, in addition, associations may be required to accept co-opted representatives on their executive committees to ensure their compliance with the terms of financial support.

Civil society associations indulge in many different types of activity which may need regulation. As indicated in Figure 5-2, the type of activities pursued range from political lobbying through the provision of public services to strikes, boycotts and demonstrations. It is contended that relevant stakeholders may be the appropriate form of accountability. As indicated in Figure 5-2, these range from sponsors, through members to the government. While the emphasis in much civil society literature is on the independence of group organization, the concern here is with the responsibility and answerability of groups and networks to the wider public and society.

Figure 5-1:   Types of Regulation of Civil Society Associations by Source of Finance

	Type of Regulation				
	General Laws (Indirect)	Specific Laws (Direct)	Taxation (Indirect)	Self-Regulation	
Associations					*Source of Finance*
Churches, Political Parties, Health care provision	X	X	X	X	State
Political Parties, Humanitarian aid, Educational institutions	X	X	X	X	Corporate Economy
Churches, Parties, Youth organizations, Sports Clubs, Environmental associations	X			X	Participants/ Beneficiaries

Figure 5-2:   Responsibility of Civil Society Organizations by Types of Activity

	Type of Activity						
	Lobbying	Media	Public Service Provision	Member Service Provision	Strikes	Boycotts	Demonstrations
Stake Holders							
Sponsors	X	X	X	X			X
Consumers			X		X	X	
Members	X	X	X	X	X	X	X
Clients	X	X	X	X		X	
Governments	X	X	X	X	X	X	X

The chart brings out the importance of government as a stakeholder in all these activities. This does not mean that government runs and controls civil society organisations but that the government has a responsibility for the provision at least of a legal environment in which activities may take place. In providing services to members (religious services) the state also has a responsibility to consider the impact on other interests; hence there is a pluralism of answerability even of church associations – to members, clients, sponsors and the state. The problem here is to maintain the autonomy of civil society organisations and concurrently provide some safeguards to stakeholders that their interests are promoted, and not infringed.

5.7. Conclusions

This chapter has shown that compared to the old members of the European Union, there is a qualitative 'deficit' in the sphere of civil society associations in the new member states. Regulation and a legislative framework can only be effective if civil society is constituted from self-sustaining associations with a viable organisational capacity. Civil society organisations as effective political inputs are concentrated in countries with high levels of economic development, and robust autonomous civil society organizations will only develop in the new states in pace with a substantial rise in economic development. Without an adequate structure of employment and personal income, the financial sustainability of civil society organizations is imperilled and their capacity to act as political inputs to the political process severely weakened. Civil society organizations are generally too weak to take over the provision of services on a substantial scale. Hence there is a danger that ad hoc development of NGOs as providers of collective services will lead to piecemeal development. For a considerable time to come, provision of services should be predicated on local and central government institutions. These in turn should be made subject to greater democratic control and answerability and in this respect civil society associations have an important role to play. Such associations may lobby governments and may promote accountability through strikes and demonstrations (or the threat of them). The post-communist societies have particularly weak civil society organisations as political inputs; most of all they need to be strengthened as a component of democratic government. Concurrently with the development of accountability mechanisms, policy needs to consider means to promote the development of associations which might articulate and defend group interests. The post-communist societies have some civil society assets, particularly in the trade union movement. In countries with a weak and often illegitimate business class, the unions might well be developed as a support for government stability. While civil society organizations require autonomy, their accountability is dependent on different kinds of stakeholders and the types of activities they promote. In addition to analyzing the answerability of civil society organization in terms of legal norms, attention should make such associations responsible to different types of stakeholders not only to those who support and constitute civil society organisations, but also to the constituencies (sponsors, consumers, clients, members, and society at large) that benefit. The accountability of civil society organisations has to strike a balance between maintaining their autonomy and ensuring that the interests of stakeholders are furthered, not infringed.

References

Anheier, H./Glasius, M./Kaldor, M. (2001): *Introducing Global Civil Society*, in: H. Anheier, M./Glasius M. /Kaldor, *Global Civil Society 2001*, Oxford University Press, Oxford.

Cohen, J.A./ Arato, A. (1992): *Civil Society and Political Theory*, MIT press, Cambridge MA.

Commission of European Communities (2001): *European Governance: White paper*, COM 428, Brussels, 25.7.2001.

EU Subcommittee Civil Society Organisations (1999): *The Role and Contribution of Civil Society Organisations in the Building of Europe*, Economic and Social Committee, Brussels, 22 September 1999, CES 851/99 D/GW.

Howard, Marc Morjé (2003): *The Weakness of Civil Society in Post-Communist Europe*, Cambridge University Press, Cambridge.

Keane, John (1988a): *Democracy and Civil Society*, Verso, New York and London.

Keane, John (ed.) (1988b): *Civil Society and the State: New European Perspectives*, Verso, New York and London.

Klon/Jawor Association (2004): *Situation of non-governmental sector in Poland in 2004*, in: http://english.ngo.pl/labeo/appcms/x/48315

Kopecky, P and Mudde, C (2003): *Rethinking Civil Society*, in: Demokratization, 10(3), pp. 1–14.

Seligman, Adam B. (1992): *The Idea of Civil Society*, The Free Press, New York and Macmillan.

US Agency for International Development (USAID): *NGO-Sustainability-Index*, in: http://www.usaid.gov/locations/europe_eurasia/dem_gov/ngoindex/index.htm

Daniela Obradovic and Redmar Damsma[1]

6. Central and Eastern European Civil Society as a Constituency in the Commission's Consultations

6.1. Introduction

The formalisation of the civil groups' involvement in EU policy conception and implementation can be regarded as part of the European Union's strategy to boost the efficiency of the new forms of governance it has introduced and to bolster its legitimacy (Commission, 2001, 11).

The Commission formalised the dialogue with civic groups by introducing general principles and minimum standards for consulting with interested parties (Commission, 2002b). The Commission defines consultations as those processes through which it wishes to solicit input from interested parties and thereby engage them in the shaping of policy prior to issuing its decisions (Commission, 2006, 11). 'Interested parties' refers to all parties wishing to participate in consultations run by the Commission, including for- and non-profit organisations as well as private citizens (ibid). National as well as EU-level associations are eligible to take part in those consultations. The participation of various parties in the Commission's consultations should also enable the Commission to uphold accountability standards.

The Commission mentions the following general principles, which should apply to the consultation process: participation, openness and accountability, effectiveness and coherence (Commission, 2002b, 16–18). It gives a very brief indication of the content of these principles. The Commission goes on to set out the following five minimum standards, which give slightly more concrete requirements for the Commission's conduct in the consultation process: A) *Clear content of the consultation process*: all communications relating to consultation should be clear and concise, and should include all necessary information to facilitate responses; B) *Consultation target groups*: when defining the target group(s) in a consultation process, the Commission should ensure that the relevant parties have an opportunity to express their opinions; C) *Publications*: the Commission should ensure adequate awareness-raising publicity and adapt its communication channels to meet the needs of all target audiences. Without excluding other communication tools, open public consultations should be published

1 This article has been prepared as a part of the research programme 'Constitutional Order and Economic Integration' of the Amsterdam Center for International Law, University of Amsterdam and the Sixth Framework Project 'New Modes of Governance' sponsored by the European Commission.

on the Internet and announced at the 'single access point';[2] D) *Time limits for participation*: the Commission should provide sufficient time for planning and responses to invitations and written contributions. The Commission should strive to allow at least 8 weeks for the reception of responses to written public consultations and 20 working days notice for meetings; and E) *Acknowledgement and feedback*: receipt of contributions should be acknowledged. Results of open public consultation should be displayed on websites linked to the single access point on the Internet (ibid, 19–22). In the following, we will refer to the whole as 'the principles and standards' or the minimum standards'. As a result of the application of these minimum standards, the involvement of all interest groups in EU governance is subject to their compliance with principles of good governance[3]: representativeness, accountability and transparency.

The Commission has emphasised that the aforementioned consultation policy is intended to ensure that all parties affected by particular EU decisions are properly addressed and consulted beforehand. The standards are also meant to guarantee that an adequate balance is struck between the various parties, depending on their societal makeup, economy, size, specific target groups and state of origin. The minimum standards are applied systematically to all major policy initiatives,[4] prior to the drafting of policy proposals by the Commission. The contribution of Obradovic and Alonso Vizcaino to this volume analyses in an extensive manner the issue of the standards for the Commission's consultations.

This paper examines interest groups from Central and Eastern European Countries (CEECs)[5] as a constituency in the Commission consultations in terms of their level of participation and the significance thereof for this process.

6.2. Input of CEEC Civil Groups in the Commission's Consultations

From the beginning of 2003, when the minimum standards entered into force, until 1 May 2007, the Commission completed approximately 455 major proposals to which the minimum standards applied: 60 in 2003, 95 in 2004, 106 in 2005, 129 in 2006 and

---

2   See http://europa.eu.int/yourvoice/consultations/index_en.htm
3   The concept of good governance entails understanding that public decision-making and implementation thereof should be conducted in accordance with particular standards comprising an efficient, open, accountable and audited public service (Harlow, 2005, 59). See also the Commission's definition of the concept of good governance in Commission 2001, 8).
4   Impact assessment website http://ec.europa.eu/governance/impact/index_en.htm. See also Commission 2002a and the latest Impact assessment guidelines in Commission, 2005.
5   The CEECs that joined the European Union in May 2004 are Hungary, Estonia, Slovenia, the Czech Republic, Poland, Slovakia, Lithuania and Latvia. Bulgaria and Romania acceded to the EU in January 2007.

65 in the first 4 months of 2007[6] (as illustrated by Figure 6-1).[7] In addition, the Commission published 33 Green Papers in the period 2003–2006, to which these standards also applied.[8]

Figure 6-1:   Number of the Commission's Impact Assessment Consultations Launched per Year in the Period 1998 – 1 May 2007

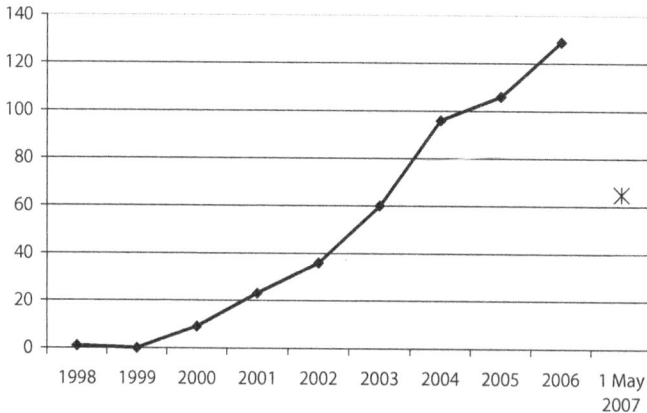

The Commission asserts that the standards for the Commission consultations over this period were properly and successfully applied by its departments.[9]

In contrast to the Commission's generally positive self-evaluation vis-à-vis the application of its minimum standards for consultations, our research shows that at present, the most important objective of its consultations, the balance between the points of view expressed with respect to their country of origin, is not being fulfilled.[10] Namely: interest groups operating in the CEECs submit far fewer contributions than their counterparts from the 15 original EU member states.

---

6   These proposals are available on the impact assessment site: http://ec.europa.eu/governance/impact/index_en.htm
7   A part of the data upon which this figure is based on is taken over from the following source: Commission 2006, 11; Commission, 2007a, 4.
8   Green Papers are available on the following site: http://europa.eu/documents/comm/green_papers/index_en.htm
9   The Better Lawmaking reports report on application of the minimum standards for consultation: Better Lawmaking 2006: http://eur-lex.europa.eu/LexUriServ/site/en/com/2007/com2007_0286en01.pdf; Better Lawmaking 2005: http://eur-lex.europa.eu/LexUriServ/site/en/com/2006/com2006_0289en01.pdf; Better Lawmaking 2004: http://europa.eu/eur-lex/lex/LexUriServ/site/en/com/2005/com2005_0098en01.pdf; Better Lawmaking 2003: http://europa.eu.int/eur-lex/en/com/rpt/2003/com2003_0770en01.pdf
10   See above.

Our conclusion is based upon the assessment of the contributions submitted by civil society groups in response to 108 Commission consultations carried out in the period January 2003 through December 2006. The number of consultations analysed per year is given in Table 6-1. The policy issues dealt with by the assessed consultations are mostly of an economic nature, as displayed in Figure 6-2.

Figure 6-2:   Policy Issues Covered by 108 Commission's Impact Assessment Consultations Carried Out in the Period January 2003 – December 2006

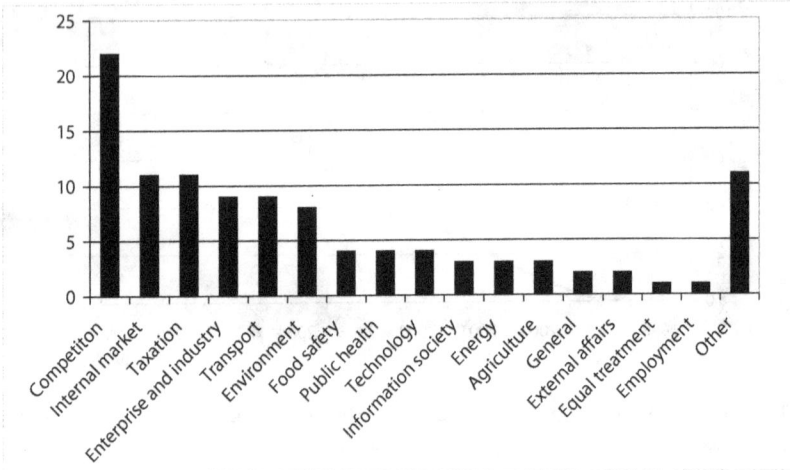

Table 6-1:   Number Of The Commission's Impact Assessment Consultations Assessed per Year in the Period January 2003 – December 2006

Year	Consultations (sample)
2003	14
2004	16
2005	31
2006	37
Total	108

We could not identify the country of origin of every contribution submitted to the 455 consultations because the input to open public consultations was not published on the Internet in every case (Commission 2006, 12) in violation of minimum standard C.[11] Furthermore, in some instances, the data are not accessible or missing. In many cases, the country of origin was simply not specified. For example, three contributors to the DG Completion consultation on Regulation 1617/93 are referred to as compa-

---

11   See above.

nies X, Y and Z.[12] The information on submissions is not uniformly presented in each consultation in accordance with the standard presentation model; the format varies from one consultation to another. Contributions are often assigned to the 'other' category, which does not specify the country of origin. Consequently, it was not possible to determine the nationality of the contributors in every case.

Our assessment of the contributions that are publicly accessible on the Internet demonstrates a disproportionately low level of input from CEEC civil groups relative to their counterparts from the rest of the member states (Figure 6-3). For example, while interest associations from Germany and France submitted 20,931 and 12,572 contributions, respectively, in response to the Commission's consultations from January 2003 – December 2006, civil groups from Lithuania and Latvia contributed 344 and 242 opinions, respectively, in the same period. Civil organisations from seven of the eight CEECs belong to the list of the 10 least active contributors. This disparity remains unchanged even when the number of contributions submitted per 10,000 inhabitants is compared, as shown in Figure 6-4 and Table 6-2. The cases of Estonia and Slovenia, as illustrated in Figure 6-4, are somewhat misleading because although they show a relatively high rate of participation, more than 50 per cent of their contributions were submitted in response to just two of the consultations examined.

Figure 6-3: Number of Contributions per Country Submitted in Response to 108 Commission's Impact Assessment Consultations Carried Out in the Period January 2003 – December 2006

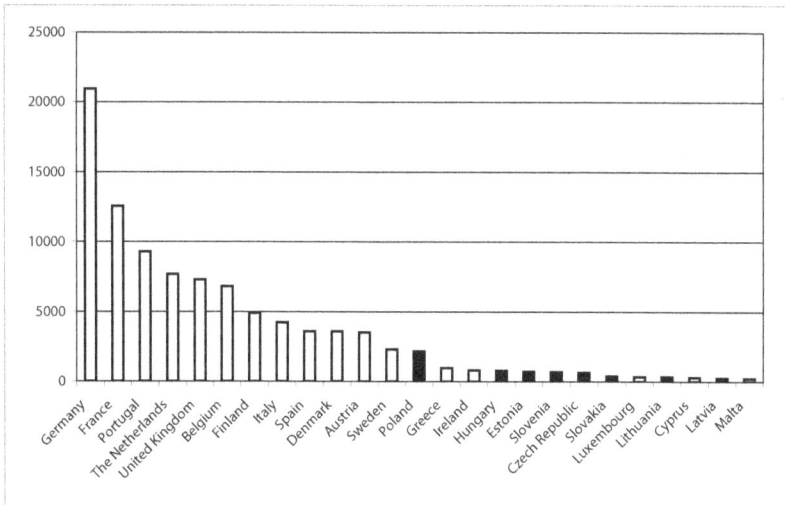

Figure 6-4: Number of Contributions per 10,000 Inhabitants per Country Submitted in Response to 108 Commission's Impact Assessment Consultations Carried Out in the Period January 2003 – December 2006

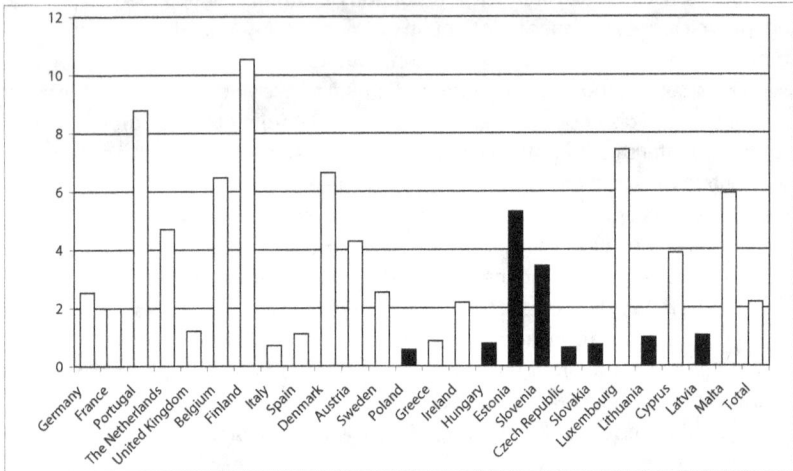

The dearth of CEEC input into the Internet-based consultations is recognised by the Commission as well. For example, in its analysis of the stakeholders' consultations on the future of EU policy concerning support for research, the Commission acknowledges that very few contributions came from the 10 new member states (European Commission 2004 4). Similarly, in its examination of responses to the consultation on research themes in the 7th Framework Programme for Research and Technological Development, the Commission stated that only 6.4 per cent of all responses came from the CEECs (European Commission 2005b, 2).

Our research shows that the CEEC interest groups have not adopted a consistent approach regarding the policy areas in which the impact assessment consultations are launched. Indeed, Figure 6-5 and Table 6-3 demonstrate that there is no discernible systematic pattern in the choice of policy area for which they submitted their opinions. Save for the areas of food safety and the internal market, interest groups operating in the CEECs do not follow the same policy area pattern displayed by the rest of the contributors. For example, while contributions submitted in response to consultations dealing with environmental matters are quite numerous overall, contributors from the CEECs are not particularly active in this area. The number of their submissions in the areas of competition, taxation, transport and budget is also extremely low (see Table 6-3). Furthermore, although the majority of the CEECs have large agricultural sectors, their submissions in this policy area are almost negligible; groups from the rest of the EU member states submit far more.

Table 6-2:   Number of Contributions per 10,000 Inhabitants per Country Submitted in Response to 108 Commission's Impact Assessment Consultations Carried Out in the Period January 2003 – December 2006

Member States	Population	Contributions	Perform./10000 inhab.
Germany	82,438,000	20,931	2.54
France	62,886,000	12,572	2.00
Portugal	10,570,000	9,276	8.78
The Netherlands	16,334,000	7,685	4.70
United Kingdom	60,393,000	7,301	1.21
Belgium	10,511,000	6,809	6.48
Finland	5,256,000	5,538	10.54
Spain	43,758,000	4,912	1.12
Italy	58,752,000	4,251	0.72
Denmark	5,428,000	3,606	6.64
Austria	8,266,000	3,543	4.29
Sweden	9,048,000	2,294	2.54
Poland	38,157,000	2,164	0.57
Greece	11,125,000	952	0.86
Ireland	4,209,000	918	2.18
Hungary	10,077,000	789	0.78
Estonia	1,345,000	714	5.31
Slovenia	2,003,000	689	3.44
Czech Republic	10,251,000	643	0.63
Slovakia	5,389,000	392	0.73
Lithuania	3,403,000	344	0.99
Luxembourg	459,000	341	7.42
Cyprus	766,000	297	3.88
Latvia	2,295,000	242	1.05
Malta	404,000	240	5.94
TOTAL	463,523,000	101,818	2.20

Figure 6-5:　Number of Contributions Coming from the CEEC's per Policy Area Submitted in Response to 108 Commission's Impact Assessment Consultations Carried Out in the Period January 2003 – December 2006

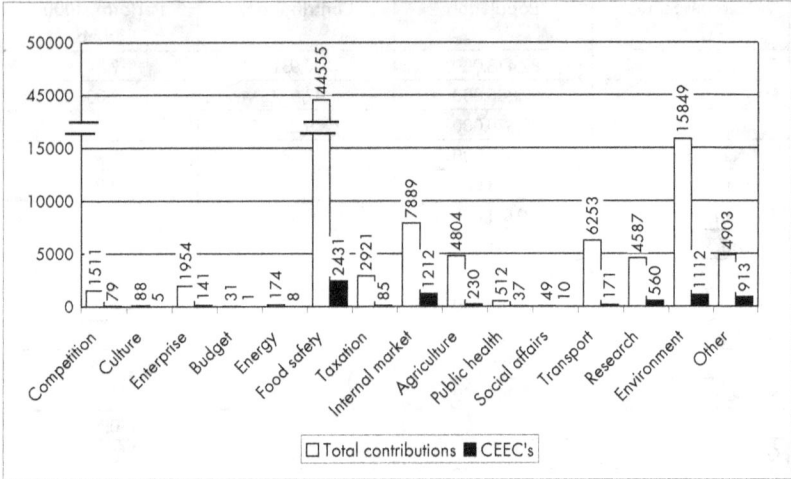

□ Total contributions ■ CEEC's

Table 6-3:　Number of Contributions Coming from the CEEC's per Policy Area Submitted in Response to 108 Commission's Impact Assessment Consultations Carried Out in the Period January 2003 – December 2006

Policy area	Total number of contributions	Number of contributions coming from the CEECs	Participation of submissions coming from the CEECs in total number of contributions
Competition	1511	79	5%
Culture	88	5	6%
Enterprise	1954	141	7%
Budget	31	1	3%
Energy	174	8	5%
Food safety	44555	2431	5%
Taxation	2921	85	3%
Internal market	7889	1212	15%
Agriculture	4804	230	5%
Public health	512	37	7%
Social affairs	49	10	20%
Transport	6253	171	3%
Research	4587	560	12%
Environment	15849	1112	7%
Other	4903	913	19%

The quality of the contributions submitted by the CEEC interest groups has yet to be evaluated, because it is currently very difficult to determine the exact extent to which their positions have been incorporated into the Commission's legislative proposals. Those data are presented in a very user unfriendly manner and systematic exploration requires a considerable investment of time. There were also cases of insufficient feedback from the Commission with respect to how the comments received in the consultations were or were not taken into account in the final policy proposal from the Commission.[13] Recently, the Commission acknowledged the need to provide better feedback and to explain how and to what extent the comments have been taken into consideration. It also recognises the need to ensure that a plurality of views and interests are expressed in the consultations (Commission 2007, 6). Those are the reasons why the qualitative effect of those submissions requires further research.

The Commission's policy is to accept contributions only from entities fulfilling the criteria of representativeness, openness and accountability (Commission 2002b, 19–22).[14] Given that the CEEC civic organisations rarely meet those requirements, it is unlikely that their submissions exert a significant impact upon the Commission's proposals. The empirical research findings show that membership in voluntary organisations in the CEECs is lower and perhaps even declining relative to the old member states; there are some exceptions, however, particularly in the trade unions (Howard 2003, 65, 66, 69, and 71). At first glance, there appears to be a great number of civil organisations in the CEECs: Hungary boasted nearly 50,000 NGOs in 2000, Poland had around 100,000 in 2002 (Rose-Ackerman 2007, 169) and in 1994–95, 30,000 NGOs were registered in the Czech Republic (Narozhna 2004, 247). However, most of these 'organisations' exist in name only or comprise a small number of individuals; some of them are actually one-person businesses (Mudde 2007; Korkut 2005, 115). Vari submits that because foundations enjoy various tax benefits in those countries, many civil society organisations are established solely for the purpose of tax evasion (Vari 1998, 19 and 30). Thus, she continues, most of those NGOs that mushroomed in the CEECs were actually for-profits in disguise, misusing their non-profit status. According to the New Europe Barometer of Winter 2004–05, roughly 16 per cent of the CEE population belongs to civil associations. The individual percentages vary enormously from country to country, from 46 per cent in Estonia to three per cent in Romania (Mudde 2007). The statistics based upon the first wave of the European Social Survey (ESS) (2002–

---

13   Commission of the European Communities (2006) 'Green paper: European Transparency Initiative', COM(2006) 194, Brussels, 3.5.2006, p. 12.In two thirds of the cases reviewed up to 2004 too little was said on how comments were taken into account in the proposals or why they were disregarded (Commission, 2005, 4).

14   See also Obradovic/Vizcaino 2006.

2003)[15] indicate that associational membership in the EU ranges between 92 per cent for Denmark and only 21 per cent for Poland (Vazquez-Garcia 2007, 10).

Apart from the problem of membership, CEEC civil organisations are hampered by the negligible level of engagement in the activities they sponsor. Active membership in civil society organisations is low and therefore strains their credibility as interest groups articulating public interests. According to the ESS (2002–2003) data, the level of participation in civil organisation activities ranges between 49 per cent in Belgium and the United Kingdom to 11 percent in Poland (Vazquez-Garcia 2007, 10). The associated empirical studies show that the internal decision-making channels of CEEC civil associations are closed to members.[16] Member participation therefore does not actually occur in practice, but remains an abstract concept. In actuality, interest associations are run by elites in a non-participatory hierarchical manner. Conferences are an infrequent occurrence for CEEC interest groups and decisions are nearly always made by unaccountable secondary bodies. Local branches, experts and ordinary members tend to be excluded from internal decision-making processes. Their influence is therefore rather indirect and consists of sending delegates to local and national conferences. However, these delegates very often do not even elect the members of the main decision-making bodies. In addition, the elites use their leadership positions in order to further their long-term career objectives.

Many civil society organisations were formed on the basis of sponsors' purses and therefore lack fiscal independence. For example, Kuti's research indicates that private contributions make up a much larger proportion of the sector's revenue than those disbursed by the government in Hungary in comparison to Germany, Italy and the United Kingdom (Kuti 1997). Awards of grants to civic associations situated in the CEECs have also figured prominently in the funding priorities of USAID, the EU's PHARE programme, the EU Stability Pact for Southeast Europe and the agendas of funding agencies like the World Bank, the European Bank for Reconstruction and Development, the Council of Europe, the Organisation for ECONOMIC Cooperation and Development and of private donors' organisations such as the Soros Foundation, etc. (Sardamov, Ivelin 2005, 379; Narozhna 2004, 250). One independent source of income, membership fees, is enjoyed by a very small percentage of CEEC NGOs, whose finances continue to depend upon private donors. A survey conducted among environmental civil society organ-

---

15   The European Social Survey (the ESS) is designed to chart and explain the interaction between Europe's changing institutions and the attitudes, beliefs and behaviour patterns of its diverse populations. The ESS is jointly funded by the European Commission, the European Science Foundation and scientific funding bodies in each participating country. In the round (2002–2003) 22 countries participated, including all 15 old EU member states as well as Poland, Hungary, the Czech Republic and Slovenia.

16   This particular research is based on the results of 62 interviews with representatives of trade unions, employer organisations and agricultural producers' associations in Hungary, Poland and Romania (Korkut 2005, 120–123).

isations operating in the Ceecs demonstrates that for 18 per cent of those organisations, the most important funding sources are national private grants from domestic foundations, while for 16 per cent, the most significant sources of income are membership fees; for 13 per cent, foreign grants are the largest source (Vari 1998, 57.).

CEEC civic groups lack regulated forms of accountability, adequate monitoring, answerability and transparency (Lane in this volume). For example, elections for presidential posts have mostly been symbolic and thus cannot really be seen as concrete proof of internal democracy and accountability (Korkut 2005, 121). A more positive picture is painted by the research conducted by CIVICUS, the World Alliance for Citizen Participation. According to their survey of civil society organisations, the situation in Central and Eastern Europe is not that bad. Though some problems remain, particularly with regard to corruption and transparency, the civil society organisations in these countries are generally reported to be internally democratic. However, Mudde warns that one has to treat these findings with some caution, since the organisations surveyed seem to constitute a particular subsection of civil society, i.e. groups integrated into what is increasingly labelled 'global civil society' (Mudde 2007).

6.3. Reasons for the Low Level of Participation of CEEC Civic Associations in the Commission's Consultations

There are several factors that explain the strikingly low level of involvement of civil organisations originating in the CEECs in the Commission's consultations.

First, there is a lack of awareness of the general participatory framework among interest groups operating in the European Union. The possibility to engage in the Commission's consultations remains largely unknown, even in the old member states (Fazi/Smith 2006, 39)

Furthermore, major European-level groups and platforms that regularly submit contributions to the Commission's consultation process have not undertaken any measures to promote the participation of their members or supporters in the preparation of those submissions (Vizcaino 2005, 64;[17] Fazi/Smith 2006, 9). Moreover, following the biggest simultaneous enlargement in EU history, a number of European-level associations are still building their membership in the new member states (Fazi/ Smith 2006, 47).

Various case studies in the literature illustrate that some types of civic organisations (such as business interest associations) from the CEECs focus on gathering material about specific legislation at the domestic level by default rather than making a

---

17   The study assesses the practices of the following European level NGOs: the Platform of European Social NGOs (Social Platform), the European Environmental Bureau (EEB), the European Youth Forum (EYF), the European Women's Lobby (EWL) and the European Public Health Alliance (EPHA).

deliberate attempt to shape legislation by accessing EU institutions and networks. Hence, we conclude that the Europeanised activities of CEEC interest groups mimic a model of interest mediation, where the exchange and ownership of information are more important than the actual impact on policy-making (Borragan 2004, 262). According to some scholars, Eastern European interest groups are dependent on Eurogroups' expertise while their own input is based on the exchange of information rather than an effective impact on policy outcomes (Borragan 2004, 252).

Linguistic problems also limit the participation of CEEC civil society organisations in the European arena. Our research demonstrates that the majority of the 54 Commission's Internet-based impact assessment consultations were launched in English, French or German (see Figure 6-6). Only a fraction was conducted in one of the languages spoken in the CEECs, such as Polish. However, English is less widely spoken in the CEECs than in the 2004 and 2007 pre-accession EU members (26 per cent versus 36 per cent). The same holds for German (21 per cent versus 12 per cent) and French (12 per cent versus 3 per cent) (European Commission 2005a, 5).

Figure 6-6: Number of Times a Particular Language was Used for a Consultation Instruction Document, Out of the 54 Sample Commission's Impact Assessment Consultations Carried Out in the Period January 2003 – December 2006

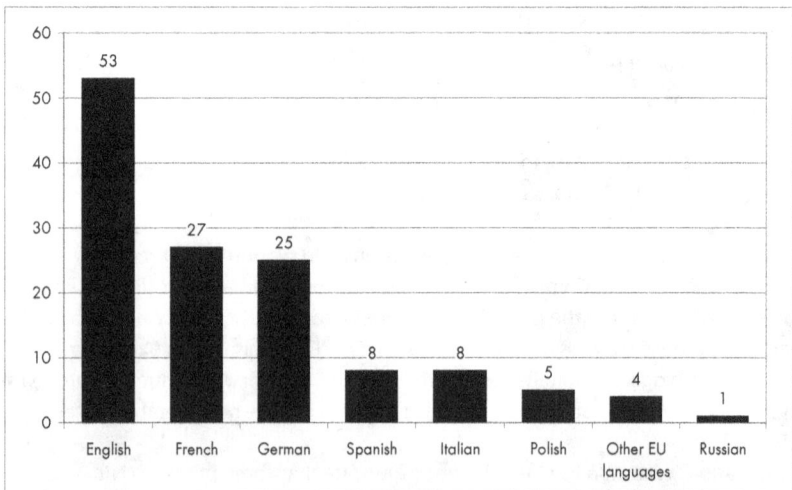

Furthermore, it seems that civil associations established in the CEECs find that participating in consultation processes at the national level is more effective for pursuing their objectives than EU consultations. The empirical research shows that the participation of those organisations in national consultations is higher in Poland than in

Germany.[18] However, those findings have to be viewed cautiously because they are based upon interviews with civil society representatives and not on an independent assessment of the actual degree of involvement in the consultations. For example, in contrast to the aforementioned findings, the Estonian case study on the engagement of domestic interest groups in national decision-making processes shows that interest groups consider their participation in national consultations inadequate and feel that their opinions are rarely taken into account (Lepa et al 2004, 49). Nevertheless, empirical research reveals that e.g. environmental organisations situated in the CEECs operate at the local rather than at the international level. About 43 per cent of those organisations are active mainly at the local level, 30 per cent operate in a particular region, 24 per cent operate nationwide and less than 3 per cent operate at the international level (Vari 1998, 55).

However, the main reason for the modest involvement of CEEC interest groups in the Commission's consultations lies in their limited organisational capacity; their relatively poor finances and lack of sustainable operational structures are very well documented empirically in the literature.[19] Their communication structure is particularly weak, and owing to the lack of technical expertise, it is used inefficiently (Vari 1998, 23). Due to budgetary constraints, those organisations simply cannot meet the costs of transnational mobilisation.

6.4. Capacity Building

Current scholarship asserts that the level of CEEC civic group participation in the Commission's communications can be increased through the provision of EU funding for capacity building. A study commissioned by the Civil Society Contact Group stresses that without such funding and capacity building, these organisations cannot effectively participate in EU modes of governance (Fazi/Smith 2006, 88). Structural funding in particular would allow civil society associations to contribute to the EU policy-making process in a meaningful way by providing them with the resources needed to develop the critical organisational structures required for active participation in EU policy-making. This approach is in concert with the EU initiatives adopted for the purpose of improving civil society input in other modes of EU governance that entail civic involvement, such as the social dialogue (which is codified by the Treaty's standardised procedure for the involvement of employers' and employees' associations in EU law-making) (Commission 2004b, 5). Structural funding initiatives have also emerged

---

18 This research consisted of 800 interviews with representatives of civil society organisations and institutional actors in Belgium, France, Germany, Greece, Hungary, Italy, Poland, Spain, Sweden and the United Kingdom (Bozzini 2007, 4).
19 See Lane 2006, 14–17.

(entailing civil society participation in the process of determining and implementing the distribution of EU resources for the purpose of regional development).[20]

Some programmes designed to support the EU's policies can be utilised by CEEC interest groups to strengthen their capability to take part in the Commission's consultations. Those include, for instance, EIDGR, the European Initiative for Democracy and Human Rights or the Daphne Programme to combat violence against children, young people and women. However, the majority of those funding initiatives were designed to support the activities of European networks (Fazi/Smith 2006, 20), or to finance public policy objectives,[21] and not to build the capacity of national CEEC interest groups to take an active part in the Commission's consultations.

Although it appears that EU funding of civil society organisations would enable them to actively participate in the Commission's consultations, one cannot deny the risks linked to an over-dependency on one main source of funding. Single funding sources lead to competition between organisations and increase the likelihood that interest associations will feel beholden to the supporting institutions' agenda and neglect their own priorities. Such efforts can in fact facilitate the proliferation of clientelist NGO-based networks without significant offsetting benefits (Sardamov 2005, 380).

Privileging a limited number of civic groups could easily create new clientelist networks that might be used to relieve groups of prospective 'multipliers' from the acute problems faced by most ordinary citizens. In this context, an excessive focus on 'civil society assistance' may paradoxically hamper the deeper, longer-term social processes necessary for the development of a vigorous associational life and of the democratic representation of differentiated social interests (Sardamov 2005, 380).[22] On the other hand, public funding can also guarantee independence by insulating the groups from private influence.

However, it cannot be expected that EU resources for capacity building would, on their own, significantly increase the participation of CEEC civil society groups in the Commission's consultations. It is well established in the literature that the major weakness of a simple resource-based perspective that ignores the structural ties of an organisation with its environment/ members/ constituencies/ sponsors (so-called critical resources dependencies) is its assumption that interest groups are always prepared to modify and Europeanise their strategies as soon as their material self-inter-

---

20 See Articles 11 and 42 of the Council Regulation EC no 1083/2006 of 11 July 2006 laying down general provisions on the European Regional Development Fund, the European Social Fund and the Cohesion Fund and repealing Regulation EC No 1260/1999, Official Journal of the European Union, L 210/25 of 31.7.2006.
21 The Commission publishes information on beneficiaries under those programmes at http://ec.europa.eu/grants/beneficiaries_en.htm and http://ec.europa.eu/public_contracts/benefi ciaries_en.htm
22 Ibid and Fagan, 2006.

ests require it or their resources enable them to do so. Such a perspective glosses over the possibility that actors might refrain from going beyond the domestic level because they are in need of, identify with or are loyal to their local or domestic resource suppliers. The empirical evidence demonstrates that it is not resources that matter most. More important is how organisations are structurally connected or tied to their environment, i.e. how strongly an organisation depends on its members/ constituencies for its survival, the sector in which its main activities are located, and how dependent an organisation is on sponsors in its immediate environment (Beyers/Kerremans 2007). In this respect, it is important to point out that the majority of civic groups in the CEECs lack any grass-roots support (Stark/Vedres/Bruszt 2005) and do not critically depend upon their supporters for funding. In all aspects of financial support, civil associations in the CEECs receive a significantly lower level of contributions (with the exception of trade unions), than do their counterparts in Great Britain and Germany, although the number of subscribers to humanitarian and environmental/peace organisations is greater in the Czech Republic. All CEECs exhibit a financial participation gap far in excess of the differences in gross domestic product relative to the rest of the EU member states. The disassociation of civic groups operating in the CEECs is aggravated by the fact that many civil society organisations were founded and financed by foreigners, especially American public and private donors (Lane in this volume). Civic organisations from the CEECs are not firmly embedded in their own environment because their membership base is extremely weak and volatile. The CEECs do not have a consolidated and sustainable civil association sector. The sustainability scores of civil society calculated on the basis of, among other factors, the financial viability, organisational capacity and infrastructure of voluntary associations by the United States Agency for International Development in 2003 are relatively low in all CEECs and reflect the weakness of civic organisations in those states (Howard 2003, 65, 66, 69, and 71).

6.5. Conclusions

The European Commission's consultations are designed to solicit input from civil society associations prior to the drafting of EU legislation and to enable the institution to take different views into account when making policy proposals. The Commission's failure to meet these objectives is reflected in the disproportionately low level of input from citizens' organisations originating in the CEECs. Our research shows that the number of submissions from interest groups operating in the Eastern European member states is disproportionately lower than the number of contributions forwarded by civic organisations carrying out their activities elsewhere in the Union. If and when the CEEC civic groups participate, they do so almost exclusively through European networks (Howard 2003, 65, 66, 69, and 71).

Our research results empirically confirmed the findings of some earlier studies vis-à-vis the dearth of direct engagement of CEEC interest groups in the Commission's consultations.[23] The empirical evidence also shows similarly low levels of participation in other forms of EU governance that formally require civil organisations' input, such as the open method of co-ordination,[24] the social dialogue (Mailand, Mikkel /Due, Jesper 2004) and EU structural funds (Harvey 2004).

References

Alonso Vizcaino, Jose M. (2005), 'European civil society organisations and the principles of participatory democracy: 'Hit-and-miss-policy?', Master thesis defended at the International School for Humanities and Social Sciences of the University of Amsterdam, 19 September 2005.

Beyers, Jan /Kerremans, Bart (2007), 'Critical resource dependencies and Europenization of domestic interest groups', *Journal of European Public Policy*, 14(3), pp. 460–481.

Borragan, Nieves Perez-Solorzano (2004), 'EU accession and interest politics in Central and Eastern Europe', *Perspectives on European Politics and Society*, 5(2), pp. 243–272.

Bozzini, Emanuela (2007), 'Why to get involved in Brussels? A cross-sectoral and cross-national comparison of the involvement of civil society organisations in EU policy processes', paper presented at the CINEFOGO Network of Excellence Mid-term Conference 'European Citizenship – Challenges and Possibilities', Roskilde, 1–3 June 2007.

Commission of the European Communities (2001), 'European governance: White paper', COM(2001), 25.7.2001.

Commission of the European Communities (2002a), 'Communication from the Commission on impact assessment', COM(2002) 276.

Commission of the European Communities (2002b), 'Communication from the Commission: Towards a reinforced culture of consultation and dialogue – General principles and minimum standards for consultation of interested parties by the Commission', COM(2002) 704.

Commission of the European Communities (2004a), 'Commission staff working paper: Social Inclusion in new member states: A synthesis of the joint memoranda on social inclusion', SEC(2004) 848.

23　For cases of Czech and Latvian civil groups, see Fazi/Smith 2006, 72–73 and 76–78 respectively.
24　See Commission 2004a, 35–36.

Commission of the European Communities (2004b), 'Communication from the Commission: Partnership for change in an enlarged Europe – Enhancing the contribution of European social dialogue', COM (2004) 557.

Commission of the European Communities (2006), 'Green paper: European Transparency Initiative', COM(2006) 194.

Commission of the European Communities (2005), Impact Assessment Guidelines, 15 June 2005, SEC (2005) 791.

Commission of the European Communities (2005a) 'Commission staff working document, Annex to the Report from the Commission "Better lawmaking 2004" pursuant to Article 9 of the Protocol on the application of the principles of subsidiarity and proportionality (12ᵗʰ report), SEC(2005) 98.

Commission of the European Communities (2007), 'Communication from the Commission: Follow-up to the Green Paper: European Transparency Initiative', COM(2007) 127.

Commission of the European Communities (2007a), 'Commission staff working document, Annex to the Report from the Commission "Better lawmaking 2006" pursuant to Article 9 of the Protocol on the application of the principles of subsidiarity and proportionality (14th report), SEC (2007) 737.

European Commission (2004), 'Analysis of the stakeholder consultation on "Science and technology, the key to Europe's future: guidelines to for future European policy to support research"', COM(353) 2004, http://ec.europa.eu/research/fp7/pdf/analysisdoc_en.pdf.

European Commission (2005a), *Eurobarometer 63.4: Europeans and Languages*: Fieldwork May – June, http://ec.europa.eu/public_opinion/archives/ebs/ebs_237.en.pdf.

European Commission (2005b), *Responses to the consultation on research themes in FP7*, 16 March 2005, http://ec.europa.eu/research/fp7/pdf/fp7themesconsultation_en.pdf.

Fagan, Adam (2006) 'Transnational aid for civil society development in post-socialist Europe: Democratic consolidation or new imperialism', Journal of Communist Studies and Transnational Politics, 22(1): 115–134.

Fazi, Elodie /Smith, Jeremy (2006), Civil Dialogue: making it work better, Study commissioned by the Civil Society Contact Group, http://act4europe.horus.be/module/FileLib/Civil%20dialogue,%20making%20it%20work%20better.pdf.

Greenwood, Justine (2003), 'The world of NGOs and interest representation, in: NGOs, Democratisation and the Regulatory State', A Collection of Papers Presented at the Conferences in London and Brussels, European Policy Forum, London.

Harlow, C. (2005), 'Deconstructing government', Yearbook of European Law, 23 (2004): 57–89.

Harvey, Brian (2004), *The Illusion of Inclusion*, ECAS, Brussels.

Howard, Marc Morje (2003), *The Weakness of Civil Society in Post-Communist Europe*, Cambridge University Press, Cambridge, pp. 57–92.

Korkut, Umut (2005), 'The position of interest groups in Eastern European democracies: Maturing servicemen or Trojan horse?', in: Rossteutscher, Sigrid (ed.), *Democracy and the Role of Associations: Political, Organizational and Social Context*, Routledge, London, pp. 113–132.

Kuti, E. (1997), *The Non Profit Sector in Hangary, John Hopkins Nonprofit Sector Series*, Manchester University Press, Manchester and New York.

Lane, David (2006), 'Civil society formation and accountability in the new post-socialist EU member states', Working papers of the Research Centre for East European Studies No. 74, Bremen, pp. 7–22.

Lepa, Reesi et al. (2004), 'Engaging Interest Groups in Decision-Making Processes', Poliitikauuringute Keskus Praxis, Tallinn, htt://www.praxis.ee/data/kaasamine_eng._9_03.pdf.

Mailand, Mikkel /Due, Jesper (2004), 'Social dialogue in Central and Eastern Europe: present state and future development', *European Journal of Industrial Relations*, 10(2), pp. 179–197.

Mudde, Cas (2007), 'Civil society', in: White, Stephen/ Batt, Judy / Lewis, Paul G. (eds), *Developments in Central and East European Politics, 4*, Palgrave, Houndmills (forthcoming).

Narozhna, Tanya (2004), 'Foreign aid for a post-euphoric Eastern Europe: the limitations of western assistance in developing civil society', *Journal of International Relations and Development*, 7, pp. 243–266.

Obradovic, Daniela /Alonso Vizcaino, Jose (2006), 'Good governance requirements concerning the participation of interest groups in EU consultations', *Common Market Law Review*, 43, pp. 1049–1085.

Rose-Ackerman, Susan (2007), *From Elections to Democracy: building Accountable Government in Hungry and Poland*, Cambridge, University Press Cambridge.

Sardamov, Ivelin (2005), 'Civil society and the limits of democratic assistance', *Government and Opposition*, pp. 379–402.

Sargenet, Jane A. (1985), 'Corporatism and the European Community', in: Wyn Grant, (ed.), *The Political Economy of Corporatism*, Macmillan, London, pp. 229–253.

Stark, David /Vedres, Balazs /Bruszt, Laszlo (2005), 'Global Links, Local Roots? Varieties of Transnationalization and Forms of Civic Integration', Working Papers Series, Center on Organizational Innovation, Columbia University.

The European Ombudsman (2005), Decision 948/2004/OV of 4 May 2005, http//www. euro-ombudsman.eu.int/decision/en/040948.htm.

Vari, Anna (1998), *Civil society and public participation: recent trends in a Central and Eastern Europe*, Community Economic Development Centre at Simon Fraser University, British Columbia, Canada, http://www.sfu.ca/cscd/research/civilsoc/vari.htm.

Vazquez-Garcia, Rafael (2007), 'Broadening European citizenship through voluntary organisations. Effects on civil society and the quality of democracy', paper presented at the CINEFOGO Network of Excellence Mid-term Conference "European Citizenship – Challenges and Possibilities", Roskilde, 1–3 June 2007.

Part III. The European Civil Dialogue. NGOs
and Economic Interest Groups

Heiko Pleines and Kristýna Bušková

7. Capacity Building for Czech Environmental Ngos to Participate in EU Governance

7.1. Introduction

Environmental Ngos are among the strongest civil society organisations in the Czech Republic.[1] In public opinion polls conducted in 2004, the year the country joined the EU, three thirds of the Czech population declared their trust in environmental Ngos, which is the second highest ranking among Czech civil society organisations. In the same poll environmental Ngos were also described as successful (Vajdová 2005, 58–60). At the same time, the European Union exerts a strong influence upon the environmental policy of the member states. Accordingly, among Czech civil society organisations environmental Ngos should theoretically have the best chances for engagement at the EU level.

In this case study we will examine how Czech environmental Ngos interact with EU bodies. In order to provide background information, we will assess their general ability to engage in political decision-making processes, focusing on the national level. After that we will describe the pre-accession capacity-building efforts made by the EU to bolster Czech environmental Ngos and groom them for participation in decision-making processes at the EU level. From there, we will examine the representation and activities of these organisations at the EU level. This will enable us to assess the impact the Czech environmental Ngos' engagement has had on the EU as well as on the Ngos themselves.

7.2. Post-Socialist Challenges to Czech Environmental NGOs

In socialist Czechoslovakia environmental organisations represented a haven for dissidents. Accordingly, the environmentalists played an important role in bringing down the regime in 1989 and influenced the new political leadership significantly. Their main success was the adoption of the law on the environment and environmental information in 1990.

However, in the independent Czech Republic Prime Minister Vaclav Klaus soon insulated his government from the influence of environmental Ngos, as well as from most other independent politically active organisations. Since then environmental Ngos have redirected their activities on their position relative to state representa-

---

1   Academic analyses of their role are provided by: Fagan 2005 and 2004; Jehlička/Sarre/Podoba 2005; Carmin 2003a and 2003b; Fagan/Jehlicka 2003; Tickle/Vavroušek 1998.

tives. They have insisted on exercising their right to access environment-related information and participate in environment-related political decision-making processes, including the right to prepare reports on state-financed projects having an environmental impact. Environmental NGOs have organised protest actions to support their positions and initiated judicial actions to thwart specific projects or to protect their rights in the political decision-making process.

The adoption of the environmental part of the EU acquis communautaire in 2001 and the signing of the Aarhus Convention in 2004 at the EU's request fortified the legal rights of Czech environmental NGOs considerably.

As a result of these developments, the environmental NGOs have generally been able to make their way back into political circles since the late 1990s. This view is supported by NGO activists as well as by public opinion (Spiralis Foundation 2005). In 2004, when the Czech Republic joined the EU, the national Ministry of the Environment already cooperated with environmental NGOs on a routine basis. Approximately 10% of the NGOs were represented in regional administrations and their committees (Nadace Partnerství 2004, 14) The political significance of environmental NGOs was strengthened by the media as well. The Czech public broadcasting TV company devotes a lot of attention to these organisations in regional news. There is also a new trend of inviting NGO activists to appear on programmes as experts (Spiralis Foundation 2005).

Accordingly, environmental NGOs had enjoyed a number of political successes in the years preceding EU accesion. In 2003 they were allowed to take part in the state-funded regional development programme Agenda 21. In 2004 their lobbying on the State Environmental Policy and Waste Management Programme as well as on the protection of Natura 2000 ecological sites had a visible impact on political decisions.

It is often maintained that these NGOs' political successes are solely dependent on their relations with specific political actors. As Adam Fagan argues:

> From the perspective of the Czech environmental movement, although over a decade of foreign assistance and know-how transfer has resulted in a tier of professional NGOs that have obtained political influence at the elite level, these organizations have made little progress in rooting themselves in society at large. (Fagan 4/2005, 528)

This view is backed by empirical data. According to the European Social Survey 2004, only 1.8% of the Czech population claims membership in environmental NGOs and a mere 1.4% active support[2]. About 2.5% of the Czech population has made donations to environmental NGOs.[3] Thus Czechs contributed 9% to the NGOs' coffers, while the share of EU support alone stood at 7%. Czech environmental NGOs are therefore

---

2   In the original wording: unpaid voluntary work.
3   European Social Survey 2004, http://ess.nsd.uib.no/nesstarlight/index.jsp.

dependent on institutional donors and commercial activities, with the latter contributing about 20% of their budget (Nadace Partnerství 2004, 12).

Accordingly, it can be argued that the environmental movement is one of the strongest elements of Czech civil society in terms of political influence. Nevertheless, their organisational capacity is limited, and in financial terms they are heavily dependent upon institutional and foreign support. Prior to EU accession they were also lacking in international experience. In the second half of the 1990s only 1.8% of Czech NGOs were working on the international level (The Regional Environmental Center for Central and Eastern Europe 1997, 43–44).

7.3.   Pre-Accession Support from the EU

In the years preceding accession, the EU strove to buttress NGOs in the candidate countries through a number of measures. For Czech environmental NGOs three aspects of EU support were of special relevance. First, the EU promoted their integration into an EU-wide NGO network. Second, the EU offered vital training to the NGOs' leading representatives. Third, the EU provided considerable financial support for the purpose of honing their organisational and managerial skills.

7.3.1.   Integration of Czech Environmental NGOs into an EU-Wide NGO Network

From 1999 to 2004 the Directorate General for the Environment (DG Environment) of the EU Commission organised an EU-NGO dialogue, in which 40 environmental NGOs from the Balkan and candidate countries (among them four from the Czech Republic) took part.[4] In addition nine major international environmental NGOs active at the EU level participated as observers.[5] The dialogue meetings were held roughly twice a year either in Brussels or in one of the candidate or Balkan countries with selected NGOs representing their respective national civil societies. The final meeting took place on 18–19 April 2004.

Until 2002 the dialogue meetings were coordinated by the Regional Environmental Centre for Central and Eastern Europe (REC). Headquartered in Hungary, the REC set up country and field offices in 15 Central and Eastern European countries, includ-

---

4   These were the Center for Community Organizing, the Rainbow Movement, the Society for Sustainable Living and ZO CSOP Veronica.
5   These were Birdlife International, the Climate Action Network, the European Environmental Bureau, the European Federation for Transport and Environment, Friends of the Earth, Greenpeace, Friends of Nature and the World Wide Fund for Nature.

ing the Czech Republic. The German Institute for Biodiversity (IBN) arranged the final meeting in 2004.[6]
According to the DG Environment, the purpose of these meetings was to:

- improve the transparency and relations between the NGOs and DG Environment,
- inform the NGOs about ongoing issues on enlargement and environmental policy developments,
- consult the civil society on new environmental policy developments in the EU, and their implications for the Candidate Countries,
- explore, with the NGOs, ways in which they can play an active and constructive role in the enlargement process ('environmental watchdog'),
- create a platform for NGOs to address their concerns to EU policy makers and to enhance cooperation among the NGOs themselves.[7]

The participating environmental NGOs from the Czech Republic saw the dialogue as an important source of information, especially on regulatory issues and funding opportunities, and as a critical opportunity to forge international contacts. Through their Czech network, the Green Circle, an NGO participating in the dialogue disseminated information from the meetings in Brussels to the other Czech environmental NGOs. As most Czech environmental NGOs lacked the necessary funding to join a Brussels-based organisation, the EU-NGO dialogue was the only chance for Czech environmental NGOs to establish regular direct contact with EU institutions prior to their country's accession.[8]

Then, in 2003, an educational mission to Brussels was organised for representatives of Czech NGOs. The Czech delegation, headed by Czech diplomat Pavel Telicka, was able to discuss the potential consequences of the country's accession face to face with representatives of the EU.

7.3.2. Training to Leading Representatives of Czech Environmental NGOs

The training of Czech environmental NGO representatives was supported by the EU, which tied many grants to the organisations' level of professionalism and further enabled many NGOs to meet professionals from the field during the EU-NGO dialogue. In

---

6   For information on the dialogue see the websites of the DG Environment, http://europa.eu.int/comm/environment/enlarg/ngodialogue_en.htm, and the REC, http://www.rec.org/REC/Publications/EC-NGO_Dialogue/Introduction.html. Now that the dialogue is over, the IBN website (www.biodiv.de) no longer contains related information.
7   DG Environment http://europa.eu.int/comm/environment/enlarg/ngodialogue_en.htm.
8   Green Circle, www.zelenykruh.cz.

addition, the EU funded training courses for Czech civil society organisations through its PHARE programme,[9] in which altogether 200 NGOs took part.[10] According to the training organisers the aims were to:

- inform NGOs about directives and regulations that governed the allocation of resources from pre-accession programmes like PHARE and from the Structural Funds of the EU,
- improve the knowledge of the IT technology and programs specifically designed for development and project management,
- make sure that other agents in the society gain knowledge and access to the EU programmes and learn how to manage projects,
- support and motivate NGOs to make contacts with the local and regional admin-istrations,
- positively influence the relationship of the Czech citizens to the EU (NROS 2003).

In addition, Czech environmental NGOs obtained EU funding for issue-specific training courses and seminars.

7.3.3. Financial Support

Prior to the EU accession of their country, Czech environmental NGOs could obtain EU funding from PHARE, ISPA, and SAPARD.[11] Thus the EU provided about 7% of their income through direct payments (Nadace Partnerství 2004, 14).

Since its 2004 accession to the EU, the Czech Republic's environmental NGOs are now eligible to apply for EU funding for member states. The most important funding opportunities are the EU Environmental Programme, Structural Funds and the Rural Development Policy within the Common Agricultural Policy. In addition, since 2007 LIFE+ offers funding exclusively for environmental projects.[12]

However, for Czech environmental NGOs this means that they no longer receive funding for capacity building, but have to engage exclusively in environmental projects. Competition tends to be stiffer in this arena and Czech environmental NGOs now have to compete with environmental-related organisations from all member states (in the case of environment-related funds) or with fellow organisations from the Czech Republic (in the case of structural funds). In addition, the EU requires that funding be matched by contributions from the organisations themselves, which can range from 20% up to 80% of the project value. Accordingly, the weak financial position of Czech environmental NGOs may paradoxically restrict their eligibility to apply for EU funding to a substantial degree.

---

9   Civil Society Development Programme 2001.
10   There is no information available on the share of environmental NGOs in this figure.
11   A comprehensive overview is given by: REC (2001)
12   Comprehensive overviews are given by: European Commission (2005) and WWF (2005)

7.4.   Engagement at the EU Level

As the EU has acquired an important role in shaping environmental regulation of member countries, environmental NGOs as well as representatives of industries having an environmental impact are active at the EU level. Environmental NGOs participate in EU expert panels and in preparatory and implementation committees, contributing to the formulation of EU policies, programmes and initiatives. In addition, NGOs regularly form part of the EU delegation to international environment-related negotiations, such as the United Nations Conference on Environment and Development (UNCED) in Rio and most sessions of the UN Commission on Sustainable Development.[13]

In order to coordinate their engagement at the EU level and to increase their impact, environmental NGOs have signed on with a number of European associations with representative offices in Brussels.[14] The biggest environmental NGOs and NGO associations active in Brussels have formed the Green 10, which consist of BirdLife International (European Community Office), Climate Action Network Europe (CAN Europe), CEE Bankwatch Network, European Environmental Bureau (EEB), European Federation of Transport and Environment (T&E), EPHA Environment Network (EEN), Friends of the Earth Europe (FoEE), Greenpeace Europe, International Friends of Nature (IFN), and the WWF European Policy Office.

According to its mission statement, the Green 10

work with the EU law-making institutions – the European Commission, the European Parliament and the Council of Ministers – to ensure that the environment is placed at the heart of policymaking. This includes working with our member organisations in the Member States to facilitate their input into the EU decision-making process.
While campaigning at EU level, Green 10 NGOs encourage the full implementation of EU environmental laws and policies in the Member States; lobby for new environmental proposals, as appropriate; work with the EU institutions to ensure that policies under consideration are as environmentally effective as possible; promote EU environmental leadership in the global political arena.
In terms of public awareness raising, Green 10 NGOs inform their members and the wider public of environmental developments at EU level, and encourage them to make their voice heard; give voice to thousands of locally-based associations, which would otherwise have no access to EU decision-makers; contribute to the strengthening of civil society across Europe through training in advocacy skills, policy analysis and the EU decision-making process.[15]

In summary, the role of environmental associations at the EU level is twofold. On the one hand they lobby EU bodies on environmental issues in order to influence related EU regulations. On the other they cooperate with EU bodies (and especially with the DG Environment of the European Commission) in order to compel their national gov-

---

13   http://europa-eu-un.org/articles/sv/article_1004_sv.htm.
14   For portraits of the leading international associations of environmental NGOs see the Green Year Book 2004, http://www.greenyearbook.org/ngo/ngo-ind.htm.
15   http://www.foeeurope.org/links/green10.htm.

ernments to implement EU guidelines. Whereas the first task requires strong representation in Brussels, realisation of the second task demands political influence at the national, regional and local levels (Wörner 2004, Greenwood 2003).

Whereas Czech environmental NGOs can boast considerable experience in national politics (having joined the fray by the late 1980s), lobbying in Brussels is a newer task (with official contacts first starting in 1999). Two years after their country had joined the EU, 13 environmental NGOs from the Czech Republic had become full members of at least one Green 10 partner; of these, four are national branches of international NGOs. As Table 7-1 demonstrates, the highest number of Czech environmental NGOs can be found in the European Environmental Bureau (EEB).

Table 7-1:   Membership of Czech Environmental NGOs in Associations at the EU Level

Czech NGO	Website	Member of
Centrum pro dopravu a energetiku (Centre for Transport and Energy)	http://cde.ecn.cz	CAN Europe CEE Bankwatch Network T&E
Česká společnost ornitologická (Czech Society for Ornithology)	http://www.birdlife.cz	BirdLife International
Český a Slovenský Dopravní Klub (Czech and Slovak Traffic Club)	http://dopravniklub.ecn.cz/	T&E
Ekologické Centrum Toulcův Dvůr	http://www.ecn.cz/yee	EEB
Ekologický právní servis (Environmental Law Service)	http://www.eps.org	EEB
EkoWatt	http://www.ekowatt.cz	CAN Europe
Greenpeace Czech Republic	http://www.greenpeace.cz	Greenpeace International
Hnutí DUHA (Rainbow Movement)	http://www.hnutiduha.cz	CEE Bankwatch Network Friends of the Earth Europe
Sdružení Duha (Friends of Nature)	http://www.duha.cz	International Friends of Nature
Společnost pro trvale udržitelný život (Society for Sustainable Living)	http://www.czp.cuni.cz/stuz	EEB
Středisko pro Efektivní Využívání Energie – "SEVEn" (Energy Efficiency Center)	http://www.svn.cz	CAN Europe
Ústav Pro Ecopolitiku (Institute for Environmental Policy)	http://www.uep.ecn.cz	EEB
Zelený Kruh (Green Circle)	http://www.ecn.cz	EEB

Source: Green 10 (http://www.foeeurope.org/links/green10.htm), May 2006.

Czech environmental NGOs can certainly be said to profit from their engagement at the EU level. First, they become integrated into an international network. This helps them to professionalise and to obtain advice. Second, they receive information and advice about funding opportunities at the EU level. Third, they acquire first-hand information about EU environmental policies, which gives them an edge in negotiations with Czech state agencies. Fourth, they have the power to monitor the activities of Czech representatives at the EU level. However, as they participate only indirectly in EU decision-making processes through their partnerships with Green 10 members, they do not have any visible impact on EU policy.[16]

Measured by the accumulated number of members in the Green 10, Czech environmental NGOs fall in the middle range. Of the post-socialist member states, only Hungary (with 19 NGOs) is better represented than the Czech Republic. However, as Table 7-2 demonstrates, the NGOs from the five most active countries account for 45% of Green 10 members, whereas NGOs from the Czech Republic have a share of only 4%.

In addition, it has to be noted that there is no shortage of tension among the Green 10 partners as they focus on different topics, exhibit varying degrees of willingness to compromise and pursue distinct lobbying strategies. WWF and Birdlife, for example, concentrate on nature preservation and are willing to join forces with businesses and politicians to reach compromises, thereby pursuing a cooperative strategy of lobbyism based on voluntary support and negotiations. Greenpeace, on the other hand, zeroes in on industry-related issues such as emissions and nuclear policy and is much more confrontational. Accordingly, its lobbying strategy is often predicated on public pressure and showdowns with business and politics.

These tensions make it even harder for smaller environmental NGOs such as those from the Czech Republic to work in Brussels. One result of the divisions within the Green 10 is that much of the environmental NGOs' work at the EU level is still being done individually by the partners. Furthermore, the internal tensions limit the ability of the Green 10 to provide adequate support to smaller member NGOs. Last but not least, involvement in the infighting makes it harder for Czech NGOs with different Green 10 affiliations to cooperate and sometimes actually ends up alienating NGO members active in Brussels from their national organisations (Wörner 2004, Greenwood 2003).

---

16   This assessment is shared by the European Environmental Bureau as well as by the major association of Czech environmental NGOs, the Green Circle. See esp. European Environmental Bureau: How the EEB works, www.eeb.org and Zelený Kruh (Green Circle): EU a životní prostředí, www.zelenykruh.cz.

Table 7-2:   Share of Countries within the Green 10

Country	Share of NGOs in Green 10
Czech Republic	4%
Estonia	2%
Hungary	5%
Latvia	1%
Lithuania	1%
Poland	2%
Slovakia	2%
Slovenia	2%
Post-socialist member states	*19%*
Belgium	10%
France	7%
Germany	8%
Netherlands	7%
United Kingdom	13%
Top 5	*45%*
Austria	3%
Cyprus	1%
Denmark	4%
Finland	3%
Greece	3%
Ireland	2%
Italy	4%
Luxemburg	3%
Malta	1%
Portugal	2%
Spain	4%
Sweden	4%
Others	*34%*
Total	*100%*

Note: The individual numbers do not add up to 100% due to rounding.
Source: own calculation based on Green 10 (http://www.foeeurope.org/links/green10.htm), May 2006.

7.5.   Conclusions

In conclusion, the EU has a much bigger impact on Czech environmental organisations than the latter have on EU decision-making processes. The EU was a strong promoter of the internationalisation of Czech environmental NGOs and has contributed to their professionalisation. In addition, EU regulation has strengthened the position of environmental NGOs within the Czech Republic. This means the EU has not only improved the EU-related capacity of Czech environmental NGOs, but has also strengthend their capacity to engage in political decision-making processes at domestic levels.

As a result, Czech environmental NGOs regularly support EU environmental policy at domestic levels. They promote and monitor the implementation of EU regulations. In this respect they cooperate with the European Commission, namely with the DG Environment. However, Czech environmental NGOs have thus far failed to gain momentum as a lobbying force capable of influencing EU decisions. They are too small to shape or otherwise make a difference in the major international environmental associations they have joined at the EU level.

Accordingly the impact of the engagement of Czech environmental NGOs at the EU level is felt primarily at the national and regional levels within the Czech Republic itself. In fact, pre-accession EU support has not so much helped to integrate Czech environmental NGOs into EU decision-making structures, but has considerably improved their capacity to influence domestic politics at home. In so doing the EU Commission has strengthened a powerful ally for the implementation of EU environmental regulation in the Czech Republic.

References

Carmin, J. (2003): *Non-governmental organisations and public participation in local environmental decision-making in the Czech Republic*, in: Local Environment, 8(5), pp. 541–552.

Carmin, J. (2003): *Resources, opportunities and local environmental action in the democratic transition and early consolidation periods in the Czech Republic*, in: Environmental Politics, 12(3), pp. 42–64.

European Commission (2005): *Handbook for Environmental Project Funding*, Brussels.

Fagan, A. (2005): *Taking stock of civil-society development in post-communist Europe. Evidence from the Czech Republic*, in: Democratization, 12(4), pp. 528–547.

Fagan, A. (2004): *Environment and democracy in the Czech Republic*, Edward Elgar Publishing, Cheltenham.

Fagan, A. / Jehlicka. P. (2003): *Contours of the Czech environmental movement: a comparative analysis of Hnuti Duha (Rainbow Movement) and Jihoceske matky (South Bohemian Mothers)*, in: Environmental Politics, 12(3), pp. 49–70.

Greenwood, J. (2003): *Interest representation in the European Union*, Palgrave Macmillan, New York, pp.186–196.

Jehlička, P. / Sarre, P. / Podoba, J. (2005): *The Czech environmental movement's knowledge interests in the 1990s. Compatibility of Western influences with pre-1989 perspectives*, in: Environmental Politics, 14(1), pp. 64–82.

Nadace Partnerství (2004). *The Czech Non-Profit Sector Before Entering the European Union: Development, Capacity, Needs and Future of Czech Environmental NGOs*, Prague, p. 14, http://www.nadacepartnerstvi.cz.

NROS (2003): *Školeni pro organizace občanské společnosti, Evropská Brána*, www.ngo-eu.cz/Prospectus.

REC (2001): *Directory of Funding Sources for Environmental NGOs in Central and Eastern Europe*, Budapest, http://www.rec.org/REC/Databases/Funders/Default.html.

Spiralis Foundation (2005): *Zpráva o neziskovém sektoru v České republice*, Prague, pp. 1–12, www.spiralis-os.cz.

The Regional Environmental Center for Central and Eastern Europe (1997): *Problems, Progress and Possibilities: A Needs Assessment of Environmental NGOs in Central and Eastern Europe*, Budapest, pp. 43–44, www.rec.org/REC/Publications/NGONeeds.

Tickle, A. / Vavroušek, J. (1998): *Environmental politics in the former Czechoslovakia*, in: Tickle, Andrew/ Welsh, Ian (eds): *Environment and society in Eastern Europe*, Harlow, Longman, pp. 114–145.

Vajdová, T. (2005): *An Assessment of Czech Civil Society in 2004: After Fifteen Years of Development*, Academic Press CERM, Brno, pp. 41–62.

Wörner, T. (2004): *Einflussmöglichkeiten von NGOs auf die Umweltpolitik der Europäischen Union*, Tectum, Marburg.

WWF (2005): *EU Funding for Environment. A handbook for the 2007–2013 programming period*, http://assets.panda.org/downloads/eufundingforenvironmentweb.pdf.

Gesine Fuchs and Silvia Payer

8.   Women's NGOs in EU Governance. Problems of Finance and Access[1]

8.1.   Introduction

EU gender policy has often been characterised as one of the most elaborated and advanced policy fields. With comparatively strong civil society participation and the recent Gender Mainstreaming strategy, it has moved beyond employment as its sole focus.[2] Does this mean that gender equality issues and with them Women's NGOs in the new Central and East European EU member states (CEECs) are gaining momentum?

The new EU members adopted the gender acquis in record time; they pushed it through much faster than the old member states did, and with a more homogeneous result (for the entire *acquis communautaire*, see Schimmelfennig/Sedelmeier 2005, 225). However, a 'Potemkin harmonisation' (Jacoby 1999) may now be emerging: Since the hurdle of membership conditionality has already been surmounted, the gap between adoption and implementation of gender equality directives is widening, and domestic political factors, including national gender regimes, adjustment costs and resistance from the bureaucracy and societal groups, are gathering steam.

Nevertheless, the European Union has proven itself as a political opportunity structure in which women's groups can affect national policy and place otherwise ignored issues on the agenda. In this context, the capacity of women's organisations from the new member states to participate in EU governance is of vital importance. This particular case exhibits complexity on several different levels, and diverse challenges are evolving for meaningful participation. To begin with, NGOs in the new member

---

1   This article is based on research on Polish women's NGOs conducted by Gesine Fuchs and on research by Silvia Payer, which is based on a survey conducted by the author in 2006 within the framework of postgraduate studies on 'International Gender Research and Female Politics in Eastern Europe'. The research was focused on Bulgaria and Slovakia. For the development of the thesis, interviews were conducted with women's NGOs, NGOs, donor organisations and government officials. A questionnaire was disseminated via email.

2   EU gender equality policy rests on three pillars: (1) Equal treatment since the 1970s: A set of directives to ensure equal treatment in the labour force (equal pay, access to training and admission to professions) was enacted in the 1970s; (2) Positive actions: 'Positive actions' further contributed to the elimination of unequal starting positions and living conditions in a patriarchal society, via e.g. women-specific legislation and support programmes or quotas and (3) Gender mainstreaming (GM): Thirdly, in 1996 the European Commission declared 'Gender Mainstreaming' as the official policy frame (see Bretherton 2001). Gender mainstreaming is the systematic integration of gender issues (priorities, needs, effects) in all policy fields and governmental institutions with the goal of promoting the equality of women and men. This objective is to be pursued during planning, implementation and evaluation phases.

states are newcomers both on the EU political scene and at home; they are not as firmly entrenched on the domestic front as their counterparts in the EU-15. The organisational and financial bases for forming and negotiating women's interests, making political claims and influencing EU governance are often weak or completely absent. Women's interests are in any case fairly marginalised in the region. To compound matters, the general public has not yet come to see the EU as a standard channel of influence. On the other hand, national and regional actors in the new member states have been increasingly directing their activities to the EU level, and have undergone political learning processes that are very useful for democratic consolidation and civil society capacity building.

Against this backdrop, we examine the capacity of women's NGOs from the Central and East European countries to engage in EU governance. It is clear that the main obstacle to this engagement is the lack of funding and access to decision-making processes; sufficient resources in particular constitute a conditio sine qua non. We will start with an assessment of the situation of women's NGOs in Central and Eastern Europe and then elaborate the problems of funding. Using Poland as an example, we will examine the extent to which women's NGOs from the new member states have become integrated into EU governance.

8.2. Women's NGOs in Central and Eastern Europe

For women living in Central and East European countries, the post-socialist transition presents a formidable challenge. Before the changes in 1989, the majority (up to 94%) of working-age women in CEECs had full-time paid employment. Their high level of participation in the labour market was made possible by several state-mandated benefits, such as paid maternity leave, annual paid leave to care for sick children and heavily subsidised child care (Bretherton 2002, 6). During the transition period, the employment rate in CEECs declined dramatically. Millions of women lost their jobs when many state industries were privatised or closed down altogether. Many others found themselves with low-paid work or exploitative jobs. Due to the dire economic situation, women continue to be in urgent need of work, and are therefore highly vulnerable to sexual harassment and exploitation (Bretherton 2002, 7). On average, women in the region earn nearly a quarter less than men (http://www.unifem.sk/). Very few women have been able to take advantage of the new opportunities provided by their changing economies (ETF 2006, 19).[3]

---

3   This recently visible feminisation of poverty in transitional countries is merely the deepening and widening of a situation that existed even prior to the changes of 1989; access to financial resources was more limited for women in socialist societies, too (Lokar, 2005, 6; Moulechkova, 2004).

One significant survival strategy for women to surmount the economic crises unleashed by the transition process was to actively participate in the development of the 'third sector'. Women created programmes for people who needed services. They worked for the community, took jobs for which they were overqualified and worked for low wages, unprotected and without legal contracts (Lokar 2005, 8).

Most women's organisations in CEECs appeared in the wake of the Beijing Conference in the second half of the 1990s;[4] few women's NGOs had heretofore existed.[5] The number of women's NGOs varies substantially from country to country, depending in part on the character of the former socialist regime. Some states permitted informal women's and feminist networks in the socialist era. Meanwhile, the presence or absence of political opportunities *after* 1989 to develop a women's agenda also influenced the formation of NGOs. Some women's groups are affiliated with political parties but have independent status by virtue of their non-political character. Women have founded mainly small and local organisations that are organised around e.g. the issues of domestic violence or human trafficking, problems that had previously received scant attention in CEECs (Bretherton 2002, 8). In relation to the overall number of women's NGOs, very few concentrate on changing the situation of women by means of political participation (Sloat 2004, 6). Women's movements and organisational networks in Eastern Europe are characterised by a special thematic profile. Work, education, the body and violence are some of the meta-issues that have surfaced during the transformation process. Nowadays, education, employment, qualifications and knowledge are necessary but by no means sufficient factors for female independence. They certainly do not guarantee a living given the rampant sex discrimination in the new capitalist economy coupled with the state's retreat from social duties and provisions. In the past few years, domestic violence has become another meta-issue, sometimes supported by state-sponsored campaigns. Activists understand domestic violence or violence against women to include not only spousal abuse but also structural or material violence in a broader sense, as illustrated by Julie Hemment in her work on Russian crisis centres (Hemment 2004, esp. 829). Women's organisations work to foster empowerment and orientation and to exert political influence; to this end, they have tended to build networks and service-NGOs rather than big umbrella organisations.

In the early 1990s, women generally founded NGOs active in historically 'gendered' fields, as they were less likely to encounter resistance from society or the state

---

4   The Fourth World Conference on Women in Beijing, China – September 1995; for achieving the stated conference goals of 'equality, development and peace for all women everywhere', the Beijing Declaration on women's rights was adopted, and the Platform for Action (PFA), one of the most progressive agendas, was generated; for further information, see: http://www.un.org/womenwatch/daw/beijing/beijingdeclaration.html.
5   IHF: 'Women 2000: An Investigation into the Status of Women's Rights in Central and South-Eastern Europe and the Newly Independent States', Nov. 2000, www.ihf-hr.org/viewbinary/viewdocument.php?download=1&doc_id=2055.

there. According to Ferree/Mc Clurg, 'Women are institutionally disadvantaged in contexts waged on men's terrain. Women are thus more likely to organize outside the formal polity, in those community and grassroots contexts that are gendered female.' (Ferree/McClurg 2004, 589) Most of those initiatives run by women and for women were active in social affairs and focused on support, consultation and training: 'Most of them play a particularly important role in the field of social protection, since they largely represent and defend the interests of specific disadvantaged groups. Because most of these NGOs are familiar with the specifics of particular communities (lifestyle, culture, religion, labour and social skills and habits, health and similar problems) they play an equal role along with the State in the development and implementation of social protection and are able to ensure that assistance will reach every single target' (Marinova/Gencheva 2003, 22–23). Subsequent women's NGOs have extended their scope of activity, but all 'women's NGOs' share the common goal of improving the situation of women. Some identify themselves as feminists, but many others explicitly do not. In recent years, when many of these NGOs relabelled their activities in order to qualify for EU funding programmes, their activities often became linked to development or human rights issues. Even today, organisations dealing mainly or exclusively with women's issues seldom identify themselves solely as women's organisations; more often, they also call themselves 'human rights' or 'development' organisations. One reason for this practice is that most databases on NGOs simply do not have categories for the topics of gender issues, women's rights or equal opportunities. Therefore, if women's groups want to be accessible, they have to choose an extant rubric. Not even the EU's CONECCS – the database for Consultation, the European Commission and Civil Society – provides any gender-related category in its search function.[6]

Accordingly, women's NGOs' charters have undergone a ,change of wording' in the past few years that has dissociated them from women's issues. One consequence is that women's NGOs have acquired substantial expertise in the human rights approach to women's issues (Ilieva/Kmetova/Delinesheva 2005, 22–26). They have participated in the monitoring of the EU Accession Plan for Equal Opportunities for women and men and taken part in Stability Pact initiatives that address political and economic empowerment, participation and decision-making for women (Marinova/Gencheva 2003, 21–22).

8.3.   Problems of Funding and the Role of EU Assistance

In the 1990s, many trans-national organisations, western states and private foundations invested in the creation of civil society with active NGOs in post-socialist states (Funk 2006, 68). For many years, grants from American foundations and the Open Society

---

6   See the list of policy areas at http://ec.europa.eu/civil_society/coneccs/listedomaine.cfm?CL=en.

Institute, historically the most important provider of funds for women's rights work in this region, were a very important source of funding for NGOs (Blister 2005, 7; Clark et al. 2006, 90). Most of the donors that supported the improvement of women's situation in the transition period later started to scale back their programmes, including foreign governmental donors. Every country in the region has been affected by this sharp decline in funding levels over the last few years, which took effect almost immediately after the European Council announced the intended entry of the particular countries into the EU.

A possible reason for the heavy decline in foreign financial support for NGOs might be the general sense among donors that due to the aid recipients' forthcoming EU membership, democratisation was already 'underway'. Therefore, the focus of the official development assistance was either shifted to anti–poverty projects or simply dried up when many donors pulled out of the region entirely. This shift has affected women's organisations dramatically. There seems to be consensus in the donor community that the EU itself is now mainly responsible for the development of civil society and funding the NGOs (Clark et al. 2006, 86).

However, one of the EU's strategies for strengthening the principle of subsidiarity has been to shift the financial aid agendas to national governments. Bilateral and multilateral aid agencies are now directing more funds to national governments rather than to the NGOs themselves (Clark et al. 2006, 2). Accordingly, the national authorities, mostly the ministries, have to build commissions, which then decide how the money will be spent. Although these commissions are required to involve representatives of NGOs, universities and local governments, someone from the relevant ministry is always in charge. Hence, women's NGOs in CEEC are often forced to look to their national governments for funding, a scenario that presents obvious challenges if they happen to take a critical stance on official policies. Moreover, the preferred topic of most Central East European governments is the reconciliation of family and working life rather than gender issues.

Thus, with waning foreign monies and limited (and sometimes politically sensitive) national financial aid, EU funding is one of the few remaining options for women's NGOs in the new member states. However, many of these NGOs lack the capacity to apply for and administer EU funding. To many of the smaller, younger and less experienced women's groups, particularly in the rural areas, the structures and funding mechanisms of the EU remain a mystery (UNIFEM 2006, 16), and the complex procedures of the EU applications and project implementations themselves very often pose obstacles. Experts estimate that, for example, only about 20% of all Polish women's organisations are capable of applying for EU-funds[7].

---

7   Personal communication between G. Fuchs and Joanna Piotrowska, feminoteka.pl, August 20th 2007.

The EU's information dissemination policy has a decisive – if not exclusionary – impact, as its lines of support often do not reach to women's NGOs. This failure is in part due to linguistic barriers (i.e. information is not always available in the NGOs' native languages), improper announcements or to the limited availability of the information (much of it is either only online or available in print only in metropolitan areas). The criteria for supportable organisations, projects and structures have their origins in the private economy, in which minimum turnover, number of staff, size, time of existence or co-financing possibilities are taken into account. These criteria tend to reinforce the traditional gender gap between men (who tend to operate in the formal sector with good access to resources) and women (who tend to operate in the informal sector with poor access to resources and different working structures).

Furthermore, the EU's accounting rules, late payment schedules (forcing NGOs to cover costs up front and await reimbursement), insistence on co-financing of project budgets, bureaucracy and inaccessibility all seriously undermine the local NGOs' access to EU funding. In addition, successful EU grants often have to be shared with foreign (NGO or for-profit) partners in EU member states (often as lead partners), which results in fewer funds for the local NGO (Funk 2006, 75–76). And as NGOs are not-for-profit, they cannot benefit when their for-profit partners profitably market the outcomes and new developments from women's NGOs later on.

As the EU's financial assistance is generally a co-support (covering 50% of supportive costs on average), women's NGOs are continually forced to look for new funding possibilities. In addition, the organisation receiving the aid is not allowed to reap any profits from EU-funded projects (Weidel 2004, 31–34), which makes it nearly impossible to accumulate savings towards the necessary co-financing. Another stumbling block inherent in EU funding is the eligibility rules for costs. It is significantly easier to raise funds for media, technology and communications work, leadership development, and linking and networking than for staff salaries, administration and capacity building (Clark et al. 2006, 12). National rules on the registration and taxation of NGOs further hamper the women's NGOs' efforts to apply for EU funding. In addition, EU monies are dispensed in Euros, which exposes recipients in Central Eastern Europe to an exchange rate risk.

It should also be noted that the overall amount of funds the EU disburses for women's issues is relatively small. In fact, in absolute and relative terms, the amount that the EU has spent on women's NGOs since the eastern enlargement is lower than in the mid-1990s, with the exception of trafficking and domestic violence grants (Funk 2006, 77). Though women's NGOs from the new member states tend to be in a precarious situation, they have formally gained access to decision-making processes at the EU level. Their actual degree of involvement in EU governance will now be examined for the Polish case.

8.4.   Gaining Access to EU Governance. The Case of Polish Women's NGOs

8.4.1.   Polish Women's NGOs

The Polish women's movement has crystallised around different issues since the demise of socialism in 1989. These include the planned ban on abortion since 1989 and the transformation of living conditions, along with issues of education, work and other gender-political conflicts. In a first phase of 'social self-defence', many informal women's groups that had already existed prior to 1989 registered themselves officially. The Federation for Women and Family Planning was founded in 1992 (www.federa. org.pl). In November 1994, twelve important women's organisations united to form the Social Committee of Non-governmental Organisations (SKOP). Until 1997 and from 2001–2005, a forum of the women's organisations co-operated with the government in the implementation of the Beijing Action Platform as well as on other questions of gender equality. Since the World Women's Conference, almost all of the women's organisations' demands have been legally legitimised. The law has in fact become the primary medium for calling attention to violence against women, forced prostitution, job discrimination and severely restricted reproductive rights.

Today, around 300 women's organisations, groups and research centres are active across the entire country, engaged in particular in the areas of employment and qualifications, social assistance, violence and health. Up to 2004, the Women's Information Centre Ośka (Ośrodek Informacji Środowisk Kobiecych, www.oska.org.pl) created vital networking and discussion opportunities in the women's political environment. Numerous initiatives, like election alliances, drafts for an anti-discrimination law, political protests sprang from this environment. Following internal irregularities and debates on strategic positioning, however, Ośka lost substantial funds and leading staff. From 2005 on, no other organisation was willing or institutionally capable of overtaking Ośka's advocacy and co-ordinating functions. Overall, the Polish feminist movement is small, though with an increasing number of sympathisers. Although the movement stages numerous (but small-scale) protests, political-strategic matters are rarely aired. Observers have even described a complete lack of alliance policies or strategies. The withdrawal of funding, especially of institutional grants, has forced feminist organisations to reduce activities, lay off staff and move to smaller offices.

The terms of Polish conservative governments from 1997 to 2001 and again since 2005 exhibited inferior co-operation with state institutions and took actual steps backwards in terms of gender policies (as evidenced in the now partially privatised social security system, to name just one instance). The leftist government of 2001–2005 appointed an equal opportunity officer in the ministerial rank, whose office launched many domestic as well as international co-operation projects. Among other things, equal opportunity officers were appointed regionally. The office was dissolved in 2005 and a subsection for family issues in the Ministry of Labour and Social Policy was established in its stead. While the chairwoman of the Women's League (the former socialist front organisation), as well as a high-profile feminist philosopher had formerly occupied the post (Izabela Jaruga Nowacka and Magdalena Środa, respectively), the conservative Joanna Kluzik Rostkowska now took office until mid-2007 (she was appointed employment minister in August). Although Rostkowska harboured traditional attitudes e. g. on homosexuality, she expressed modern Christian-Democratic views in terms of economic opportunities – namely, that the gainful employment of women must remain a component of modern societies (see Gazeta Wyborcza of 8 November 2005). She earned respect and recognition for her activities to promote female employment and entrepreneurship, mainly with EU funds.[8] Many women's organisations now engage in employment projects in order to obtain EU funds; these projects do not necessarily reflect their previous focus vis-à-vis their activities or political priorities.

8.4.2.   Adopting the EU as a Master Frame

Up until roughly 1998, women's organisations usually deployed the 'international commitments' master frame to mobilise followers and legitimise their goals in the public eye (on framing in general, see Snow/Benford 1988 and 1992; for the international women's movement, Joachim 2003). In framing the issues, the Polish women's movement built upon the fact that the relevant political forces in Poland had affirmed their affiliation with the European value system and had pledged adherence to international norms. The Polish opposition had cited European values to challenge the socialist state since the 1970s. Now that Poland has acceded to the EU, these norms and values apply directly. After all, if Poland is part of Europe, then it must adopt and obey the obligations resulting from international and European agreements. This is particularly important in terms of the civil rights of inviolability and individual freedom of choice, especially regarding the abortion question.

More systematic references to 'European regulations' began in 1998 with the accession negotiations. Little by little, women's organisations began to decry the nation's failure to adopt the 'gender acquis'. They proceeded to inform themselves about the gender equality policies of the EU and launched their own projects with EU support. In addition, they networked on the EU level. They stressed the need for political action via comparison with other EU states. This strategy can be seen as a consequence of the political learning process: Political changes do not come about via appeals to political

---

8   See personal communication between G. Fuchs and Beata Kozak, eFKa Kraków, August 17th 2007.

decision-makers, but require self-initiative (especially if misleading information policies are to be improved).[9] The women's organisations' own information policy offensives ('Europe Supplement', 'European Travel Kit for Women', etc.) were a step away from the state-society antagonism in Polish political culture. The state is no longer the sole addressee for political demands; society as a whole is increasingly seen as an invaluable participant in social change.

While the concepts of direct and indirect discrimination were finally embodied in the labour code after numerous protests and appeals (just prior to the conservative-liberal coalition's exit from office in 2001), women's rights nevertheless remained controversial in the Polish public sphere. The fate of the 'Letter from 100 Women' ('list stu kobiet') of February 2002 illustrates the limitations of an appeal strategy and dependence upon external allies. The letter was addressed to the European Parliament and the Commissioner for Employment and Social Affairs, Anna Diamantopoulou. In it, prominent personalities (e.g. Wisława Szymborska) and the most important women's organisations expressed their concern about the course of the accession debate in Poland. Due to numerous public declarations, it could be inferred that a pact between the Catholic Church and government had been established: The Church would support the accession in exchange for the renouncement of a recent liberalisation debate on abortion. In a prime example of an emotional public debate, Bishop Pieronek criticised the equal opportunity minister by calling her 'feminist concrete that does not melt even under hydrochloric acid'[10] because she had flatly demanded this particular liberalisation as well as matter-of-fact sex education in schools. In her reply two months later, EU commissioner Diamantopoulou asserted that the abortion question was a 'difficult topic' and was the exclusive legislative jurisdiction of the member states.[11] A letter from January 2003 demanding that the European Parliament reject the Polish 'Declaration on Morality, Culture and Sanctity of Life' as part of the treaty of accession experienced a similar fate. This demonstrates that references to EU regulations and requests for direct support from EU officials had a very limited impact on Polish gender policy prior to accession[12].

---

9   In April 1999, the Ośka Conference on 'Government Politics vs. Women' wrote an open letter to the Integration Committee; it may strike its brochure 'European Union – Women' (Unia Europejska – kobiety). Its incorrect, distorted contents exemplarily demonstrate that the importance of independent information, particularly in the climate of the reactionary gender politics of the conservative government at that time, can hardly be overrated.

10 In reaction, T-shirts which read 'More feminism, less hydrochloric acid' soon emerged.

11 Text via www.oska.org.pl/infopage.php?id=41, available on 8 March 2002; reply by Diamantopolous in Chołuj 2003, 224.

12 In this context, Western European solidarity with gay parades in Eastern Europe and attempts at re-politicising Christopher Street Day with slogans like 'homo europaeicus – walk upright' in Cologne seem to be a big success.

Over the course of the accession negotiations, the Polish public became increasingly critical and sceptical of the European Union. The information politics of the government improved only haltingly (see Grabowska 2001, 34). During the preparation for and the negotiations themselves, gender issues and gender mainstreaming were not addressed (see Bretherton 2001, 69–72). Implementation of the 'gender acquis' was not of paramount concern for either side. In 2007, a young male student was the first to sue employers for discriminating against men, as reported in the press (Newsweek Polska 28/2007, 72–75).

8.4.3. Joining the EU-Level Umbrella Organisation

When Poland joined the EU, Polish women's NGOs became directly involved in EU governance. Their main line of access was through the European Women's Lobby. The European Women's Lobby, or EWL (www.womenlobby.org), was founded in 1990 on the initiative of the European Commission and, according to its own data, represents over 2700 organisations. It is thus the largest women's NGO on the European level (Schmidt 2000, 211). The EWL is a member of the European Advisory Committee on Equal Opportunities for Women and Men and is represented on the Social Platform. About 80% of its budget comes from Commission funds; a small part comes from membership dues.[13] The EWL takes a stand only on 'non-controversial' topics in order to represent as many member organisations as possible. These include the struggle against violence against women (including all forms of prostitution), increasing women's role in decision-making processes, fighting discrimination on the job market and in employment policy, combating multiple discrimination and enlargement issues. Preparing dossiers for the Councils of Ministers constitutes a substantial part of their work. In light of this agenda, the question arises whether the EWL is in fact the Commission's alter ego. The EWL worked for the new directive for the same access to services. It was also successful with the codification of gender equality and mainstreaming in the Treaty of Amsterdam (Schmidt 2000, 218–220).

Women's NGOs that are active in at least four member states can join the EWL, while smaller groups can affiliate with national co-ordinating groups. These in turn send members to the EWL General Assembly, which elects the executive committee. Organisations from candidate countries have only been able to join since January 2003. An important step for Polish women's NGOs in terms of European networking was the establishment of a co-ordinating group in Poland in the summer of 2004.[14]

---

13 A reason for the European Commission's support surely was the fact that it saw women's politics as an important tool for the expansion of its own authority and was able to legitimise it via the establishment of the EWL (Schmidt, 2000, 222).

14 The following description is based on minutes and reports for the establishment of the Polskie Lobby Kobiet (Polish Women's Lobby), which was available under www.oska.org.pl in October 2004.

Nearly all major organisations took part in it, but not without controversy: The EWL had apparently not been interested in co-operating with women's organisations from the accession states for quite some time. There were and continue to be numerous political reservations, e. g. regarding the EWL's conservative attitude towards the prohibition of prostitution. The idea of a platform of Eastern-Central European women's organisations for the European level was ultimately rejected in order to avoid accentuating or perpetuating the East-West divide.

The 'Polish Women's Lobby' was set up with an open, co-operative formula; it was not an umbrella organisation. At a nationwide meeting, statutes, authorities and spheres of activity were discussed. It was emphasised that Polish organisations should be represented in the EWL as well as in the EU's control and advisory committees (e. g. for structural funds). About three dozen organisations signed the co-operative protocol, but discord was quick to surface. The Coalition for Gender Equality (Karat) had not participated in the preparations at all and the Family Planning Federation later withdrew. This fallout was reportedly due to large discrepancies between the agenda and key activities of the European Women's Lobby compared to the main concerns of Eastern European or Polish organisations (see Aigner 2007, 80–82). In particular, questions concerning women's health and reproductive rights, namely access to legal and safe abortion, are simply non-issues for the EWL. For the Polish women's movement, however, the abortion question is *the* focal point. The issues of economic and social rights beyond the labour market, such as future EU enlargements and new dividing lines between EU and non-EU states, are likewise ignored.

The representation of Polish women's organisations at the EU level has proved tricky. The Polish Women's Lobby was closely affiliated with Ośka, whose former director was elected delegate to the Executive Board of the EWL. The quality of exchange of information between the EWL and Polish organisations was deemed very bad by the latter. This resulted in the dissolution of the Polish Women's Lobby. Aigner reports that the expectations of the Polish organisations and networks vis-à-vis the EWL are slated to be introduced to relevant actors and integrated into governance processes in Brussels (Aigner 2007, 81).

In 2006, some women's organisations mainly from outside Warsaw took the initiative to re-establish the Polish Women's Lobby, this time as a federation (see www.polskielobbykobiet.pl). They did not consist of outspoken feminists, but were rather traditional or conventional women's groups, including post-communist organisations. The Polish Women's Lobby was founded at the end of 2006. Renata Berent, chairwoman of the Democratic Union of Women, hopes that the number of member organisations will rise to 46. There are clear political motives for this second attempt at establishing a Polish Women's Lobby: the wish to make the voices of Polish women's organisations heard in Poland and the EU and to take an active part in umbrella organisations like the EWL.[15] The situation of the whole milieu of women's organisations has been assessed critically, with emphasis on the lack of organisational consolidation and strategic activities.

The attempts to create a second Polish Women's Lobby seem to have gone on without the participation of feminists. Some feminists are very sceptical about the post-communist organisations involved; they also question the Lobby's information policies and the very sense of lobbying at the EU level.[16] It remains to be seen if feminist organisations will join the second Polish Women's Lobby. In our opinion, this situation emphasises the difficulties of the women's movement to negotiate interests and political demands and to ultimately act strategically. Obviously, this is not simply a matter of interest or willingness, but it shows the necessity for stable and institutionally funded organisations that can afford to occupy themselves with capacity building.

8.4.4. Building Alternative Networks

On the European level, the EWL holds a quasi-monopolistic position, which weakens the legitimisation opportunities of other actors. For local women's organisations and those that are not members of the national EWL coalition, the hurdles to direct influence are thus very high (Schmidt 2000, 222). However, some alternative routes to participation in EU governance have been carved out through international women's organisations. In three of them, women's NGOs from the post-socialist member states play an important role.

Since the early 1990s, regional networks of women's organisations reaching from Central Eastern and South Eastern Europe to the CIS have been emerging. Karat, or 'Coalition for Gender Equality', was officially established in Warsaw in 1997 as a result of discussions among regional organisations during the Women's World Conference in Beijing (see Marksová-Tominová 2006). Karat consists of about 30 women's organisations and focuses on the UN level, but addresses the EU as well. It monitors the implementation of international agreements, lobbies for national gender equality mechanisms and supports the political participation of women leaders in the region. Since 2002, Karat has issued repeated warnings against a new division in Europe due to the accession processes of CEEC states. It has emphasised the importance of considering the viewpoints, achievements and problems of non-candidate countries. In other words, enlargement must not be allowed to lead to a widening of the economic

---

15   Personal communication between G. Fuchs and R. Berent, August 20th 2007.
16   See also personal communication between G. Fuchs and Joanna Piotrowska, feminoteka.pl, August 20th 2007.

gap in the region or to the breaking of ties between member and non-member countries.[17]

Karat builds strategic partnerships with other organisations, e.g. with the Stability Pact Gender Task Force for South Eastern Europe or the German NGO Women's Forum (Karat 2006, 2) for campaigns on specific issues. Since 2001, Karat has concentrated on economic issues (including economic empowerment) and literacy in the context of EU enlargement. It is important to note that Karat addresses the negative impacts of globalisation and neo-liberal reforms on women's social and economic status as well as the feminisation of poverty. The group integrates economic rights into the human rights discourse. These activities somewhat counter the frequently expressed criticism that feminist women's organisations in post-socialist Europe have ignored the burning questions of economic transformation and social inequality, concentrating instead on a classic liberal agenda of individual freedoms (e.g. Miroiu 2006).

Established in 1991, the Network of East-West Women (www.neww.org.pl) is an international network of resources and communication. Its aim is to promote dialogue, information exchange and activism between all actors who want to improve the situation of women in Central and Eastern Europe and the NIS. NEWW supports independent women's organisations and their capacities to influence policies relevant to women. Since 1994, they have improved their online communication and news network. NEWW has recently started to organise regional conferences on gender politics, such as 'women and economy'. In 2004, its headquarters moved from Washington to Gdańsk. NEWW has members in over 30 countries.

A third important regional network worthy of mention is Astra, which advocates sexual and reproductive health rights (SRHR) as fundamental human rights (www. astra.org.pl/articles.php?id=127, 26.06.06). Astra is engaged in awareness-raising and elevating SRHR to the top of the agenda, particularly in the EU and UN. Instruments for this mission include monitoring and reporting on the status of implementation of SRHR and gender-related policies. The network organises public events, conferences and workshops. In February 2006, Astra and the Polish Delegation of the Socialist Group held a hearing in the European Parliament. Its goal was to draw the European policymakers' attention to their obligations in this area. If, as Astra argues, SRHR are human rights, then EU institutions (which are fundamentally committed to the guarantee of human rights) are obliged to develop policies that secure these rights (www. astra.org.pl/news.php?id=21, 26.06.06).

Karat and NEWW try to get permanent access to EU governance and the EWL has expressed the wish for more women's rights organisations on the EU level. But there is rarely any co-operation between them. Heidrun Aigner argues: 'Concerning the

---

17   See www.karat.org/eu_and_economy/regional_contribution.html, available on 12 October 2004, as a letter to the Convent for the Future of Europe in 2002.

co-operation between the EWL and the Poland-based networks Karat and NEWW, there seems to be a discrepancy between the latter's expectations and the former's perceptions vis-a-vis their roles. NEWW and Karat expect the EWL to usher them into the EU governance arena and to furnish access to its lobbying structures. The EWL, however, sees the groups merely as regional networks and does not consider them equal partners. In addition, one wonders whether the EWL really wishes to have organisations representing differing opinions on specific issues next to it.' (Aigner 2007, 83, own translation)

8.5. Conclusions

The current situation of women's NGOs in the new CEEC member states is precarious at best. Due to the fallback of the historically important private, independent and bilateral donors, the EU, with its policies and supportive measures, is becoming more and more decisive for the survival of the working activities of women's NGOs. Small NGOs and those located in rural areas have an especially difficult time meeting the EU's application and project requirements as well as the eligibility criteria. They often lack the capacity for participation. The application procedures and project rules for EU funding are often very complicated and lengthy. As such, they do not seem to have been designed with the smaller women's NGOs in mind. The co-financing rules and eligible costs criteria bar many women's NGOs from applying for EU funding.

Furthermore, the EU's lines of support rarely extend to women's NGOs; allotments for equal opportunities and women's rights constitute less than 0.1% of the EU's overall budget. At the time of the eastward enlargement, the EU switched to the subsidiarity system, which means that most EU funding is now allocated directly by the member states' national governments, whose first priorities are clearly not gender issues. Thus, NGOs that take a critical stance towards their own government might find themselves at a disadvantage when it comes to procuring funding. As a result, women's NGOs have started to apply and work under different names, avoiding terms like 'women', 'gender' and 'equality'. In summary, because women's NGOs constantly have to fight for funds, they are vulnerable to the influence and agendas of their donors. Their ongoing lack of money, time and resources severely limits their ability to shape their own agendas and organisational development.

As the example of Poland shows, women's NGOs have had to fulfil several conditions and overcome numerous obstacles in order to influence the European Union as civil society actors. This has included the colossal undertaking of creating a civil society with the associated movements and NGOs, acknowledging the relevance of the EU for their own agenda and development of their own country. At the time, 'Europe' was used as an argument, image and master frame. This analysis has underscored how important involvement in EU civil society is for newcomers and marginalised interests like Polish women's organisations. We have shown that the Polish women's movement has been learning by doing: Step by step, from appeals for information to fundraising and networking, it has become clear just how important and effective political activism can be in multilevel governance. Civil society has succeeded in making a critical step towards the elimination of the gap between political actors and European policy. It has contributed, not least with spreading information about funding opportunities, to the popularisation of the EU. The organisations have since learned to move into the institutions and set the agenda. Building capacities and alternative networks has been crucial for gathering momentum. This is why all successes are preliminary and precarious. As soon as funds are slashed, the capacity to act politically deteriorates.

The Polish women's movement's emphasis on Europe, the EU and European regulation was a useful political strategy, but one that nonetheless has clear limits. Joining the European Women's Lobby was therefore a logical next step towards Europeanisation, one that took place after a lengthy deliberative process and was linked to compromises. The failure in 2005 reflects structural – not personal – deficiencies in the movement. The Women's Lobby itself appears to be a prime example of a European umbrella organisation that is already well integrated into the negotiation system and can definitely boast successes. However, the exclusion of minority interests is also clearly illustrated by the principle of the 'smallest common denominator'. This dilemma can partly be resolved by the activities undertaken by alternative networks and coalitions, such as NEWW, Karat or Astra, which also wish to exert influence on the EU. Whether this should be considered a division of labour or organisational competition is an open question.

However, it is difficult to assess if Polish women's organisations have benefited from European integration, especially if one takes funding policies into account. Generally speaking, gender policies in the new member states now rely more on European regulations, but are still contested, and without ongoing political pressure, backlashes are probable.

Moreover, the 'Europeanisation' of Polish women's organisations analysed here clarifies the contradictions of the European Commission's rules for consultations with civil society groups. It is implicitly assumed – erroneously – that interests within a single group are harmonised, and that despite barriers, all interests can be organised. As a moderate, overarching and big lobby, the European Women's Lobby is essential, but since women do not constitute a monolithic group, the need for strong lobbies for other groups whose agendas differ from or contradict the EWL's is clear.

We see the present precarious capacities to participate in EU governance as a result of the developments since 1989. Donor policies (predominantly private) for the nascent civil society emerged incrementally and were not co-ordinated. Small organisations that emerged were supported, however. Although the big donor organisations expressed their preference for umbrella organisations, these were not established; due to the experience with state socialism, civil society organisations were reluctant to relinquish their new independence by joining such federations. The result is that no strong lobby for women's organisations now exists and that isolation and competition prevail. The withdrawal of funds, especially for small organisations or those in disadvantaged and remote areas came suddenly, often before organisational stability had been achieved. The difficulties in acting and participating in EU governance are directly linked to the competition for funds and jobs. We conclude that interests cannot be negotiated or formed without enough money, space and trust for debate. And without interest formation, interest representation – be it on a local, national or supranational level – seems paradoxical.

References

Aigner, Heidrun (2007): *Die Europäische Beschäftigungsstrategie. Gleichstellungspolitische Konzeptionen und Einbindung ost-westeuropäischer Frauennetzwerke*, Masterthesis, Rosa-Mayreder-College, Vienna.

Blister, Anita (2005): *Development NGOs in the Slovak Republic*, in: TRIALOG Project report: Development NGOs in the enlarged EU, Oct. 2005, Vienna.

Bretherton, Charlotte (2002): *Gender Mainstreaming and Enlargement: The EU as Negligent Actor?*, in: National Europe Centre Paper No. 24, presented to conference on The European Union in International Affairs, National Europe Centre, Australian National University, 3–4 July, 2002.

Bretherton, C. (2001): *Gender mainstreaming and EU enlargement: swimming against the tide?*, in: Journal of European Public Policy 8(1), 1, pp. 60–81.

Chołuj, B. (2003): *Die Situation der Frauen-NGOs in Polen an der Schwelle zum EU-Beitritt*, in: Miethe, Ingrid / Roth, Silke (eds): *Europas Töchter: Tradition, Erwartungen und Strategien von Frauenbewegungen in Europa*, Leske + Budrich, Opladen, pp. 203–224.

Chołuj, B./ Neusüß, C. (2004): *EU Enlargement in 2004. East-West Priorities and Perspectives from Women Inside and Outside the EU*, Discussion Paper written with support from Unifem, Warszawa, Berlin.

Clark, Cindy / Sprenger, Ellen / VeneKlasen, Lisa / Alpizar Duran, Lydia / Kerr, Joanna (2006): *Where is the money for women's rights?*, Assessing the resources and the role of donors in the promotion of women's rights and the support of women's rights organisations, published by the Association for Women's Rights in Development (AWID), Mexico.

Europäische Kommission (2001): *Weißbuch Europäisches Regieren*, Brussels.

Europäische Kommission: *KOM(2002) 704 endg. Mitteilung der Kommission. Hin zu einer verstärkten Kultur der Konsultation und des Dialogs – Allgemeine Grundsätze und Mindeststandards für die Konsultation betroffener Parteien durch die Kommission*, Brussels.

European Training Foundation (ETF 2006): *Looking for a fair deal for women in the workplace*, in: Women in Education and Employment 2010, Report of the Conference on Women in Education and Employment 2010, 6–7 March 2006; Turin, Italy.

Ferree, Myra Marx / Mc Clurg Mueller, Carol (2004): *Feminism and the women's movement: a global perspective*, in: Snow, David A./ Soule, Sarah A./ Kriesi, Hanspeter: *The Blackwell Companion to Social Movements*, Blackwell Publishers, Oxford.

Funk, N. (2006): *Women's NGOs in Central and Eastern Europe and the Former Soviet Union: The Imperialist Criticism*, in: femina politica 15(1), pp. 68–83.

Gal, S./ Kligman, G. (2000): *The Politics of Gender after Socialism*, Princeton University Press, Princeton.

Geringer De Oedenberg, Lidia Joanna (2006): *'Re: Komisja Praw Kobiet i Równouprawnienia'*, E-mail to the author, 4 July.

Grabowska, M. (2001): *Euroskeptyczki i euroentuzjastki*, in: Ośka Pismo : Pismo Ośrodka Informacji Środowisk Kobiecych No. 16, pp. 33–38.

Greboval, C. (2004): *Author's telephone interview with the policy coordinator of the European Women's Lobby*, 9 January 2004.

Hadj-Abdou, L. / Mayrhofer, M. (2006): *FEMMinistische Politik nach der EU-Erweiterung*, in: femina politica 15(1), pp. 58–67.

Holz, A. (2006): *Vorwärts oder rückwärts? Die Entwicklung der Frauen- und Geschlechterpolitik in Polen, Tschechien und Ungarn*, in: femina politica 15(1), pp. 48–57.

IHF-International Helsinki Federation for Human Rights (2000): *Women 2000: An Investigation into the Status of Women's Rights in Central and South-Eastern Europe and the Newly Independent States.*

Ilieva, Gergana / Kmetova, Tatjana / Delinesheva, Magdalena (2005): *Equal Opportunities for Women and Men – Monitoring Law and Practice in Bulgaria*, Open Society Institute / Network Women's Programme.

Jacoby, W. (1999): *Priest and Penitent: The European Union as a Force in the Domestic Politics of Eastern Europe*, in: East European Constitutional Review 8, No. 1–2, www.law.nyu.edu/eecr/vol8num1-2/special/priestpen.html.

Joachim, J. (2003): *Framing Issues and Seizing Opportunities: The UN, NGOs, and Women's Rights*, in: International Studies Quarterly 47(2), pp. 247–274.

Karat/NRO-Frauenforum (2003): *Rechte erweitern, Handlungsspielraum schaffen? Die EU-Reform und der Erweiterungsprozess aus der Geschlechterperspektive*, Positionspapier des NRO-Frauenforums und der Karat-Koalition. Ms. Berlin.

Karat; Stability Pact Gender Task Force (2005): *Gender Equality. Social and Economic Justice*, Position Paper to the 49th UN CSW, www.karat.org, section publications, accessed 26 June 2006.

Lemke, C. (2003): *Die EU-Verfassung: Eine Chance für nachhaltige Gleichstellungspolitik?*, Ms. Berlin.

Liebert, U. (ed.) (2003): *Gendering Europeanisation*, Peter Lang, Bruxelles.

Lokar, Sonja (2002): *The Relationship between Transition and Globalization*, in: Fair Play No. 7, pp. 4–9 (This article was first published by B.a.B.e. – Be active, Be emancipated, in: Women & Work, 2000).

Marinova, Jivka / Gencheva Mariya (2003): *Gender Assessment of the Impact of EU Accession on the Status of Women in the Labour Market in CEE – National Study: Bulgaria*, Bulgarian Gender Research Foundation, Sofia.

Marksová-Tominová, M. (2006): *Die Koalition KARAT: Ein Zusammenschluss von Frauenorganisationen der ehemaligen sozialistischen Länder*, in: femina politica, 15(1), pp. 115–117.

Miroiu, M. (2006): *A Mayflower turned Titanic: The Metamorphosis of Political Patriarchy in Romania*, in: femina politica, 15(1), pp. 84–98.

Moulechkova, Irina (2004): *EU candidate countries. In: WIDE Information Sheet: The enlarged EU and its agenda for a wider Europe: What considerations for gender equality?*, December 2004.

Pollack, Mark A. / Hafner-Burton, E. (2000): *Mainstreaming gender in the European Union*, in: Journal of European Public Policy, 7(3), pp. 432–456.

Schimmelfennig, F. (2004): *Starke Anreize, ambivalente Wirkungen: Die Europäisierung Mittel- und Osteuropas*, in: Leviathan, 32(2), pp. 250–268.

Schimmelfennig, F./ Sedelmeier, U. (eds.) (2005): *The Europeanization of Central and Eastern Europe*, Cornell University Press, Ithaca.

Schmidt, V. (2000): *Zum Wechselverhältnis zwischen europäischer Frauenpolitik und europäischen Frauenorganisationen*, in: Lenz, Ilse et al. (eds): *Frauenbewegungen weltweit. Aufbrüche, Kontinuität, Veränderungen*, Leske + Budrich, Opladen, pp. 199–230.

Sloat, Amanda (2004): *Legislating for Equality: The Implementation of the EU Equality Acquis in Central and Eastern Europe*, Jean Monnet Working Paper, New York.

Snow, D. / Benford, R. D. (1988): *Ideology, Frame Resonance, and Participant Mobilization*, in: Klandermans, B./ Kriessi, Hanspeter / Tarrow, Sidney (eds): International Social Movement Research, Vol. 1, J. A. Press, London, pp. 197–217.

Snow, D. / Benford, R. D. (1992): *Master Frames and Cycles of Protest*, in: Morris, A. D. / McClurg Mueller, C. (eds): *Frontiers in Social Movement Theory*, Yale UP, New Haven, London, pp. 133–155.

Thiel, A. (2006): *Zwischen Lissabon und Tallinn – Europäische Beschäftigungsstrategie und Frauenerwerbstätigkeit nach der EU-Osterweiterung*, in: femina politica, 15(1), pp. 20–34.

UNIFEM (2006): *Annual Report 2005–2006*.

Weidel, Christiana (2004): *EU Förderungspolitik und NGOs*, in: Glocalist Review – Sondernummer.

Wobbe, T. (2001): *Institutionalisierung von Gleichberechtigungsnormen im supranationalen Kontext: Die EU-Geschlechterpolitik*, in: Heintz, Bettina (eds): Geschlechtersoziologie, KZfSS Sonderhefte, Westdeutscher Verlag, Opladen, pp. 332–355.

Zimmer, A. (2003): *Der Dritte Sektor als organisierte Zivilgesellschaft im politischen System der EU* (Lerneinheit 'Interessenvermittlung in der Europäischen Union', Kapitel 5), www.politikon.org, 30 September 2004.

Iglika Yakova

9. The Czech Agricultural Lobby in EU Governance

9.1. Introduction

Regulation of agriculture is one of the policy fields, where the European Union has a significant impact on member states. The Common Agricultural Policy (CAP) of the EU consists mainly of market regulation and income support, which amounts to more than 40% of the total EU budget; it also includes accompanying measures and, since 1998, rural development regulations mainly in the form of agri-environmental aid. In the decision-making pertaining to the CAP, the Council of Ministers and the European Commission are the most important institutions, whereas the European Parliament is still only a marginal actor. The Council of Agricultural Ministers decides on the main policy line.

The new member states were forced to adjust their agricultural policy to the CAP and had to accept less favourable terms than the old member states. Accordingly, the agricultural lobbies from the new member states should have an interest in defending their position at the EU level. In this context this chapter will explore if and how EU accession negotiations have influenced interest groups, in particular in their capacity to take part in EU governance. Specifically, it will focus on the case of the Czech Republic through the analysis of the main farmers' associations there.

During the past decade, Central and Eastern European countries (CEECs) have undergone dramatic changes. Two events are particularly important. First, with the collapse of state socialism, most of these countries became committed to the liberalisation of their political and economic systems. Another important event was the accession of CEECs to the European Union (EU). It brought challenges in terms of conditionality and asymmetrical relationships between old and new member states (Grabbe 2003). As such, accession to the EU has been presented as an incremental process, a tool for reform and an objective for candidate countries (Agh 2004). In this context, the process of accession to the EU has greatly influenced not only the development of institutions and policies, but also the evolution of actors, including special interest or civil society groups (Saurugger 2003; Perez-Borragan 2004). This was performed through the rapid adoption of new, Western types of institutions and the adoption and implementation of the common EU legislative body, the *acquis communautaire* (Dakowska 2003; Dakowska and Neumayer 2005).

Agriculture in the Czech Republic bears the legacy of a typical large, collectivised sector. During the era of state socialism, the most common type of professional organisations was corporatist (Skilling and Griffiths 1971). Over the years, their roles were transformed into those of negotiation agents within the central planning framework. State-run associations held a monopoly position. Consequently, the intermediation of economic and social interests was not totally absent.

During the transformation period in the 1990ies, it was possible to build new institutions, but these too were influenced by the legacy of the previous system (Stark and Bruszt 1998; Ekiert and Hanson 2003). They had implicit links with the state, which had organised their structures and often determined the limits of their political role. Accordingly professional associations had to adapt to new rules and gain credibility in a new political system. The rapid changes that interest groups have undergone in the past fifteen years of political and economic transformation not only shows their former degree of dependence on the state, but also highlights the weakness of their structures and their lack of resources and capital. New and old associations often engaged in mutual ideological sparring on the basis of their links to the state-socialist regime.

Czech agriculture, with its small share in national GDP, dual farm structure and competing agricultural associations, is an ideal case for analysing the Europeanisation of agricultural interest groups in the new EU member states. It can serve as an example for the problems of capacity building for the participation of interest groups from the new post-socialist member states in EU governance.

9.2. Main Actors in the Domestic Context

The creation of professional associations followed a path of duality according to specific patterns of agricultural transformation, i.e. representation of big entrepreneurial companies versus small, family or semi-subsistence farms. Indeed, other forms of ownership have since emerged from the former co-operatives and state farms. Nowadays, farmland is distributed as follows: corporate farms – 44%, co-operatives – 26.3%; individual private farms – 27.4% (Ministry of Agriculture of the Czech Republic 2003). More than 80% of agricultural land is cultivated by large farms (500 ha and more), representing only 7.5% of the total number of farmers. Representation of these economic entities has been organised though the Agrarian Chamber, the Agricultural Association (which represents mostly large-scale agricultural enterprises of more than 500 ha) and the Association of Private Farming (representing smaller individual farms consisting of approximately 100 ha). Table 9-1 gives an overview of the main agricultural associations, which will be portrayed in this chapter.

Table 9-1: Main Agricultural Associations in the Czech Republic

Association	Type of association	Territorial specificity and perception of EU in 2004
Agrarian Chamber / Agrární komory České republiky (CAC)	Semi-public agency whose institutional structure is copied from Western models	• Euro-sceptic at the local level • Euro-pragmatic at the national level • Euro-active at the EU level
Agricultural Association / Zemědělský svaz ČR (AA)	Post-communist association transformed into a modern agricultural lobby group	• Delegitimised at the local level • Euro-active at the national level • Euro-active at the EU level
Association of Private Farming / Asociace soukromého zemědělství ČR (APF)	Copied institution that resulted from the alliance of several small associations	• Pro-European at the local and national levels • Anti-communist • Pro-European at the EU level

9.2.1.   The Agrarian Chamber

In 1991, the Czech Parliament passed a law on professional chambers of commerce, industry and agriculture. Under this law, the new Chamber took over many tasks formerly distributed among various government agencies (e.g. registration, regulation and training). While membership in the Agrarian Chamber (CAC, http://www.agrocr. cz) is voluntary today, it was compulsory during the first two years after its inception. The Chamber encompasses 71 district agrarian chambers and 59 professional organisations, which include approximately 77,000 physical entities (entrepreneurs) and 7,600 legal entities (farming companies). The Chamber was modeled after the Austrian/ German system, with compulsory membership and strong regional representation. However, it also reflects an old pattern of elite participation on the regional level and is reminiscent of a recent socialist model of top-down control of authoritarian/ state-corporatism (Ingleby 1996). The CAC is the main actor involved in constant negotiations with government officials, research institutes, universities, parliamentary committees and the Ministry of Agriculture. The Chamber is interested in increasing agricultural production. It aims to negotiate better quota limits and to obtain equal rights to the subsidies enjoyed by other EU farmers. One of its main goals is to obtain EU or national funding for the sector. It lobbies for an increase of direct payments rather than rural development measures. The Chamber seeks to convey itself as a leader, a unifier and a representative of the Czech Republic's entire agricultural community.

9.2.2.   The Agricultural Association

The Agricultural Association of the Czech Republic (AA, http://www.zemsvazpraha.cz) was officially founded under this name in 2001. It is the successor of the big and powerful Association of Co-operative Farming. The AA's success was guaranteed through the careful provision of domestic and external resources. European influence was combined with social capital and ex-communist elite networking. The Association has been transformed several times since the 1990s. During the socialist era, the association promoted the State's policies and communicated State decisions to the farmers. It has close links with the Chamber of Agriculture at the local, national and EU levels. As a result, both organisations are often associated with one another. In the first years after 1990, the AA did not succeed in influencing agricultural policy-making. However, the election of the Czech Social Democratic Party (CSSD) in 1998 and the subsequent appointment of Jan Fencl (the former chair of the Association) as Minister of Agriculture made it possible for the association to shape agricultural policies. The Association is also a member of the tripartite body for social partnership, which represents employers in the agricultural sector. As a lobby, the AA defends employers while also functioning as the voice of agriculturalists; it is also the most powerful association in terms of economic impact. In 2004, AA members cultivated 1,349,000 ha of agricultural area, which represented 37% of the total agricultural area in the Czech Republic.[1] The association has about 1,018 members, half of which are co-operatives; approximately one third are joint-stock companies and around 15% are limited liability companies (Bavorova, Curtiss and Jelinek 2005).

Representing large entrepreneurial entities, the Agricultural Association and its members are nowadays the winners in terms of agricultural privatisation and consolidation. The Association managed to restructure successfully and changed its name, removing the words 'co-operative' and 'collectivised'. It is now a modern EU-type lobby whose organisational structure is based on the National Farmers' Union in the UK and Northern Ireland.[2] However, as the main partner of the Chamber of Agriculture, the Association faces a crisis of legitimacy at the local level. The AA has very strong links to the ministry and parliament, but it is not specialised enough and often lacks 'added value' for those farmers who are not directly involved as leaders. Its ideology and interests often mirror those of the Agrarian Chamber, but the AA has considerably less presence in the countryside. Its members are very large agricultural companies, some of whose executives and leaders live in big cities. They are the most influential political entities, and yet they are absent from the social activities in the countryside.

9.2.3. The Association of Private Farming

The Association of Private Farming (APF, http://www.asz.cz) is the only association that was created from the bottom up, with roots in local initiatives and with the help of political interests. The APF was established in 1998 as the successor to three small

---

1   Interview with an AA official, December 2002, Prague.
2   Presentation brochure of the Agricultural Association 2000.

associations defending the interests of small restituted land owners and victims of land collectivisation. The Association strives to promote family farming in modern agriculture and the countryside. The APF has a conservative orientation and ties with the right-wing Civic Democratic Party and its MPs. The members of the APF owned a combined 300,000 ha of agricultural area in 2003, or 7% of all agricultural land. It represented approximately one third of the area cultivated by individual farmers. The association has about 3,100 members, which means that the average cultivated area per member farmer is approximately 100 ha. However, many small individual farmers are not even registered in the local 'Agricultural Register' as food producers. The number of those who are and who can be counted as market-oriented farmers exceeds the number of APF members by tenfold (Bavorova, Curtiss and Jelinek; 2005). Thus, free-riding is a big problem for the Association; it has few members, yet a majority of Czech farmers can take advantage of its policy achievements.

The APF is not a member of the Agrarian Chamber. This reduces its political and economic impact. Its members left the Chamber and adopted an outsider strategy because of ideological competition between the leaders and rival interests in the policy-making process. The leader of the Association is ideologically opposed to the president of the Chamber, who represents big agricultural structures and the former co-operatives. Important disputes have arisen on issues regarding decollectivisation, former links with the communist party and the co-operatives' debts. The APF has also protested against the big farms, which are considered the winners of the privatisation process. APF members are very active in local politics, but have difficulty accessing the national policy-making arena. Their main strategy consists of dredging up the past, specifically by condemning the communist elite, through effective media presence. The leaders of the APF see their role as a balancing power against the big farms and co-operatives in general. They highlight their distinctiveness in relation to the controversial communist past.[3] APF is based at the local level and receives its legitimacy from its role as a representative of small farms whose concerns are rural social issues.[4] At the local level, this agricultural association has found a new role as a translator and mediator of European norms and legislation.

This and its relatively large membership notwithstanding, the APF is less influential in the parliament and ministry due to its members' lack of economic strength. Their efficacy is also lessened by the conflicting political and personal orientations of its leaders. Yet even if members of the APF are often excluded from the policy-making process because of political agendas and alliances, they have nonetheless gained a certain amount of legitimacy through their European activities and their readiness

---

3   Interview with APF activist in June 2005, Kladno.
4   Interviews and meetings with farmers and activists from the APF showed that some of its active members are involved in politics and hold municipal jobs: they include vice mayors, experts, consultants and local activists.

to implement EU programmes locally (SAPARD in particular[5]). The main beneficiaries of the programmes have been municipalities engaged in co-operation projects and big agricultural companies. Small farms, meanwhile, have had difficulty in securing funds.

9.3.   Integration into EU Governance

9.3.1.   Path Dependent Institutions and New, Copied Structures

During the period of the economic transformation in the 1990s when agricultural groups were established, some copied new Western types of structures while others were based on old patterns of elite participation and past legacies. After 2004, accession to the EU triggered another role for professional associations that allowed them, via the diffusion of EU norms, to participate in the policy-making process at the domestic and EU levels. Building new interest groups in a new economic system is a learning experience. During international meetings, conferences and seminars, agricultural associations copied models and exchanged knowledge and experiences with their Western counterparts, most importantly from the neighbouring countries Austria and Germany.

During the first post-socialist years of social and economic change, collectivised Czech agriculture struggled for survival under dire economic conditions. Competing rural and agricultural associations represented the different interests involved in the restitution of collectivised land and property, privatisation and the transformation of co-operatives or state farms. Hence, agricultural interests were articulated around the issue of land and property, or the issues of losers and winners of the agricultural reforms after decollectivisation, and they were later confirmed around the issue of competition for SAPARD funds (Hudečková and Lošták 2003). The struggles over land and property in the post-socialist countryside are not only about material resources but also concern social and moral values (Sikor 2005, 189). Actors motivate their claims by asserting primacy over historical justice, symbolic compensation for victims or the efficiency of 'the market' and their role as 'entrepreneurs'. Throughout the period of

---

5   SAPARD: Special Accession Program for Agriculture and Rural Development. This programme has helped CEECs to prepare for their participation in the CAP and internal markets as well as the implementation of the EU regulatory framework. This is accomplished through a range of 15 measures intended to support the competitiveness of their agriculture and the development of their rural areas. The management of SAPARD has been fully decentralised to the candidate countries. As such, it has provided them with the opportunity to gain experience in applying the mechanisms for agricultural management and rural development in advance of EU membership. If this programme initially targeted big farming structures, municipalities have also taken advantage of it. It would be interesting to examine the exact role of APF members in the local distribution of funds and projects more closely.

decollectivisation, privatisation and consolidation of land rights, a dual structure of farms was put into place (Doucha 2004). Even if big companies or co-operative farms were not competitive enough, they managed to restructure successfully through copying. Austria and Germany's models inspired the most copies.

For instance, the Czechs adopted an Austrian model for their Chamber of Agriculture and Institute for Research in Agrarian Economics. The Austrians had been interested in presenting their model of agricultural intermediation and recommended its implementation in the CEECs at several transnational conferences.[6] Their eagerness not only reflected the conviction that corporatist structures better respond to the needs of these new free market societies, but also indicated a desire to introduce small-scale family farming into CEECs.[7] This was influenced, among other things, by a growing concern about rural development, the values of family farming and the social role of farmers.

Some Agrarian Chambers in other CEECs also took a cue from their German neighbours: a regional structure was created and local representatives were put into place where none had existed before. However, the first model did not correspond to the situation of agricultural entities in Czechoslovakia, especially to those in the Czech Republic. The Czechs chose it during the creation of the Chamber in 1991, but modified it so that compulsory membership was quickly replaced by voluntary membership. In addition, there are no elections based on the local distribution of farmers; instead, the Chamber works through its local offices (similar to the situation in Hungary).[8] The first experts to arrive in Prague were German. In the second tour of the EU twinning programmes, Czech associations chose to have Irish experts as partners. One of the reasons given for this was that they wanted to learn from another newer member state how to use EU funding. Moreover, the other European experts had already shown a preference to establishing links with Polish and Hungarian partners, relishing the prospect of tighter trade relations. They were less interested in Czech farming.[9]

---

6   At meetings at the Council of Europe. These conferences were organised by COPA-COGECA.

7   Speech by Gottfried Holzer, Agrarian Chamber or the Lower Austrian Region: 'Our model could be used by former communist countries as an example to reorganize their agriculture'. p. 11. CEA, COPA, COGECA, 'Séminaire paneuropéen sur le rôle des agriculteurs et des organisations professionnelles agricoles dans l'élaboration et la mise en œuvre des politiques pour le développement agricole et rural', Congress of European Agriculture, Council of Europe, Strasbourg, 14 September 1995. In Croatia, a similar system has been put into place. M. Jankovoi,: 'Today we copied the Austrian model and our cooperatives are doing better and better'. *op.cit*. Also, starting in 1995, the German Chambers of Agriculture cooperated with Hungarian and Kazakh partners., *op.cit*.

8   *Op.cit*.

9   Interview with Strategy Director, COPA-COGECA, June 2004.

9.3.2. The Pre-Accession Process: Asymmetric Relations between Czech and EU Agricultural Lobbies

The relation of Eastern and Western associations was asymmetrical during the first years of transformation (copying of structures, procedures and behaviour), but later on, the relationship became more balanced and mutually beneficial. I argue that the PHARE programme (Poland and Hungary: Assistance for Restructuring their Economies)[10] has been used for the transfer of informal norms from EU member states representing their sectoral and professional domestic cultures. During the EU negotiations, coercion mechanisms widely contributed to the inclusion of associations in the domestic poli-cy-making process, thus transforming their collective strategies, directing their interest towards EU policy-making and guaranteeing their role as legitimised partners.

Since the official launching of EU negotiations, the transfer of national versus EU models of interest representation in the field of agriculture has been linked to the increased role of the European agriculture confederations during the twinning pro-grammes financed by PHARE. Contacts with agricultural associations were organised through COPA-COGECA (the Committee of Professional Agricultural Organisations in the European Union, the General Confederation of Agricultural Co-operatives in the European Union), and it was implemented almost exclusively within the framework of twinning programmes between different partners, national administrations and experts in neighbouring countries.[11] The first part of the PHARE twinning project was signed in 1996. The second part continued from 1998 for another two years within the framework of technical assistance in the field of institutional reforms in the agri-cultural and agro-food sector. COPA and two experts' institutes prepared a project within the framework of the 'Business Support Programme', which created initiatives for the unification of professional agricultural associations in each post-communist country[12]. Thus, a horizontal network was built among professional associations. Some partners were included in the process, and thus became legitimised by the selec-tion process. Others were not considered representative and could not take part. But most of all, this facilitated the transfer of informal norms to organisations evaluated as being representative of a certain type of farmers or rural population. Also, each gov-ernment agreed to implement models that would better supervise and control their

---

10   The PHARE programme, initially created to foster reforms in Poland and Hungary, had become the main financial instrument of the European Community in the field of external cooperation with all Central and Eastern European Countries. The other two financial instruments, ISPA and SAPARD, financed investments in the environmental and transportation sectors in order to ensure better conformity with European legislation and also helped secure the implemen-tation of the acquis concerning the CAP and other agricultural priorities.
11   Evidence from interviews with officials in charge of the enlargement process, from COPA-COGECA, 2003.
12   Interviews with EU administrators from DG AGRI, DG ENLARG and experts from Eurogroup COPA-COGECA, Brussels 2003.

professional elites, in particular in the event of an agricultural crisis. Indeed, this was not a bottom-up process[13].

Priority has been given to bilateral exchanges between two partners, but the first round of partner selection was conducted with the help of national ministries of agriculture and the European delegation in the country concerned.

9.3.3. Joining EU Associations

The first European agricultural organisation representing farmers from EU member states was created in 1958. In 1962, COPA (Committee of Professional Agricultural Organisations) merged with COGECA (General Confederation of Agricultural Co-operatives). From its very inception, the Euro-confederation has had privileged relations with EU policy-makers. COPA has always been well represented at the Consultative Committees in the related department of the European Commission, DG AGRI. Members of COPA are also members of the European Parliament and the European Economic and Social Committee. COPA-COGECA sought to keep its privileged position after the fifth enlargement. Indeed, COPA had anticipated the enlargement since 1995 and aimed to consolidate agricultural associations in Central and Eastern Europe in order to better integrate them afterwards.[14] The above-mentioned associations were in a crisis situation, threatened by the enlargement of the EU, while the Eastern Europeans also faced a crisis of representation and reconstruction. Socialisation of Eastern and Western associations through a common model of behaviour was asymmetrical during the first years of transformation, but later became more balanced, with both sides operating as equals.

When COPA was founded, there were 13 member organisations from 6 member states. Later, COPA came to represent 27 organisations from 15 EU states. Currently, however, COPA has 58 member organisations from 27 EU countries, and 7 partner organisations from Iceland, Norway, Switzerland and Turkey.[15] This very large membership hinders its activities. Although the Euro-confederation's power stems from its unique 'bargaining position' based on representativeness (Jones, Clark 2001: 84), it is

---

13   More about this issue in INGLEBY, Susan J., 'The role of indigenous institutions in the economic transformation of Eastern Europe: The Hungarian Chamber System – one step forward or two steps back?, *Journal of European Public Policy*, (3)1 March, pp. 102–121. 1996.

14   CEA, COPA, COGECA, Report, 'Séminaire paneuropéen sur le rôle des agriculteurs et des organisations professionnelles agricoles dans l'élaboration et la mise en œuvre des politiques pour le développement agricole et rural', Congress of European Agriculture, Council of Europe, Strasbourg, 14 September. 1995

15   COPA in numbers: 11,000,000 agricultural entities. 15,000,000 agricultural employees. 30,000 agricultural cooperatives employing more than 700,000 people, and almost always in rural areas. 300 meetings per year organised by the Secretariat of COPA/COGECA. 45 people working at the secretariat 53 member organisations. 5 working languages. Source: http://www.copa. be/fr/copa_objectifs.asp.

problematic to represent both the general and specific interests of such a large membership base. Even though COPA now represents a unified European agricultural front
from West to East, its influence has dramatically decreased since 1992 (Grant 1995;
Clark and Jones 1999).[16]

COPA-COGECA made the choice to integrate several associations per country. In
the case of the Czech Republic, there were four associations, including the three profiled above, which were designated as representative partners. They were expected to
represent Czech agriculture under the umbrella of the Chamber or within the framework of a platform. However, the unified Czech Platform failed, as did most of its counterparts in other CEECs.

The Europeanisation of associations in CEECs was certainly vertical in that the process came from a higher EU authority. However, it was also horizontal by virtue of its
basis upon a common learning process vis-à-vis lobbying techniques, access to information, influence and repertoires of action. Social learning (Checkel 1999) is possible
in groups where individuals share a common professional background, as was the
case with Czech agricultural associations. Learning is facilitated when the group feels
it is in a crisis or faced with clear evidence of policy failure (challenges of COPA and
transformations in CEECs). Furthermore, learning is more likely to occur when a group
meets repeatedly and where there is a high level of interaction among participants (for
instance, through twinning initiatives or conferences, workshops and exchanges).

In the case of agriculture priority has been given to bilateral exchanges between
two partners. The result is visible in terms of access to power, the creation of alliances
(e.g.: the new Visegrad initiatives and alliances of small farmers across the EU), learning of a specific behaviour in Brussels, improved knowledge of the specificities of each
partner and also challenging the monopoly of COPA-COGECA. A reciprocal relationship was thus imposed. 'COPA cannot afford to lose us. This is a political question of
representativity. [...] COPA would no longer be speaking on behalf of all EU member
states.'[17] This attitude was considered a pedagogical lesson towards organisations
in CEECs: how to work together and co-operate at the EU level. However, the CEECs'
organisations were not willing to simply unite into national alliances, as distinctions
between old and new types of organisations persisted and were even accentuated.

---

16   Jones and Clark identify different stages of this process in change of relationship. Since 1975,
     relations between DG AGRI and COPA have not been the same, in particular because of the
     incapacity of the Euro-confederation to give an adequate response to the incentives for reform
     of the CAP.
17   Interviews with representatives of the Czech Agricultural Association and the Czech Association
     of Private Farming, Brussels, December 2003.

9.3.4. Usage of Europe: Czech Lobbies at the Copenhagen Summit

Observing interest groups' repertoires of action at different levels of governance during the EU accession negotiations allows us to identify to what extent there is a learning process in terms of common behaviour through the usage of EU mechanisms.

On 10 December 2002 the Czech government announced the successful conclusion of negotiations with the EU on the agricultural chapter. Three days later, as representatives from existing and prospective EU member states gathered at the European Council meetings in Copenhagen to ratify (among other things) the new agriculture programme, hundreds of outraged Czech farmers parked tractors and heavy equipment across key border crossings into Austria and Germany to protest being sold out to Europe by their government.

At the EU Summit in Copenhagen on 12 and 13 December 2002, administrators from various Czech agricultural associations were invited to participate in the technical team during the final negotiations. The invitation was hailed as a victory for the invited parties, which included the Chamber of Agriculture, the Chamber of Food Industry, the Agricultural Association and the Association of Private Farming. They were the only agricultural lobbies invited to participate from the candidate countries. Now was their chance to help defend domestic agricultural interests and try to negotiate better conditions. This was a double-edged game, however: the government needed a partner and an expert in order to collect information. By organising a press conference with them in Copenhagen, it also wanted to associate them with the results. The interest groups were 'easier to work with as they did not have their members behind them. Doing the same thing in Prague would have been difficult'.[18]

At the domestic level, the repertoires of action used – public demonstrations, media slogans, blockading national borders, even hurling produce at government buildings – have been borrowed from the EU 15 and are commonly deployed in other EU countries. In fact, the components of the agricultural protests in the Czech Republic were reminiscent of those seen in campaigns mounted by farmers in other EU member states concerning the development of the Common Agricultural Policy (CAP). These kinds of actions are highly visible and easy to understand, which appeals to public opinion. The Czech farmers therefore imported and performed similar actions in their domestic context. Their tactics are very theatrical; they engage both government and public opinion in an interaction involving participation in the streets. They emphasise the importance of the media and the public in an emotional give and take.

The growing distance between the location where political decision-making takes place (Brussels, or Copenhagen for instance) and the sites of farmers' protests reflects

---

18   Interview with former Chief negotiator for the accession of the Czech Republic (1998–2002), Brussels, 13 June 2006.

an increasing trend in Europe. Contention is expressed within the traditional confines of domestic and national political space. While the Czech Ministers travelled to Copenhagen to sign the agricultural agreements, Czech farmers stayed at home and expressed their anger in the context that was available and familiar, the domestic political space. The farmers were also confined to a narrow geographical niche: they came from the countryside to protest in Prague. Last but not least, they further limited the scope of their protests by addressing agricultural issues according to their domestic policy priorities.

9.4. Conclusions: Problems of Capacity Building

EU membership (and in particular, prospective EU membership) has had a mixed impact on interest group representation, providing both new opportunities and pitfalls. It is clear however that the capacity of Czech farmers' groups to take part in EU governance has greatly increased during the process of EU accession negotiations.

Related to this, we can identify three periods of EU capacity building of actors in Czech agriculture. First, foreign partners were identified and selected. Partnerships were then mainly build in the twinning context. In a second step channels of communication were opened through participation in mutual socialisation. The result was an adaptation to multi-level governance which triggered differentiations according to the repertoires of action used. The third step, the transfer of repertoires of action towards Brussels, is limited for the moment. It so far mainly concerns the collection of information.

To sum up, the Czech farmers' lobby groups have developed general capacity to take part in political governance. At the national and sub-national levels they are able to communicate efficiently with political decision-makers and within in the public sphere. As a result Czech farmers' groups gradually became reliable partners and mediators. In terms of specific capacity to engage in decisions making at the EU level, the Eurogroup COPA-COGECA provided the Czech farmers with channels of communication, recognition and accountability. Membership in the umbrella group ensured improved skills (language, EU jargon, advocacy techniques, network building etc), increased voice in EU agricultural politics and more expertise. At the same time, the capacity of Czech farmers' groups to take part in EU governance has increased their legitimacy and impact at the domestic level. At the local and regional level farmers' groups learned to communicate policy-related information, to convey opinions, to make alliances with local and regional decisions makers and to secure EU and national funding for the agricultural community.

However, this process of integration into EU governance is clearly limited. At the EU level Czech actors focus more on information gathering and learning than on coalition building and policy-making. Moreover, there is a visible trend towards the creation of islands of expertise, exclusion of some actors and an emphasis of differences. The third phase of capacity building, the assumption of an active role at the EU level, has just started.

References

Ágh, A. (ed.) (2004): *Post-accession in East Central Europe : The emergence of the EU 25*, Demokrácia Kut, Alapítvány, M. Közp.

Bavorova, M. / Curtiss J. / Jelinek, L. (2005): *Czech agricultural associations and the impact of membership on farm efficiency*, Paper presented at the EAAE Seminar on Institutional Units in Agriculture, held in Wye, UK, April 9–10.

CEA, COPA, COGECA (1995): *Séminaire paneuropéen sur le rôle des agriculteurs et des organisations professionnelles agricoles dans l'élaboration et la mise en œuvre des politiques pour le développement agricole et rural*, Congress of European Agriculture, Council of Europe, Strasbourg, 14 September.

Checkel, J. (1999): *Social construction and integration*, Journal of European Public Policy, 6(4), pp. 545–560.

Dakowska, D. (2003): *Usages et mésusages du concept de gouvernance appliqué à l'élargissement de l'Union européenne*, Politique européenne, No. 10, pp. 99–120.

Dakowska, D. / Neumayer L. (2005) : *Introduction : Repenser l'impact de l'adhésion*, Politique européenne, no. 15.

Doucha, T. (2004): *Nová struktura zájmů v českém zemědělství jako důsledek jeho reformy po roce 1989*, Paper presented at a seminar in 2003, Prague.

Doucha, T. (2002): *Czech Agriculture and EU accession*, Institut de Recherche d'Economie Agraire, RIAE, Prague.

Ekiert, G. / Hanson, S.E. (eds.) (2003): *Capitalism and Democracy in Central and Eastern Europe: assessing the legacy of communist rule*, Cambridge University Press, Cambridge.

Hudečková, H. / Lošták, M. (2003): *Preparation and Implementation of the Programme SAPARD: Who might be winners and losers*, Agricultural Economics (Zemědělská ekonomika), Vol. 49, No. 12, pp. 547–556.

Grabbe, H. (2003): *Europeanization Goes East: Power and Uncertainty in the EU Accession Process*, in: Featherstone, K. / Radaelli, C., *The Politics of Europeanization*, OUP, Oxford, pp. 303–325.

Jones, A. / Clark, J., (2001): *The modalities of the European Union governance: New institutionalist explanations of agri-environmental policy*, OUP, Oxford.

Ingleby, S. J. (1996): *The role of indigenous institutions in the economic transformation of Eastern Europe: The Hungarian Chamber System – one step forward or two steps back?*, Journal of European Public Policy, 3(1), pp. 102–121.

Ministry of Agriculture of the Czech Republic (2003): *Summary Report*.

Perez-Borragan N. (2004): *EU Accession and Interest Politics in Central and Eastern Europe*, Perspectives on European Politics and Society, 5(2), pp. 243–272.

Petrick, M. / Weingarten P. (Eds.) (2004): *The Role of Agriculture in Central and Eastern European Rural Development: Engine of Change or Social Buffer?*, Studies on the Agricultural and Food Sector in Central and Eastern Europe, Institute of Agricultural Development in Central and Eastern Europe IAMO, Kiel.

Saurugger, S. (2003) : *Européaniser les intérêts ? Les groupes d'intérêt économiques et l'élargissement de l'Union européenne*, L'Harmattan, Paris.

Sikor, T. (2005): *Property and Agri-Environmental Legislation in Central and Eastern Europe*, Sociologia Ruralis, 45(3), pp. 187–201.

Skilling, H. G. / Griffiths F. (eds.) (1971): *Interest groups in Soviet politics*, Princeton University Press, Princeton.

Stark, D. / Bruszt, L. (1998): *Postsocialist pathways : transforming politics and property in East Central Europe*, Cambridge University Press, Cambridge.

Yakova, I. (2007): *Who are Europe's Farmers? Accession to the EU and Organized Professional Interests: Evidence from the Czech Republic*, International Journal for Sociology of Agriculture and Food, 15(1), pp. 47–58.

Heiko Pleines

10. Interest Representation of the Polish Agricultural Lobby at the National and the EU Level

10.1. Introduction

With the demise of the socialist planned economy and the liberalisation of prices at the expense of agricultural products, Polish agriculture fell into a crisis. Over the course of the 1990s, its share in GDP sank from 7% to 3%. As no alternative employment was created in the countryside, the agrarian crisis exacerbated over-employment in the agricultural sector and at the same time led to high (though often hidden) unemployment in rural areas and corresponding social problems (see e.g. Ingham/ Ingham 2004; Gorlach/Drąg/Nowak 2004; Gorton/Davidova 2004; Petrick et.al. 2001).

Concurrent to the EU accession negotiations, Poland began to align its national policy with the EU's Common Agricultural Policy in 2001. During this process, trade barriers were dismantled while market price support became less important in comparison with direct payments of subsidies. Many Polish farmers viewed these measures sceptically and feared further losses in income as a consequence of entering the EU (See e.g. Czernielewska 2000; Rieger 2004; Wrobel 2004).

Polish farmers responded to the deterioration of their situation with repeated and occasionally violent mass protests. At the same time, representatives of the agricultural sector were able to win up to 28% of the seats in the Polish parliament. This enables the farmers to exert considerable political pressure. Meanwhile, Polish agricultural interest groups became active at the EU level when their country joined the EU in May 2004.

This case study starts with an analysis of the Polish agricultural lobby and its general capacity to engage in political decision-making processes, focusing on the national level. In the second part, the way in which the domestic agricultural lobby's structure and strategies differ from those of its representation at the EU level will be examined. This includes an analysis of the capacity to engage at the EU level. At this juncture, it will be possible to draw preliminary conclusions about the political impact of the lobby on EU policy-making and to address related questions of capacity-building.

10.2. The Polish Agricultural Lobby

Contrary to all other socialist planned economies in the Soviet-dominated Council for Mutual Economic Assistance (CMEA), no comprehensive collectivisation of agriculture was implemented in Poland. Although the state-run large-scale agro-industrial

enterprises were indeed given preference over the privately-run farms up to the beginning of the 1980s, their share of cultivated land nevertheless amounted to less than
one quarter.¹ As a result, Polish agriculture remained characterised by small family-run
farms, which, due to the mandatory sale of their entire output to state-run commercial enterprises and the overall regulation of the entire economic sector, were tightly
bound to the planned economy. (Wilkin 1988; Szurek 1987)

Relatively low acreage, coupled with relatively little specialisation, further contributed to the Polish private farms' low productivity. However, the distinctive historical
development of individual Polish regions has resulted in substantial regional differences. The majority of the private farms can be found in central and eastern Poland.
After the Second World War, most large-scale agro-industrial enterprises took root in
western Poland via the conversion of former German farms. In southern Poland, on
the other hand, small farms dominate due to the commonplace practice of the division of estates under the Habsburg monarchy. Due to their size, however, they are frequently run only as a supplementary source of income (Buchhofer 1998).

While Poland's private farms survived beyond the end of the socialist planned
economy largely intact, the state-run large-scale agro-industrial enterprises meanwhile underwent extensive restructuring. Since their high debts precluded privatisation, they were handed over to the State Agency for Agricultural Property, which sold
a few and leased the rest. The tenants invested in operational modernisations and
dismissed a large number of employees in order to boost efficiency. Due to the preponderance of private farms, however, Polish agriculture consists of many actors. The
largest 10% of the agricultural enterprises manage only 40% of the farmland (Lerman/
Csaki/Feder 2002, 110).

Polish agriculture is therefore becoming dominated by unprofitable family businesses that regard state subsidies, immunity from restructuring and protection against
competition as necessary for survival. While part-time farmers, who are by and large
isolated from the market, depend on state aid, commercial farms, including many representatives of the large-scale enterprises, have a keen interest in erecting barriers to
competition. These different agendas also explain the lack of a uniform stance towards
the European Union. While the subsistence farmers seemed particularly hopeful for
larger transfer payments, many of the commercial enterprises feared intensified competition within the common European Union market and the loss of the CIS market.²

These divergent interests are probably one of the major reasons the farmers' level
of organisation is comparatively low despite widespread discontent with national

---

1   In all other CMEA states, the percentage of state–run enterprises on agriculturally utilised land
     was approximately 85%.
2   Overviews of representative polling of Polish farmers are given in (in chronological order):
     Nawojczyk, (1996, 71–76); Szafraniec, (1998, 49–64, here: 58–59); Bieńkowski, (2000, 176–188);
     Wilkin, (1999, 75–86, here: 80–83, 86); Ingham/ Ingham, (2004, 213–234, here: 229–230).

agricultural policy. In 1999, fewer than 20% belonged to a political party or lobby organisation (Petrick 2001, 24).

The oldest organisation of the agricultural lobby is the Polish Farmers' Party (PSL), which emerged from the communist United Farmers' Party (ZSL). The ZSL was created in 1949 as official representation for the farmers and was intended to integrate the farmers as a communist sister party into the socialist system. Just as the National Union of Farmer Cooperatives and Organisations (KZKiOR), established in the 1970s and which functioned as both a trade union for those employed in agriculture and an umbrella organisation for private farmers, the ZSL was dominated by the communist party until the end of the 1980s with very limited room for manoeuvre. In defiance of the communist party, starting at the end of the 1970s, some of the private farmers formed opposition groups which organised public protests. At the beginning of the 1980s, three factions of the Solidarity (Solidarność) movement dominated the rural opposition (Gorlach 1989; Halamska 1988).

Before the 1991 parliamentary elections, the pro-Solidarity farmers' movements joined forces and established the Polish Farmers' Party-Farmers' Alliance (PSL-PL). As the Solidarity-led government introduced free market reforms in 1989 as part of their 'shock therapy' (which triggered the dramatic collapse of agricultural incomes), the ZSL exploited the farmers' discontent in order to establish itself in the post-socialist party landscape. It renamed itself the Farmers' Party (PSL) in 1990 and incorporated the Wilanów Farmers' Party from the anti-communist opposition in order to win legitimacy. Meanwhile, the PSL took over both the infrastructure and the membership of the ZSL, thereby taking the reins of a nationwide organisational foundation.

The 1990s were shaped by the tension between the leftist camp that emerged from the communist parties (to which the PSL and KZKiOR belonged among the farmers' parties), and the conservative camp which evolved from the Solidarity opposition movement. The latter was represented first by the PSL-PL and later by the SKL. As a populist organisation, the Samoobrona or 'Self-Defence' movement does not fit neatly in this ideological spectrum.

In terms of their positions on agricultural policy, two major groups can be differentiated. The anti-reformers were represented by KZKiOR and Samoobrona. The moderate reformers, who wanted to receive far-reaching subsidies and trade restraints on agricultural imports in the context of a free-market economy, were represented by the PSL and the PSL-PL respectively SKL (Krok-Paszkowska 2003; Szczerbiak 2002; Gorlach/Mooney 1998).

While the farmers' organisations in their entirety represented the interests of the majority of the agricultural enterprises in the political arena into the 1990s, a smaller group of farmers repeatedly resorted to public protests. Two waves of protest can be differentiated. The first lasted from 1989–1993; the second peaked in 1998–1999.

Although several farmers' organisations mounted protests and negotiated with the government towards the end of the 1990s, Samoobrona increasingly proved itself to be the driving force. Starting in March 1999, Samoobrona acted primarily alone. As a consequence, the PSL could profit only in a limited way from the farmers' discontent with the conservative government. In a 1999 poll, only 9% of the farmers believed that the PSL would defend their interests. Samoobrona meanwhile weighed in at 27%. This signified a fundamental shift in the balance of power among agricultural parties (Foryś/Gorlach 2002; Plazynski 2006; Marks 2000; Gorlach 2000).

10.3. The Farmers' Parties Participation in National Politics

It can safely be stated that the Polish farmers' parties, with a combined vote share of 15% to 20% in the 1991–2005 parliamentary elections, represent an important political force in Poland.[3] Depending on how many parties failed to overcome the minimum percentage hurdle, their share of the vote in the Sejm fluctuated stronger and climbed as high as 28%, as shown in Table 10-1.

Table 10-1: Farmers' Parties in the Polish Parliament 1991–2005 (Share of Factions in Total Votes)

	I. Sejm (1991–93)	II. Sejm (1993–1997)	III. Sejm (1997–2001)	IV. Sejm (2001–2005)	V. Sejm (2005–2007)
PSL	11%	28%	6%	9%	5%
PSL-PL	5%	-	-	-	-
SKL	-	-	6%	2%	-
Samoobrona	-	-	-	10%	12%
Total	*16%*	*28%*	*12%*	*21%*	*18%*

Note: The average percentage of votes for the entire legislative term is given.

Sources: Sejm (www.sejm.gov.pl) and State Election Commission (www.pkw.gov.pl).

The farmers' parties' power of assertion was compromised, however, by their affiliation with rival political camps, which made co-operation impossible. Accordingly, one cannot speak of a collective agrarian lobby in the Polish case. At the same time, the strong fluctuations in the balance of power among the farmers' parties indicate relatively weak voter loyalty across the board.[4] A major tendency in parliamentary elections was thus dramatic losses in votes for whichever farmers' party happened to be involved in the government coalition.

---

3   The combined farmers' parties received more than 80% of farmers' votes in all parliamentary elections.
4   Due to its takeover of the socialist party organisational infrastructure, the PSL is the strongest Polish party in terms of membership and is represented nationwide. It appears to be the only farmers' party with a base constituency greater than 5%.

Traditionally involvement in the government coalition for a farmers' party means control over the ministry of agriculture. From the end of 1991 until spring 2003 and again from May 2006 until August 2007, the Polish Minister of Agriculture is a representative of a farmers' party, as Table 10-2 shows. As representatives of a coalition party, the agricultural ministers were always in a position to influence government policy. The farmers' party thereby had a stronger position in the left-wing coalitions, since the PSL possessed greater voting power. This is also evidenced in the fact that agricultural ministers from the PSL were always simultaneously appointed to the position of Deputy Prime Minister. The same applies to the head of Samoobrona, Andrzej Lepper, who joined a government coalition with the conservative populists of the Law and Justice Party (PiS) and the League of Polish Families (LPR) in May 2006.

Table 10-2: Polish Agricultural Ministers 1992–2007

Agricultural ministers	Party	Term	Government coalition
Gabriel Jankowski	PSL-PL	12/1991 – 10/1993	pro-Solidarity parties
Andrzej Smietanko	PSL	10/1993 – 3/1995	SLD, PSL
Roman Jagielinski	PSL	3/1995 – 4/1997	SLD, PSL
Jaroslaw Kalinowski	PSL	4/1997 – 10/1997	SLD, PSL
Jacek Janiszewski	SKL	10/1997 – 3/1999	AWS, UW
Artur Balazs	SKL	3/1999 – 10/2001	AWS (UW)
Jaroslaw Kalinowski	PSL	10/2001 – 3/2003	SLD, UP, PSL
Adam Tánski	unaffiliated	3/2003 – 6/2003	SLD, UP
Wojciech Olejniczak	SLD	7/2003 – 5/2005	SLD, UP
Józef Jerzy Pilarczyk	SLD	5/2005 – 10/2005	SLD, UP
Krzysztof Jurgiel	PiS	10/2005 – 5/2006	PiS
Andrzej Lepper	Samoobrona	5/2006 – 8/2007	PiS, LPR, Samoobrona

Sources: Office of the Prime Minister (www.kprm.gov.pl); EIU Country Reports Poland, London 1996–2004.

At the same time, however, there were other governmental actors possessing agrarian authority besides the Ministry of Agriculture. Agricultural departments existed in both the Ministry of Finance and the Treasury. In the negotiations over the EU accession, the Ministry of Agriculture had to co-ordinate its position with the entire government. Among the pro-Solidarity conservative-liberal coalitions in particular, there arose a regular conflict between the proponents of a free market liberalisation in the Ministry of Finance and the Treasury and the representatives of the farmers' parties in the Ministry of Agriculture. The Prime Minister could mediate between the two camps. Meanwhile, both camps could try to advance their position by exerting influence on the parliament during the legislative process. The resulting conflict led to numerous coalition crises.

The increasing load on the agrarian lobby from the EU accession negotiations, distinctly sinking farm subsidies due to a high budget deficit and populist pressure from Samoobrona led, in spring 2003, to the resignation of a farmers' party from the government for the first time. Thus, for the first time since 1991, the Polish Minister of Agriculture was not a representative of the agrarian lobby. Instead, the post went to Adam Tánski, a politically unaffiliated expert, whose objectives nonetheless quickly failed due to political resistance. Up to the parliamentary elections in October 2005, the Ministry was led by representatives of the SLD, who had forged their careers as party politicians in the parliament and as bureaucrats in the Ministry of Agriculture. In the PiS minority government, a professional politician with a technical education became minister for agriculture.

However, when Samoobrona became part of the governing coalition in spring 2006, the head of Samoobrona, Andrzej Lepper, became minister of agriculture and deputy prime minister. With that a representative of the agrarian lobby again gained responsibility for the government's agricultural policy. For the first time a representative of the more radical protest wing of the agricultural lobby assumed political responsibility. This was generally interpreted as an attempt by Samoobrona to react to the rising satisfaction of farmers with EU policies and to broaden the party's electoral base.

10.4. The Influence of the Agricultural Lobby at the National Level

The interests of the agricultural sector were represented by a multiplicity of rival farmers' parties and protest movements. The channels of influence of the representatives of the agricultural sector are correspondingly different. The protest movements, most prominently represented by Samoobrona, were by and large isolated in the 1990s. Their only hope of forcing their way into political decision-making processes was via the successful initiation or orchestration of mass protests. Samoobrona established itself as a permanent political force only upon its entry into parliament following the 2001 elections.

The PSL, along with the conservative Farmers' Party, could only hope to implement its strategy of government involvement successfully if its political camp won the elections. The elections of 1991 and 1997 were granted to the conservative Farmers' Party, while the 1993 and 2001 elections went to the PSL. In all cases, an intra-governmental conflict developed due to the Farmers' Party's involvement in the government. While the representatives of the agricultural sector dominated the Ministry of Agriculture, other government parties occupied the Ministry of Finance and Treasury and demanded a reduction in state support for agriculture. This conflict provoked mass protests at the beginning and end of the 1990s and led to the break-up of the government coalition in 2003. As a result agricultural lobbyists remained outside the government for about three years until Samoobrona joined the government coalition in spring 2006. With that it may change from a protest strategy to meaningful government participation and thus replace the Farmers' parties of the conservative camp, which lost political representation in the 2005 parliamentary elections.

The representation of Polish agriculture's interests is thus characterised by changing constellations. Therefore, the degree of success in exerting political influence was also subject to substantial fluctuation. In the agrarian lobby's case, the main indicator for success is the extent of state subsidies, since government support has always been the overarching demand of all representatives of Polish agriculture.

In order to facilitate the quantification of state support for the agricultural sector, the OECD has developed a system which determines the monetary effect of all measures taken by the state and then sets it in relation to the market price of the entire agricultural production. This producer support estimate (PSE) indicates, which part of the gross proceeds of agricultural enterprises was financed directly (e.g. via subsidies) or indirectly (e.g. via price regulation) by state measures.

The 1989–1990 price liberalisation led to a clear breakdown of the PSE in Poland, as indicated in Table 10-3. Since the prices for basic food were kept artificially low, agriculture in fact subsidised other sectors of the national economy, in particular private households. In 1990, the PSE in Poland hovered at around -18%. The government arranged a subsidisation system relatively quickly, which led to a positive PSE. However, the extent of the subsidies varied substantially according to the power constellation in agricultural politics.

Table 10-3: Farm Subsidies 1986–2003 (PSE in %)

	1986–1988	1990	1991	1992	1993	1994	1995	1996
Poland	10	-18	7	9	16	21	16	19
OECD	37	37	37	35	35	34	31	29

	1997	1998	1999	2000	2001	2002	2003	2004
Poland	18	28	24	15	15	19	8	N/A.
OECD	28	33	35	32	31	31	30	30

Source: OECD: Agricultural Policies in OECD countries, Paris 2005, 39; OECD: Agricultural Policies in OECD countries, Paris 2004, 64.

The PSL's strong government involvement from 1993–1997 resulted in the stable subsidisation of agriculture. On average, support for the agricultural sector, measured as PSE, was more than twice as high during the PSL's term in office than during those of the preceding conservative governments. At the same time, the extent of the subsidisation tended to vary only by a maximum of 5 percentage points, while the fluctuation was around 34 percentage points from 1990–1993 and 13 percentage points from 1998–2001.

Following the PSL's loss of power at the end of 1997, the potential success of a conflict strategy suggested itself. The highest PSE by far in post-socialist Poland was reached

when mass protests were organised against the agricultural policy of the conservative government. Only in the protest years of 1998–1999 did the Polish farm subsidies
(in their relative extent) come close to the average level of the OECD countries.

Once the protests died down, however, the liberal-conservative government immediately abandoned its subsidisation policies. In the framework of an agreement
with the European Union from September 2000, trade in agricultural products was
liberalised. All in all, the PSE sank to its lowest level since 1992. In 2002, the coalition
with the PSL, which came to power in autumn 2001, increased the farm subsidies to
the level attained during its previous term of office during the mid-1990s. As a consequence of the Polish budgetary crisis and the EU accession negotiations, the new government's room for manoeuvre was limited. At the Copenhagen Summit in December
2002, guidelines for the subsidisation of Polish agriculture were agreed upon with the
European Union. Together with a clear decrease of the PSE to a mere 8%, this sparked
the PSL's resignation from the government in the spring of 2003.

10.5. Poland and the EU's Common Agricultural Policy (CAP)

The Common Agricultural Policy (CAP) of the EU consists mainly of market regulation and income support, which accounts for more than 40% of the total EU budget.
It also includes accompanying measures and, since 1998, rural development regulations mainly in the form of agro-environmental aid. In 2003, the EU agreed on a major reform of the policy that introduced the Single Payment Scheme and shifted funds
from price and income support (Pillar 1) to rural development (Pillar 2).

The EU enlargement of 2004 entailed an eastward expansion of EU bureaucratic
procedures. The CAP was non-negotiable for the accession countries at the time. Their
role was to merely implement the decisions made in Brussels (Rieger 2004). However,
Poland forced through a compromise in last-minute negotiations, which allowed for
an expansion of Polish farm subsidies. While they were supposed to initially amount
to no more than 25% of the average of the old EU countries, upper limits of 55% for
2004, 60% for 2005 and 65% for 2006 were ultimately agreed upon. The additional
subsidies, which surpassed the EU's original recommendation, had to come solely from
the Polish national budget.[5]

In the decision-making pertaining to the CAP, the Council of Ministers and the
European Commission are still the most important institutions. In terms of agricultural
policies, the European Parliament remains a marginal actor. The Council of Agricultural
Ministers decides on the main policy line (Meester 2000). Therefore, it is the focal point

---

5   In this instance the state may also utilise EU structural funds. In terms of the agrarian lobby's
     role, the decisive factor is not the origins of the aid, but the fact that the government decides
     autonomously on the level of additional subsidies and that all additional monies allotted to
     farm subsidies must come out of the national budget.

of intergovernmental bargaining on decision-making. Three groups of actors are involved in the decision-making process: the EU member states, the Directorate-General (DG) for Agriculture and Rural Development of the European Commission and agricultural interest groups (Grant 1997, 147; Meester 2000, 48).

During the 1970s, the DG and the association of European farmers' organisations (COPA – Comité des Organisations Professionnelles Agricoles de l'Union) enjoyed unmatched power in finessing proposals through the system. COPA, which merged with the General Committee of Agricultural Co-operatives (COCEGA – Comité Général de la Coopération Agricole de l'Union Européenne) in 1962, was most frequently cited as the most powerful of all European-level interest groups (Sidjanski 1967; Grant 1997, 170–171).

However, this position has started to erode since the 1980s for three reasons. The first is the increased strain placed on the CAP as its budgetary costs became unsustainable. Second, the circle of actors involved in agricultural policy formation has since widened. Budgetary pressure and international trade negotiations brought in what is now the Directorate-General for Economic and Financial Affairs (Swinbank 2006). Additional agricultural interest groups active at the EU level are the European Council of Young Farmers (CEJA), the Confederation of the Food and Drink Industries of the EU (CIAA) and the European Trade Union for Agricultural Workers (EFFAT). External oppositional interest groups (such as consumer and environmental groups) have also been established. Third, the divergence of interests within COPA has increased after several EU enlargements. The competitive nature of its relationship with a number of national members has resulted in the establishment of their own offices in Brussels (Grant 1997; Greenwood 2007).

10.6. The Participation of the Polish Agricultural Lobby at the EU Level

The representatives of Polish farmers' parties in the European parliament have no relevant influence on the EU's agricultural policy for a number of reasons. First, they are split among three factions and therefore unable to present a common position.[6] Second, there is no organised agricultural pressure group within the European parliament. Third, the European parliament is only marginally involved in the CAP. As a result, contrary to the situation in Poland, political parties cannot help to promote agricultural interests at the EU level.

---

6   Samoobrona became a member of the socialist faction. The PSL has joined the conservative Christian Democratic faction EPP-ED. However, in early 2006 a group within the PSL lobbied for a move to the Union for Europe faction. As a result, three PSL deputies of the European parliament were excluded from their party and became members of the Union for Europe faction.

Instead, agricultural interest groups, which have been sidelined by political parties in Polish politics, are rather active at the EU level. Eight different Polish agricultural interest groups are members of four different European-level agricultural lobby associations, as Table 10-4 indicates. However, again the distinction between political party and lobbying group is blurred in the Polish case. Samoobrona has members in the Polish and European parliaments and also acts as lobby group through COPA.

Table 10-4: Membership of Polish Agricultural Interest Groups in Associations at the EU Level

Polish interest group	Website	Member of
FBZPR – Federation of Agricultural Producers' Unions (Poland)	Na	COPA
KRIR – National Council of Agricultural Chambers	www.krir.w.pl	COPA
KZKiOR – National Union of Farmer Cooperatives and Organisations	www.kolkarolnicze.pl	COPA
NSZZ RI Solidarity	www.solidarnosc.org.pl	COPA, EFFAT
PFPZ – Polish Federation of Drink Producers	www.pfpz.pl	CIAA
ZMWZK – Polish Rural Youth Organisation	Na	CEJA
ZZ CNMR – Trade Union – National Centre of Young Farmers	Na	CEJA
ZZR Samoobrona	www.samoobrona.org.pl	COPA
ZZPR – Union of Professional Agricultural Workers	http://zzpr.org.pl	EFFAT

Sources: CEJA (www.ceja.org), CIAA (www.ciaa.be), COPA (www.cogeca.be), EFFAT (www.effat.org), IFAP (www.ifap.org).

Main agreements concerning the integration of Polish agriculture into the CAP were made before Poland joined the EU and could therefore not be influenced by Polish agricultural lobbies in Brussels (Rieger 2004). Moreover, the agricultural lobbies of the old EU member states mainly see Poland as a rival, as Polish demands for agricultural subsidies reduce their share in EU payments.

> The prospect of accommodating the poorer agricultural economies of the former communist countries within the CAP has always appeared nigh-on-impossible, and the alternative of cutting benefits to those who currently receive them has long been deemed politically unacceptable. (Rumford 2002, 78)

As a result, the Polish agricultural lobby has not been able to promote its interests through European agricultural associations either.

10.7. Conclusions

In Polish national politics, the agricultural lobby has been and still is a highly visible and rather influential actor. Its influence is based on a strong position in parliament and on the high protest potential of farmers and the rural population in general. Neither factor is relevant at the EU level. The share of Polish agricultural parties in the European parliament is negligible, and the parliament itself only marginally involved in agricultural policy. The Polish agricultural lobby has no real incentive to stage protests in Brussels, especially as Polish farmers' fears about heavy losses after EU accession have not materialised.

In the multinational agricultural interest associations at the EU level, the Polish agricultural lobby is not only marginal but also rather isolated, as most interest groups from the old member states see Poland as a main rival for EU subsidies. Accordingly, the Polish agricultural lobby has no way of direct meaningful participation in EU decision-making processes. Its general capacity to influence political decision-making processes at domestic levels does not at all translate into the more specific capacity to engage at the EU level.

Nonetheless, the Polish agricultural lobby can use its influence on the national government to promote its interests. First, as a result of the pre-accession compromise with the EU, a large portion of Polish agricultural policy, including decisions on substantial subsidies, will be made in Warsaw. The Sejm will therefore remain the stage for the representation of rural interests for the time being. Second, the final decision on the CAP rests with the Council of Ministers. As representative of a member state, the Polish government now has the power to block decisions. As a result, influence on the national government is sufficient for the agricultural lobby as long as EU decision-making procedures remain unreformed. Accordingly, the incentives for the Polish agricultural lobby to engage in EU-related capacity building are very limited.

References

Bieńkowski, A. et.al. (2000): *Opinions of owners of family farms on the problems of integration of our agriculture into the European Union*, in: Comparative Economic Research. Central and Eastern Europe, 1–2, pp. 176–188.

Buchhofer, E. (1998): *Agrarsoziale Veränderungen in Polen seit 1988 in ihrer regionalen Differenzierung im Überblick*, in: Buchhofer, Ekkehard / Quaisser, Wolfgang (Ed.), *Agrarwirtschaft und ländlicher Raum Ostmitteleuropas in der Transformation*, Marburg, pp. 35–58.

Czernielewska, M. (2000): *Measuring the effects of integration of the Polish agriculture with the European Union*, in: Comparative Economic Research. Central and Eastern Europe, 1–2, pp. 195–213.

Foryś, G. /Gorlach, K. (2002): *The dynamics of Polish peasant protests under post-communism*, in: Eastern European Countryside, 8(1), pp. 47–65.

Gorlach, K. / Drąg, Z. / Nowak, P. (2004): *Ku wsi zdezagraryzowanej? Ludność wiejska i rolnicza w świetle wybranych danych spisu powszechnego*, in: Studia Socjologiczne, 172, pp. 31–45.

Gorlach, K. (1989): *On repressive tolerance. State and peasant farm in Poland*, in: Sociologia Ruralis, 2(1), pp. 23–33.

Gorlach, K. (2000): *Freedom for credit. Polish peasant protests in the era of communism and post-communism*, in: Polish Sociological Review, 1(2), pp. 59–83.

Gorlach, K. / Mooney, P. (1998): *Defending class interests. Polish peasants in the first years of transformation*, in: Pickles, John / Smith, Adrian (Ed.), *Theorising transition. The political economy of post-communist transformations*, London, pp. 262–283.

Gorton, M. / Davidova, S. (2004): *Farm productivity and efficiency in the CEE applicant countries. A synthesis of results*, in: Agricultural Economics, 3(1), pp. 1–16.

Grant, W. (1997): *The Common Agricultural Policy*, Macmillan, Basingstoke.

Greenwood, J. (2007): *Representing Interests in the European Union*, Macmillan, Basingstoke.

Halamska, M. (1988): *Peasant movements in Poland 1980–1981. State socialist economy and the mobilization of individual farmers*, in: Kriesberg, Louis u.a. (Ed.): *Social movements as a factor of change in the contemporary world*, Greenwich / CT, pp. 147–160.

Ingham, H. / Ingham, M. (2004): *How big is the problem of Polish agriculture?*, in: Europe-Asia Studies, 56(2), pp. 213–234.

Krok-Paszkowska, A. (2003): *Samoobrona. The Polish self-defence movement*, in: Kopecky, Petr / Mudde, Cas (Ed.), Uncivil society? Contentious politics in post-communist Europe, London, pp. 114–133.

Lerman, Z. / Csaki, C. / Feder, G. (2002): *Land policies and evolving farm structures in transition economies*, World Bank Working Paper, Washington, 2794.

Marks, B. (2000): *Trzy wymiary Samoobrony czyli źródła sukcesu partii Andrzeja Leppera*, in: Studia Polityczne, 14, pp. 7–33.

Meester, G. (2000): *EU Institutions and the Decision-making Process for Agricultural Policy*, in: Burrell, A. /Oskam, A. (Ed.): *Agricultural Policy and Enlargement of the European Union*, Wageningen Pers, Wageningen, pp. 37–52.

Nawojczyk, M. (1996): *Facing the new challenge. Polish villagers on European integration*, in: Eastern European Countryside, 2(1), pp. 71–76.

Petrick, M. et.al. (2001): *Poland's agriculture. Serious competitor or Europe's poorhouse? Survey results on farm performance in selected Polish voivodships and a comparison with German farms,* IAMO Discussion Paper, 37.

Plazynski, J. (2006): *Public protests. Legal regulation and legal responsibility in the Polish case,* in: Arbeitspapiere und Materialien der Forschungsstelle Osteuropa, 75.

Rieger, E. (2004): *Wohlfahrt für Bauern? Die Osterweiterung der Agrarpolitik,* in: Osteuropa, 54(5–6), pp. 296–315.

Rumford, C. (2002): *The European Union. A Political Sociology,* Blackwell, Oxford.

Sidjanski, D. (1967): *Pressure Groups and the European Community, Government and Opposition,* 2(3), pp. 397–416.

Swinbank, A. /Daugbjerg, C. (2006): *The 2003 CAP reform. Accommodating WTO pressure,* in: Comparative European Politics, 4(1), pp. 47–64.

Szczerbiak, A. (2002): *The Polish Peasant Party. A mass party in post-communist Eastern Europe?,* in: East European Politics and Societies, 16(3), pp. 554–588.

Szurek, J.-C. (1987): *Family farms in Polish agricultural policy 1945–1985,* in: East European Politics and Societies, 1(2), pp. 225–254.

Wilkin, J. (Ed.) (1988): *Gospodarka chlopska w systemie gospodarki socjalistycznej,* Warsaw, (English as: Wilkin, J. (Ed.) (1989): *Peasant farming in the system of the socialist economy,* Warsaw).

Wilkin, J. (1999): *Rural Poland in the process of systemic transformation. Attitudes of the rural population towards the market, state and European integration,* in: Emergo, 4, pp. 75–86.

Wrobel, R. M. (2004): *Gemeinsame Agrarpolitik und EU-Osterweiterung. Strukturpolitische Konsequenzen für die Landwirtschaft in Polen,* in: Osteuropa-Wirtschaft, 49(2), pp. 140–161.

Part IV. The European Social Dialogue

Zdenka Mansfeldová

11. Czech Trade Unions and Employers' Associations in the European Social Dialogue

11.1. Introduction

In democratic societies, interest organisations and political parties are key actors in the structured process of mediating interests. In a system of multi-level decision-making and governance, intermediary organisations are often ascribed the function of bridging between the citizenry and the European level. The process of interest mediation has become an important part of the functioning of modern democratic societies. In market-economy pluralistic democracies, there are always social and interest groups with differing interests and expectations, at least in the short-term. The Czech Republic's accession to the EU on 1 May 2004 created a new situation in many respects, including changes on the national political stage as well as entry into the European political arena as an equal member. This development has also brought other, multi-layered possibilities of interest representation. In order for organised interests to be able to take advantage of this potential, they have to be both ready and mature. Are the entities representing organised interests indeed sufficiently ready in this case? Do they have the capacity for it?

Among the large number of interest organisations and civic associations active in the Czech Republic, there are trade unions and organisations representing employers and businesses. Thanks to their prominent position and permanent access to political decision-makers, they have a tremendous chance to influence the shape of public policies. They played an important role during the transfer to a market economy in the process of economic restructuring, and their importance has increased as a result of both, the accession of the Czech Republic to the European Union and their subsequent contributions to the European social dialogue.

It is in the public interest for interest differences in the sphere of labour and capital to be resolved democratically, peacefully and without disrupting basic social functions and values. Such a solution is offered by social dialogue involving various forms of communication between social partners, employers and employees (or, more precisely, organisations representing their different and often antagonistic interests); at the top level, the dialogue would include the government. Social dialogue helps to create conditions for seeking consensus in the traditional conflict line between labour and capital (including decent solutions to collective disputes) while simultaneously preserving social peace.[1]

Social dialogue and its institutionalised form – the Council for Economic and Social Agreement (CESA) – were established in the Czech Republic at the beginning of the 1990s. Its initiators built on the practical experience in Western Europe with social dialogue. Since the start, three partners have been involved in the CESA: the State (represented by the government), employers [represented by the Confederation of Industry of the Czech Republic (Svaz průmyslu a dopravy ČR) and the Confederation of Entrepreneurial and Employers' Unions (Konfederace podnikatelských a zaměstnavatelských svazů, KZPS)] and employees [represented by trade unions (the strongest trade union centre is the Czech-Moravian Chamber of Trade Unions (Českomoravská komora odborových svazů, ČMKOS) and the Association of Independent Trade Unions (Asociace samostatných odborů, ASO)].

Social partnership and its institutionalised form – the tripartite/CESA – have contributed to the transformation while developing in changing political, economic and social conditions; meanwhile, the social partners themselves have been 'maturing.' During the negotiation period and after the accession of the CR to the European Union, the social partners' activities assumed a supranational and European dimension. On the one hand, the number of levels of potential interest representation has multiplied and the possibilities for social partners have expanded, on the other hand, the gap between the top representation and the membership base has widened.

11.2. The Main Actors and Their Capacity to Participate in the European Social Dialogue

Existing top centres among associations and the unions represent consensus achieved through negotiations within organisations, sectors, fields and regions. The functioning of these structures is not, of course, unproblematic, especially when it comes to relationships between representatives and the represented along fixed vertical axes that are also supposed to foster the member organisations' autonomy. The function of interest articulation is closely linked to democratic intra-union communication processes, which should convey the information from the bottom up about differing interests necessary to shape the concrete demands for the leadership to represent. In practice, the situation is often reversed, the leadership represents the interests of members without having any immediate feedback from the membership base. It may also lack a generally formulated mandate to represent the interests of members of a concrete

---

1   The definition of the term 'social dialogue' is ambiguous; generally, in the Czech Republic it is regarded as communication between social partners. Usually, however, it is reserved for negotiations at the supra-enterprise level and especially for tripartite negotiations [Kroupa et al., 2002, Mansfeldová, 2005a].

organisation in the decision-making sphere, political institutions or the public arena, or the capacity to mobilise its members to support these demands. Interest articulation thus includes processes that allow individuals to become aware of their interests as common collective interests (Wessels /Paschen, 2004).

The CESA working teams play an important and growing role, they are permanent expert bodies ensuring and drafting expert opinions and other documents for CESA bodies. Their activities concentrate on wages, salaries and related issues, social issues, public services and public administration, work safety, the development of human resources and education and the position of the Czech Republic in the EU. The Working Team for European Integration (WTEI CESA) has been active in the CESA since 1998. From the very beginning, this team has been presided over by the deputy minister of foreign affairs for EU affairs. The team brings together seven representatives of the government, trade unions and employers and also includes the Economic and Agrarian Chambers (albeit on a different principle). Their participation was especially important during the screening process, when it was occasionally necessary to obtain their expert opinion. As the regular members are not able to cover the broad spectrum of problems, the participation of both Chambers continues to be necessary. The CESA Working Team for European Integration is a platform for information and consultation on important matters related to the activities of the Czech Republic in the EU, and the output of the team is presented at CESA plenary sessions.

Trade unions have actively contributed to the process of institutional inclusion of the Czech Republic in the EU and have helped to co-ordinate decision-making. During the pre-accession period, a Committee for European Integration was set up on the governmental level at the Ministry of Foreign Affairs and in each department an office was established dedicated to issues concerning European integration and to the preparation of directives. This system is still in place, and the largest trade union confederation, ČMKOS, has been a member from the start. The trade unions are interested in the broadest possible participation in policy document preparation. For trade unions, the co-ordination commission at the Ministry of Labour and Social Affairs, as well as at the Ministry of Industry and Trade, is of paramount importance. The strong involvement of the unions in the process of institutional inclusion should not be credited to Czech corporativism but rather to the trade unions themselves, which have managed to push their interests in an environment that can hardly be said to favour corporativism. This system of participation is different from CESA, it is another channel for promoting the interests of trade unions.

Employers were active in European structures long before the EU accession, forming institutional representation of their interests. The basic agenda of employers and entrepreneurs is quite clear, generally, it involves the achievement of conditions for maximising Czech companies' profits, via, for example, low total taxation, the minimisation of interventions in labour law relations by the government or trade unions, the absence of regulations in production or business activities, protection and support for the domestic market, etc. The manner of interest promotion and the efficiency of lobbying, however, depend largely on the type of organisation (Kunc / Hartoš 2005,159).

In 1990, a common umbrella organisation was created in the Czech Republic which was to bring together all major business and employers' associations and represent them at negotiations with the government and the unions. In 1993, the organisation adopted its current name, the Confederation of Employers' and Entrepreneurs' Associations of the Czech Republic (Konfederace zaměstnavatelských a podnikatelských svazů, KZPS). Although originally only an umbrella organisation, it saw its membership base erode over the years (and, subsequently, its prominent position). In 1995, its largest member, the Confederation of Industry of the Czech Republic (Svaz průmyslu ČR), left the Confederation, and later, its second largest member, the Czech Confederation of Commerce and Tourism (Svaz obchodu a cestovního ruchu), followed suit. In comparison to the original organisation, the Confederation is weaker today, but nonetheless still brings a lot of utility to its members. It takes part in the tripartite and is a member of the Council for Economic and Social Agreement.[2]

The Confederation is not a member of any European association of employers (unlike its member associations, which are often members of these federations). Through its members, the Confederation is represented in the European Economic and Social Committee (EESC), which associates representatives of employers and of trade unions as well as representatives of various civil associations. A representative of the KZPS in the EESC is employed and paid by the Union of Czech and Moravian Producer Cooperatives and not by the Confederation, although this representative is expected to be active on its behalf (e.g. when submitting comments on European directives).

The Confederation serves primarily as a co-ordinating body harmonising the approach of member organisations to negotiations in the tripartite or comment procedures. The Confederation co-operates with the Confederation of Industry of the Czech Republic (Svaz průmyslu a dopravy ČR), the Union of Commerce and Tourism of the Czech Republic (Svaz obchodu a cestovního ruchu ČR), the Economic Chamber of the

---

2   Today KZPS associates seven entities: the Employers' Union of Mining and Oil Industries (Zaměstnavatelský svaz důlního a naftového průmyslu), the Association of Textile, Clothing and Leather Industry (Asociace textilního-oděvního-kožedělného průmyslu), the Union of Czech and Moravian Producer Cooperatives (Svaz českých a moravských výrobních družstev), the Association of Entrepreneurs and Traders of the Czech Republic (Sdružení podnikatelů České republiky), the Association of Building Industries of the Czech Republic (Svaz podnikatelů ve stavebnictví v České republice), the Union of Employers' Associations of the Czech Republic (Unie zaměstnavatelských svazů České republiky) and the Union of Agriculture of the Czech Republic (Zemědělský svaz ČR).

Czech Republic (Hospodářská komora ČR), the Agrarian Chamber of the Czech Republic (Agrární komora ČR) and other organisations. The need to co-ordinate approaches and activities resulted in 2002 in the formation of the Entrepreneurial and Employers' Council of the Czech Republic (Podnikatelská a zaměstnavatelská rada ČR), which integrates representatives of the Confederation, the Agrarian Chamber of the Czech Republic, the Economic Chamber of the Czech Republic and the Confederation of Industry of the Czech Republic in a voluntary grouping.

The Confederation strictly represents its members in the tripartite, it does not concentrate on lobbying in the Parliament, and its activities are more or less reactive with respect to governmental bills of laws, especially those that are debated in the tripartite. Lobbying activities and initiatives are left to its members and their individual courses of action. The most influential entity representing employers' and entrepreneurs' interests, the Confederation of Industry of the Czech Republic, opts for a different strategy. Thanks to a large membership base (including around thirty associations), it is the largest employers' union in the Czech Republic, it therefore also represents Czech entrepreneurs' and employers' associations at the European and global levels. Unlike the Confederation, it does not concentrate only on the tripartite, but is active along other lines as well. The union defines itself as a voluntary organisation associating employers and entrepreneurs in the Czech Republic in the field of industry and transport and, as a non-governmental organisation, is independent of the government, political parties and trade unions. The Union is a member of the International Organisation of Employers (IOE), the Union of Industrial and Employers' Confederations of Europe (UNICE) and the Business and Industry Advisory Committee to OECD (BIAC).

Today, thirty independent sectoral unions are associated in the Confederation of Industry of the Czech Republic, which represents approximately 1,660 companies, the number of members has been falling in recent years, however. The Union strives to represent larger industries rather than companies or unions active in business and services. It does co-operate with other employers' organisations that are not members with which it can push certain concrete interests. The most important companies, creating up to 85% of the GDP in industry, are associated in the Union through membership in sectoral associations (Kunc /Hartoš 2005,160–161). The Czech Confederation of Industry is active at the European level especially through CEBRE (Czech Business Representation), which the Association established with the Confederation of Employers' and Entrepreneurs' Associations (KZPS) and the Economic Chamber of the Czech Republic with the goal of defending Czech business interests directly in Brussels. CEBRE offers a large number of paid services, such as information services, news and legislation monitoring, analyses, trainings and fellowships, consultations on project preparation and mediation of contacts and lobbying meetings. Co-operation between foreign associations and representatives of Czech industry at the international level also occurs through the Union of Industrial and Employers' Confederations of Europe (UNICE), where the Czech Confederation of Industry has a delegate. In addition to this, the Confederation of Industry has ten representatives in European Commission advisory bodies. It strives to create an institutional base for mediating information, contacts at the national and European levels and for consultation. One example is the Contact Point for Industrial Research and Development in the Czech Republic (Oborová kontaktní organizace pro průmyslový výzkum a vývoj v ČR, OKO SPČR, www.okospcr.cz), created in 2000 under a programme funded by the Ministry of Education, Youth and Sports. The goal of the organisation is to create an information infrastructure for industrial research and development in the Czech Republic, make information on research programmes of the European Union accessible and mediate contacts and expert consulting to Czech entities wishing to become involved in the programmes. Another institutional basis for co-operation is the Council for the Development of the Business Environment (Rada pro rozvoj podnikatelského prostředí), which associates representatives of ministries, the CzechInvest and CzechTrade agencies and representatives of entrepreneurs, the Confederation of Industry of the Czech Republic, the Economic Chamber of the Czech Republic, the Association of Entrepreneurs of the Czech Republic, the Association of Entrepreneurs in Civil Engineering and other interest groups (Kunc /Hartoš 2005).

Regardless of the various focal points and strategies of the two centres of employers' associations (as described above), purpose-driven liaisons are formed to strengthen the negotiation potential of employers' associations. In May 2006 the largest employers' union, the Union of Industry of the Czech Republic, signed an agreement on co-operation with two other important entrepreneurial unions: the Association of Textile, Clothing and Leather Industry and the Association of Building Industries of the Czech Republic, a member of the Confederation of Employers' and Entrepreneurs' Associations. Together, they represent the employers creating the majority of jobs in industry and transport. The agreement concerns the promotion of the interests of employers and entrepreneurs in the preparation of bills of laws and joint procedures when negotiating with the cabinet, trade unions and interest organisations. As the president of the Union of Industry, Jaroslav Míl, emphasised:

> Our goal is to create one lobbyist group which will be strong enough during tripartite negotiations and in the Chamber of Deputies of the Parliament to manage to influence economic and legislative conditions for enterprising in this country. We absolutely need a joint representation of employers. Especially recently we can see that some politicians do not realise that it is not themselves but employers who create economic values and give people jobs.[3]

Another goal is to react jointly to demands coming from the European Union.

---

3   http://www.spcr.cz/cz/dynamic/article.php?artid=827.

Social partners – both trade unions and employers' associations – take their participation in the European social dialogue very seriously. Both of them have long prepared for this task. The largest trade union confederation, Czech-Moravian Chamber of Trade Unions (ČMKOS), established its European Integration Team (Evropský integrační tým ČMKOS – EIT) in 1996, a multi-disciplinary group consisting of representatives and experts of ČMKOS and its member trade unions. The team was set up based on an initiative of ČMKOS and the European Trade Union Confederation, of which ČMKOS is a member and which has helped the activities of the EIT since the beginning. Until May 2004, the EIT concentrated mostly on the preparations for the CR's accession to the EU, its mission has since expanded. Its main tasks consist of ensuring that trade unions are consulted at the national level as a social partner during preparations for all major steps and documents concerning activities of the CR in the EU, and co-ordinating representation of the CR in national structures related to the EU and European bodies where social partners are represented.

The main tasks of the EIT include:

- working towards including trade unions as social partners to be consulted during preparations of all major steps and documents concerning the activities of the CR in the EU and co-ordinating the representation of ČMKOS in national structures related to the EU and European bodies where social partners are represented;
- drafting proposals for union positions on issues related to the EU for ČMKOS bodies and contributing to strengthening the European dimension of ČMKOS activities;
- collecting and disseminating information about the European Union and its policies and the positions of the Czech Republic, ČMKOS and European trade unions on debated policy proposals among member trade unions as well as regional councils of trade unions. The EIT fulfils this task especially by publishing a bulletin entitled 'Information of the ČMKOS European Integration Team,' of which more than twenty issues per year have been published since 1997. ČMKOS EIT members also serve as lecturers on European integration in the ČMKOS trade union education programme. EIT also has a group for project preparation and participation in European programmes.

The European Integration Team also drafts proposals of expert opinions on issues related to the EU for ČMKOS bodies and collects and disseminates information in trade unions about the EU and its policies, opinions about the CR, ČMKOS and European trade unions on debated policy proposals. It also concerns itself with the development of cross-border contacts with trade unions in neighbouring countries (Germany and Austria) within inter-regional trade union councils.

An important aspect of the participation in policy formation is the formalisation and structuring of consultation. An example of participation in policy formation is the

National Strategic Reference Framework (NSRF) (Národní strategický referenční rámec ČR, NSRR), formulated in relation to the general strategic principles of the Communities and worked out in detail for the years 2007 to 2013. The ruling and co-ordination committee of the NSRF is governed by the Ministry for Regional Development and drafts national reference frameworks for the spending of European funds. Trade unions, representatives of employers' and business interest associations and non-governmental non-profit organisations can participate in these preparations and influence the formulation of programme documents. These organisations, especially the trade unions, actively take advantage of this possibility.

No organisation has been established in the Czech Republic to harmonise the interests and intensify the dialogue between economic and social partners conceptualized in the broader sense at the national and European levels. There was none during the preparations for the accession of the CR to the EU, nor is there a need for one now. Such a forum – the national-level Economic and Social Council (ECOSOC) – was created in Slovakia in 2000 during the pre-accession preparations, however. It was established based on a decision of the Consultation Committee of the Ministerial Council of the Government for European Integration, and brings together both representatives of the tripartite and social partners as well as members of academic and non-governmental institutions.[4] The goal of ECOSOC in Slovakia as an independent body was to contribute to the integration process in Slovakia. Since its accession to the EU, its activities have focused primarily on European funded programmes.

When studying the manner in which consensus is reached and support sought for opinions at the national and European levels, we concentrated in particular on network strategies. For network strategies, direct contact of individual actors and exchange of information (in the widest sense of the word) is crucial. In view of the fact that decision-making in the EU is a multi-level process, a multiplicity of approaches and contacts is important. It is also necessary to take into account that EU institutions prefer co-operating with supranational organisations and European-level organisations, national interest groups thus enjoy limited influence and access to decision-makers (Mohr/ Wessels/ Beyers /Kerremans 2005). Therefore, national interest groups seek access to supranational groups as well as support at the supranational or European levels. They seek this support directly or indirectly through supranational networks of interest organisations.

The European parliament, co-operation with Czech members of European Parliament (MEP) and other MEPs provide alternative avenues for networking. Though experience is still limited, first assessments indicate that ČMKOS does not value co-operation with Czech MEPs very highly. Although at the national level it often finds support in its natural partner, the social democrats, only a few MEPs provide individual

---

4   These were the Slovakian Rector's Conference and the Committee for the Third Sector.

support at the European level. ČMKOS has striven to explain its policy to Czech MEPs and to debate their positions with them, but the interest proved to be one-sided.5 Trade unions therefore rely more on the lobbying activities of the European Trade Union Confederation in the EP. Sometimes they use their networks and the unions and MEPs of other countries. A great weakness of the union representation at the European level is that ČMKOS does not have permanent representation or an office in Brussels. Representation would contribute greatly to interest promotion, obtaining information and functioning in the network. However, the Czech trade unions have thus far not found this to be necessary.

At the EU level, trade unions, like representatives of employers' associations, participate in social dialogue. Representatives of ČMKOS are members of the European Economic and Social Committee (EESC), the Committee for the European Social Fund, the Committee for Social Dialogue, advisory groups of the European Commission where social partners are represented, and other bodies.[6]

11.3. Problems of Representativeness

One important practical as well as theoretical problem of social dialogue is the representativeness of the representatives of individual parties. This concerns both the choice of associations or societies representing interests as well as the choice of concrete individuals to represent the different associations. The issue of representativeness is related to the plurality of trade unions and employers' organisations. CESA statutes have contained the criteria of representativeness since 1995. Besides the focus of activities, the required organisational structure and sphere of activity, the statutes also define a minimum number of organised members. In view of the demand for opening democratic social dialogue, such a restrictive quantitative criterion is considered to be problematic by those trade unions thus excluded from participating. The application of the representativeness criteria, especially the minimum number of members, leads to the exclusion of some influential trade organisations and places great demands on the trade union centres represented in CESA as far as the aggregation of union interests is concerned.

The Czech tripartite has preserved – and we can say suffers from – a tendency to define which groups may or may not become members of the tripartite according to their nature (provided that they meet the other criteria of representativeness given in the statutes). This especially concerns the Economic and Agrarian Chambers.[7]

---

5   In 2005 ČMKOS invited all Czech MEPs to a discussion, but 90 % apologised and did not come despite originally having expressed interest.
6   http://www.cmkos.cz/eit.php.
7   Chambers, Economic or Agrarian, have never been represented in the delegation of employers. This is the case in some post-communist countries because they were established later, by

At the national level, this may well be justified, but where there are more partners to social dialogue, it poses a problem. Moreover, after the accession to the EU it is no longer possible to cleanly delineate the national and supranational levels. The tripartite must adopt positions on issues that are not covered by its members. This leads to wider co-operation at the level of the tripartite's working bodies, the working teams and groups.

Another issue is the co-operation with civil society organisations. Because civil organisations representing various interest groups are included in the European social dialogue, and here we concentrate primarily on the European Economic and Social Council, more attention should be paid to the organised segment of the civil society, especially non-governmental organisations. In modern democracies, NGOs play a most important role or, more precisely, roles. The first is a participative role. Through participation in non-profit organisations, citizens strive to express their common interests and needs, they create associations with the aim of addressing common issues. In this way, citizens can participate actively in the decision-making processes of, for example, a community, region, or the government, and at the same time assume their share of responsibility for decisions taken by public authorities. Such co-operation between the non-profit sector and state administration or local governments is beneficial for both parties, as NGOs are often much closer to the reality on the ground and therefore may be helpful in identifying what problems need to be addressed. Apart from this, there are specialists in NGOs whose expertise and comments in the public debate also contribute to perfecting proposed solutions (Rakušanová 2005a, b; Mansfeldová 2005b).

Although there are no institutionalised links between social partners and civil society organisations, we have been witnessing an increase in contacts and the use of their expertise in formulating opinions on draft directives, etc. In light of the fact that various NGOs and civil society groups are active in the third group of the EESC, representatives of employers and above all employees consult these civil society groups. Harmonisation of interests is connected with specific tasks, such as working hours, environment, etc. Undoubtedly, there is sufficient cause to talk about the influence of the expansive understanding of social dialogue at the European level and its impact on the national level.

11.4. European Economic and Social Committee (EESC)

The European Economic and Social Committee (EESC) is a non-political body that gives representatives of Europe's socio-occupational interest groups and others a formal platform on which to express their views on EU issues. Its opinions are forwarded to

---

law, in 1992, and it was never foreseen that they would participate in social dialogue.

larger institutions – the Council, the Commission and the European Parliament. It thus has a key role to play in the Union's decision-making processes. Members belong to one of three groups: employers, employees and various interest groups. The 317 members of the EESC are drawn from economic and social interest groups across Europe. Members are nominated by national governments and appointed by the Council of the European Union for a renewable 4-year term of office. In the EESC, the Czech Republic is entitled to twelve positions in its three groups (three times four positions). In addition to representation in these three groups, social partners are represented in all sections of the EESC and attribute a high level of importance to it.

In the first group, employers are represented by representatives of following organisations: the Confederation of Industry and Transport of the Czech Republic; Union of Czech and Moravian Producer Cooperatives (member of Confederation of Employers' and Entrepreneurs' Associations of the Czech Republic). Unlike the national tripartite, employers are also represented by the Economic Chamber at the European level. It can be said that the representation at this level is not restricted by the narrow definition of representativeness that applies at the national level; it remains to be seen to what extent the European level will influence the national level. The effects of the European social dialogue on social partnership in member countries have been thus far little studied even in the old EU member states, and it is too early for such analyses in the new member states. We can expect the strengthening of the position of social partners, as experience in the old member states shows (Leiber /Falkner 2005,160).

The second group – employees – is made up of members with a background in national trade union organisations, both confederations and sectoral federations. The Czech Republic is represented by representatives of the larger confederation Czech-Moravian Confederation of Trade Unions (ČMKOS).

To the 3rd group, which covers various interest groups like farmers organizations, small businesses, foundations, co-operatives and non-profit associations, consumer organizations, environmental organizations, belong members representing NGOs in social and health care, in the Czech Council of children and youth, Charity organisations etc.

All these members of individual EESC groups belong to one of the six sections of the EESC. Trade unions and employers strive to represent their interests, promoting them at the European level through various bodies. The number of existing bodies is often subject to critique; some authors are critical about the 'fragmented forms of representation' as well as their sheer number (Magnette 2005, 38). Despite this fragmentation, and perhaps even because of it, the European Economic and Social Council is one of the most important bodies.

11.5. Participation in European Sectoral Dialogue

For trade unions, but perhaps even more so for employers, representation of interests in the European social dialogue at the sectoral level is very important. The sectoral dialogue is usually criticised for falling short of the expectations placed on it, including its limited impact. The outcomes of the European social dialogue strive to influence joint European policies rather than to create agreements whose content is labour relations. One of the reasons for this is a lack of interest on the part of national trade unions as well as employers to organise and carry out social dialogue at the European level (Veverková 2006a). De Boer et al. (2005,5) caution, that social dialogue in the individual EU countries takes place in different ways, organisations in the individual nations participating therein have different structures and interests and have gone through different types of development, build on different traditions, have various member ratios in terms of employees and employers, etc. If their goals are not in synch, it is difficult to organise social dialogue anywhere other than at the national level. This is also the confirmed case in the Czech Republic, there are differences among individual sectors (a phenomenon which is not unique to the Czech Republic, however).

The favourable or reserved relationship to the European sectoral dialogue is not manifested only by the development at the European level but also by the strategy of national associations, which give priority to the national level even when the sectoral dialogue at the European level is functioning well. One reason for this is the necessity of respecting the preferences of the membership base and the capability of functionaries to persuade members of the importance of international co-operation. For example, the chairman of the Trade Union in Energy and Chemistry (ECHO), Zdeněk Černý, emphasised the importance of international co-operation at the annual conference in the following words:

> I believe that it is not a secret that the opinions about the activities of our union in this respect differ. What is important is that experience forces us to this and after the accession of the CR to the EU this is true even more so, that it is necessary to continue the commenced international activities, even despite the fact that such activities place high demands on the expenditures of the budget and unfortunately despite the fact that it may sometimes seem that these activities do not have an immediate, tangible result for the union. I personally believe that it is necessary to support international activities but only such that are efficient and necessary for the activities of the union.[8]

An opposite example is the Association of Building Industries of the Czech Republic, which, although a member of the European Construction Industry Federation (FIEC), does not develop any special activities. Furthermore, the expression 'European social dialogue' is alien to some representatives (Veverková 2006b).

---

8   See Report on the activities of the ECHO trade union (Zpráva o činnosti Odborového svazu ECHO), page 5, >http://www.os-echo.cz/data/files/konference_1/Zprava_o_cinnosti.doc<

Veverková, who analysed the subjective view on the part of Czech social partners of the European social dialogue, reached the conclusion that representatives of employers' associations and trade unions particularly positively evaluated the possibility of sharing information that is otherwise hard to come by and the potential for consultations in European social dialogue; furthermore, they appreciated the opportunity to voice their opinion on European legislation in their sectors. Trade unions also highlighted the possibility of forming joint strategies vis-à-vis employers – especially in sectors where supranational companies predominate. At the same time, representatives of employers and employees harbour a number of reservations about the ESD:

- For some trade unions and employers' unions, membership in European organisations is quite costly.
- As part of the membership, it is necessary to consult and comment on European legislation, contribute to drafting documents concerning the sector, etc., but for various reasons, a number of trade unions and employers' unions do not take advantage of this option and thus remain passive members. This is most often due to insufficient human and financial resources for active membership (i.e., experts knowledgeable in issues of social dialogue in the sector in the Czech Republic who are also capable of negotiating in English; furthermore, they do not have the funds for the frequent foreign trips which active membership would necessarily require, etc.).
- Organisations participating in the European social dialogue demand that their members submit various documents and reports on developments in the sector; the drafting of such documents is, however, administratively demanding and strains human resources, not to mention that in some cases the data is hard to come by.
- Few problems that the sector perceives at the national level about which consensus can be reached can be addressed at the EU level.
- The development of the ESD in any given sector is also complicated by varying degrees of development and different historical evolution of social dialogue in general. In the EU there are countries with a high quality of social dialogue and countries (especially post-communist countries) where it is still developing. In such conditions it is difficult to negotiate at the EU level, and only some member states participate actively in the ESD.
- Neither members of trade nor of employers' unions appear interested in topics addressed at the EU level; they do not request information about them. Furthermore, the ESD appears to be too distant, and is thus becoming an elite body of trade unions and employers' unions without links to the needs and opinions of the membership base (Veverková 2006b).

11.6. Inclusion in Supranational Horizontal Structures

Accession to the EU has facilitated the development of cross-border contacts with trade unions in neighbouring countries (Germany and Austria) within inter-regional trade union councils. Trade unions struggle with social dumping at border regions. Cross-border contacts with trade unions in neighbouring countries are forged either as part of inter-regional trade unions (Meror) active thanks to the support of European Trade Union Confederation and the EU, or as part of bilateral cross-border co-opera- tion. Czech trade union organisations are members of three inter-regional trade unions – 'Boba' (Western Bohemia / Bavaria), 'Elbe/Nisa' (Northern Bohemia / Saxony /Jelenia Góra) and 'Moldau / Danube' (South Bohemian region / Upper Austria).

Another example of supranational dialogue is the inclusion in the social dialogue of trans-national enterprises through membership in the European Works Councils (EWC). EWCs are a sign of the Europeanisation of labour relations and they are sup- posed to function as intermediaries between Eastern and Western Europe, they do so in the Czech Republic. The growing volume of foreign investment in the CR is cer- tainly a significant phenomenon from the perspective of the Czech economy. In 2003, for example, the numbers of companies under foreign control grew to over 21% of the total number of companies operating in Czech industry, with foreign firms post- ing almost 50% of the total returns from industrial activities and accounting for a 70% share of returns from direct exports.[9]

In scientific and political debates, the EWCs are seen as a mediator between the East and West, as a bridge arching over existing differences between the parent com- pany and its subsidiaries. According to current findings (Tholen et. al. 2006), three developmental levels of the EWCs have been identified:

- EWCs as information bodies. For Central European and Eastern European repre- sentatives, the EWCs are places where they can obtain information on the gen- eral developments in a company and thus develop their economic-political com- petences. For Western European representatives, they are sources of information about labour relations from their branches in Central and Eastern Europe and places to develop their intercultural competences. The EWCs served as informa- tion bodies as early as the pre-accession period because some companies granted the status of an observer to representatives of their subsidiaries in the associated countries.[10]

---

9 http://www.eiro.eurofound.eu.int/2005/11/word/cz0508103s.doc.
10 For example, in the KOVO trade union 200 large companies – subsidiaries of foreign compa- nies met the criteria for a membership in the EWC as early as during the pre-accession period. Of these forty had a representative-observer in the EWC.

- EWCs as integration bodies. Secondly, the EWCs integrate central and eastern European representatives in this body as equal members; this happened after the accession of these countries to the EU.
- EWCs as mediators between the East and West. At this stage it is possible not only to discuss existing differences in wages, working conditions, etc. but also to seek a European solution.

At present, most EWCs are between the first and the second developmental stage. There are still several barriers to the third stage. Western and especially German interest representatives advocate a rapid wage levelling, if possible, in order to create certain competitive conditions that would benefit the sites of their companies. In contrast, Central and Eastern European union enterprise representatives (who often enter into collective wage agreements with management) have an interest in maintaining indefinitely wages that represent a competitive advantage for them. The classic conflict between increasing wages on the one side and maintaining a comparative competitive advantage on the other comes into play in this case as well. Another problem is the ambiguity of the election of representatives for the EWCs in companies with no institutionalised representative of employees' interests, i.e., no trade unions or works councils. Based on our research findings, we can say that trade unions in foreign companies in the Czech Republic that have a representative in the European Works Councils are better informed about developments in the company as a whole and about its intentions. They are then better equipped with information to negotiate with their own management.

11.7. Conclusions

The goal of this case study was first – to show how the process of European integration has affected organised interest groups and interest representation in the Czech Republic, especially in the field of social dialogue; second – to analyse the capacity of civil society organisations to successfully engage in EU governance. Accession to the EU has opened up a new space for social partners and representatives of interests of employers and employees, giving them new options and putting them face to face with new challenges. This concerns not only activities at the supranational level, but also the creation of new activities at the national level with the goal of implementing European policies and the use of European funds. The need to co-ordinate the approaches and activities leading to the promotion of members' interests has resulted in the formation of various voluntary groupings that should strengthen negotiating power during the drafting of legislation vis-à-vis the government, social partners, and interest organisations. In view of the wider understanding of the social dialogue at the European level compared to the national level, we are seeing co-operation with entities that up to now have not been included in the formal structures of the national social dialogue, such as the Economic Chamber, the Agrarian Chamber, and NGOs. Three major prerequisites determine the capacity of civil society organisations to successfully engage in EU governance. The first is a general ability to engage in political decision-making processes. The second is the capacity to engage at the EU level and the third is the fulfilment of EU eligibility criteria regulating access to different consultation processes in EU governance.

Looking at the development in the Czech Republic over the last several years, we can say that the capacity of civil society as defined in the introductory part of this book has increased. According to our analysis the acting power as well as the maturity of the actors has increased. The internal structures have adapted to the new requirements by creating committees specialised in EU matters. The success of this process is due to the human resource and infrastructure capacities of the actors as well as their attitude towards the process of integration and their assessment of the importance of the potential impacts. As stated above, trade unions at the national level have assessed the importance of the integration process well and have created conditions for wide and co-ordinated participation.

The favourable or reserved attitude toward interest representation at the European level and to the European social dialogue is a result of trends at the European level as well as the strategies of national organisations, which can give priority to the national level even if social dialogue at the European level is working well. One reason for this is the necessity of respecting the preferences of the membership base.

References

De Boer, R. / Benedicturs H. / van der Meer, M. (2005): *Broadening without Intensification: The Added Value of the European Social and Sectoral Dialogue*, European Journal of Industrial Relations, vol. 11, No. 1.

Kroupa, A. / Hála, J. / Mansfeldová, Z. / Kux, J. / Vašková, R. / Pleskot, I. (2002): *Rozvoj sociálního dialogu v ČR*, Research Institute for Labour and Social Affairs, Prague.

Kunc, S. / Hartoš, P. (2005): *Zaměstnavatelské svazy – Svaz průmyslu a dopravy ČR a Konfederace zaměstnavatelských a podnikatelských svazů*, in: Mansfeldová, Zdenka / Kroupa, Aleš (eds.), *Participace a zájmové organizace v České republice (Participation and interest organisations in the Czech Republic)*, Sociologické nakladatelství SLON, Prague, pp. 159–182.

Leiber, S. / Falkner, G. (2005): *Sozialer Dialog der EU und nationale Sozialpartnerschaft: Chronik einer paradoxen Beziehung*, in: Karlhofer, Ferdinand / Talos, Emmerich (eds.), Sozialpartnerschaft. Österreichische und Europäische Perspektiven, LIT Verlag, Wien, Münster, pp. 159–183.

Magnette, P. (2005): *Zastupitelská demokracie a Evropská unie*, in: Lequesne, Christian / Rovná, Lenka (eds.), *Zastoupení Evropské pětadvacítky v Evropském parlamentu*, Cefres, Praha, pp. 31–46.

Mansfeldová, Z. (2005a): *Sociální dialog a jeho budoucnost (Social Dialogue and its Future)*, in: Mansfeldová, Zdenka / Kroupa, Aleš (eds.), *Participace a zájmové organizace v České republice (Participation and interest organisations in the Czech Republic)*, Sociologické nakladatelství SLON, Praha, pp. 105–128.

Mansfeldová, Z. (2005b): *Case Study: Czech Labour and Capital Interest Representation. The Social Dialogue at the National and EU Level*, in: Pleines, Heiko (ed.), *Participation of Civil Society in New Modes of Governance. The Case of the New EU Member States. Part 1: The State of Civil Society*, Forschungsstelle Osteuropa an der Universität Bremen, Bremen, pp. 40–50.

Mohr, S. / Wessels, B. / Beyers, J. / Kerremans, B. (2005): *Zugang und Legitimität in der EU. Vorläufige Ergebnisse der Befragung deutscher Interessenverbände, politischer Parteien, Ministerien und politischer Stiftungen zur Außenhandelspolitik in der Europäischen Union*. Diskussion Paper Nr. SP IV 2005-403, Wissenschaftszentrum Berlin für Sozialforschung (WZB), Berlin.

Rakušanová, P. (2005a): *Civil Society and Participation in the Czech Republic*, Sociological Studies 05:05, Institute of Sociology AS CR, Prague.

Rakušanová, P. (2005b): *Is there a viable democracy in the Czech Republic? Internal/External Efficacy and Trust – the Czech Case*. Paper presented at the PhD Summer School on Governance and Democracy in Central and Eastern Europe, Lüneburg, Germany, 16th August 2005, 2nd session 'Which type of Democracy in Europe? Public Support for Liberal and Social Democracy'.

Tholen, J. / Czíria, L. / Hemmer, E. / Kozek, W. / Mansfeldová, Z. (2006): *Direktinvestitionen deutscher Unternehmen in Mittel- und Osteuropa. Fallstudien zu den Auswirkungen auf die Arbeitsbeziehungen in Polen, Tschechien und der Slowakei*. Rainer Hampl Verlag, München und Mering.

Veverková, S. (2006a): *Evropský sociální dialog. Praha: Výzkumný ústav práce a sociálních věcí*. Unpublished Manuscript.

Veverková, S. (2006b): *Reflexe evropského sociálního dialogu na sektorální úrovni v ČR*. Praha: Výzkumný ústav práce a sociálních věcí. Unpublished Manuscript.

Weßels, B. /Paschen, F. (2004): *Das Verbändesystem der Bundesrepublik Deutschland*. http://www.politikon.org.

Joanna Einbock

12. The Participation of Polish Trade Unions in EU Governance

12.1. Introduction

Trade unions played a significant role during the historic processes of economic and political transformation in Poland. Their influence may have waned since then, but as social partners with regulated access to political decision-makers at the national level, trade unions are still among the most influential actors in civil society. Thus, considering the growing and already far-reaching regulatory powers of the European Union (EU) in the areas of the trade unions' interests, it is not surprising that Polish trade unions are becoming increasingly active at the European level. They seem to be following the maxim once cited by Mazey and Richardson: 'You need to shoot where the ducks are.'[1] As a consequence of Poland's accession to the EU in 2004, the Polish trade unions' spheres of influence have widened considerably; European bodies are now among their addressees and they have found allies in European trade union organisations, such as the European Trade Union Confederation (ETUC) and the European industry federations, in their pursuit of interest representation.

The focus of this chapter is on the largest Polish trade union federations and their capacity to engage in EU governance. The first group of factors to be analysed is changes in internal structures and the incorporation of European issues into the federations' work programmes. In addition, various indicators, such as formal representation and activities undertaken as single interest groups or within umbrella organisations at the European level, will be taken into consideration. The crucial question discussed is: How are Polish trade unions managing to engage at the EU level more than three years after Poland's accession to the EU?

The first trade union federation to be analysed here is the Independent and Self-Governing Trade Union Solidarity (NSZZ Solidarność).[2] Founded during the worker protests on the basis of the Gdańsk Accords of August 1980, the union consists of around 14,000 local organisations from 37 regions. The local entities are organised into national branch sections, forming 16 national branch secretariats. The second federation, the Polish National Association of Trade Unions (OPZZ),[3] was founded in November 1984 as a state-run trade union federation. It consists of 90 national federations and trade

---

1   Mazey, S. /Richardson, J. (1996): *The Logic of Organisation: Interest groups*, in: Richardson, J. (Ed.), *European Union. Power and policy-making*, Routledge, London, p. 200.
2   See: http://www.solidarnosc.org.pl.
3   See: htpp://www.opzz.org.pl.

unions from various industries. The third largest Polish trade union federation, which will be discussed only in passing, is the Trade Union Forum (FZZ).[4] Established in April 2002, it currently has nearly 60 affiliates. All three federations are recognised as representative employees' organisations under Polish law and actively participate in the social dialogue at the national level via the Tripartite Commission for Social and Economic Affairs.

12.2. European Issues as a Framework

Of the international issues that have occupied Polish trade unions for the last few years, those concerning Polish EU membership and the adoption of European social standards at the national level have played major roles. The unions' previous aims, orientations and modes of action have all been challenged by new political constellations. The entire trade union movement has thus been forced to work out new approaches, undertake structural changes and place greater focus on activities at the international and European levels.

The movement's new orientation is readily apparent in the current Programme Resolutions of NSZZ Solidarność, adopted by the 15th National Congress of Delegates held in Warsaw in September 2002.[5] The Congress addressed the various challenges to the Polish as well as the international trade union movement posed by the ongoing effects of globalisation and European integration. According to the resolutions, co-operation with the International Confederation of Free Trade Unions and the World Confederation of Labour will comprise the focal point of NSZZ Solidarność's international activities in its next terms of office. The resolutions call for the further democratisation of the world economy as well as the establishment and growth of independent union movements worldwide. NSZZ Solidarność has been placing consistent pressure on the Polish government to ratify ILO conventions, EU directives and the Social Charter.

To NSZZ Solidarność, the EU is not merely a treaty or constitutional commonwealth, but an entity based on a common European identity consisting of shared roots, heritage and values, including Christian traditions. On questions of European integration, the Programme Resolution cites the words spoken by the late Polish Pope John Paul II in front of the Polish Parliament on 11th June 1999:

> We must build new European unity, if we want it to be a lasting one, on the spiritual values that once shaped it; and the richness and diversity of cultures and traditions of individual nations must be taken into account. It must be a great European Spiritual Community.[6]

---

4   See: http://www.fzz.org.pl.
5   See: http://www.solidarnosc.org.pl/dokumenty/xv_kzd/u_prog.htm.
6   Source: http://www.solidarnosc.org.pl/english/docs/15eng_pr.pdf, viewed on 25. August 2007..

Two National Commission Departments of NSZZ Solidarność became particularly active in the international and European arenas: the International Department, which handles the trade union's foreign affairs, such as its relations with international bodies, foreign trade union centres and other international organisations, and the Commission for European Integration, which concentrates more strictly on European issues. The federation has subsequently published various working papers and statements to both communicate its position regarding the EU integration to the Polish government and to raise its members' awareness on many critical issues.

In its Programme Resolution, NSZZ Solidarność underlines the necessity to strengthen international co-operation, to exchange experience, information and expertise and further develop joint programmes with trade unions from other EU member states and EU-level trade union organisations. As far as activities planned at the European level are concerned, the ETUC plays the most pivotal role. NSZZ Solidarność therefore wants to actively participate in the European social dialogue through the ETUC and the European industry federations. The strengthening of the European social model, including the common policy on employment, working conditions and social protection, is among the most important issues. NSZZ Solidarność formulated its further aims in the Resolution of the 16th National Congress of Delegates on International Co-operation. Chief among these was obtaining constitutional guarantees in the EU for the right to organise cross-border trade unions and negotiate cross-border collective agreements. Implementing the social model based on the dialogue of the social partners, improving its access to information, participating in consultations and exercising co-decision-making power were some of the federation's other stated goals on the European level. Also called for were the democratisation of EU institutions through the strengthening of the role of representative bodies, more transparency in the decision-making processes and the limitation of the unanimity principle to constitutional matters.[7] With respect to Polish affairs, the Resolution contained a provision to broaden the mandate of the European Social Charter in Poland, especially to include the right to fair remuneration.[8] This objective was reintroduced at the 20th National Congress of Delegates in September 2006.[9]

OPZZ has dealt with similar issues and challenges during its last few terms of office. In the preamble of the work programme for the 2002–2006 period adopted during the 5th Congress of OPZZ in Spala in May 2002, OPZZ stressed its commitment to Poland's integration with the EU and confirmed the objectives of the previous programme, which had identified integration with the EU as Poland's highest priority. At the same time, however, OPZZ demanded a public debate regarding the conditions for Poland's

---

7   See: http://www.solidarnosc.org.pl/dokumenty/xvi_kzd/uchw.htm, viewed on 25 August 2007.
8   See: http://www.solidarnosc.org.pl/dokumenty/xvi_kzd/uchw.htm, viewed on 25 August 2007.
9   See: http://www.solidarnosc.org.pl/dokumenty/xx/dokumenty/uchw.htm, viewed on 25 August 2007.

membership in the EU and the potential consequences of accession, especially concerning social policy. Similar to NSZZ Solidarność, OPZZ challenged the Polish government to present appropriate position papers involving the participation of social
partners. Accordingly, OPZZ organised various conferences and lectures addressing
these issues prior to the accession referendum. In a later chapter of the programme
committed to social policy, OPZZ also exhorted the Polish government to align Polish
employment and social laws with the standards of the ILO conventions, the European
Social Charter and the EU Directives. These demands were elaborated upon in a separate chapter on OPZZ's international activities. In light of growing globalisation and
industrial integration, OPZZ stresses the necessity of co-operation with international
trade union movements for establishing a stable social model. The commitment to
the idea of a 'social Europe' plays an important role in this context, a goal that can
be reached, according to OPZZ, through close co-operation with the European trade
unions and social organisations as well as through bilateral partnerships with trade
unions from other countries. Stepping up Polish trade unions' active participation in
the EU social dialogue is one of OPZZ's major priorities. In the current work programme
for the 2006–2010 period adopted by the 6th Congress of OPZZ in May 2006, Poland's
accession to the EU was lauded as the government's major success. At the international level, the programme aims to meet several objectives, including tightening the
co-operation with the European social partners (especially with the ETUC) influencing
the decision-making processes in the EU through active participation in the European
Economic and Social Committee (EESC) and raising support for the European Social
Model and the European Work Councils. The programme also underscores the necessity for active participation in EU-funded projects, including those underwritten by
European Structural Funds.[10]

In its work programme adopted by its 2nd Congress in April 2006, the Trade Union
Forum (or FZZ) expressed support for Poland's further integration into the EU, including the adoption of European regulations concerning social standards at the national
level. At the same time, the Forum stresses Poland's need to participate in the international social dialogue.[11]

12.3. Engagement at the European Level

The Polish trade unions' activities with the European Economic and Social Committee
(EESC) constitute their most significant engagement at the European level. The EESC
is a consultative body providing direct access for representatives of national socio-

---

10 See: http://opzz.org.pl/assets/File/vi_kongres/Program_i_Uchwaly_VI_Kongres.pdf, viewed on
    25 Augsut 2007.
11 See: http://www.fzz.org.pl/serwis2/index.php?option=com_content&task=view&id=61&Itemi
    d=86, viewed on 25 August 2007.

occupational interest groups (including social partners and other major players in civil society) to a formal platform for voicing their opinions at the European level. It also plays an important role in the EU decision-making process and has since become one of the major European avenues for the representation of the Polish trade unions' interests. The EESC had maintained relations with Polish interest groups even prior to the EU eastern enlargement, however. In 1997, for example, the Polish Committee for European Integration established a joint committee with the EESC. Aimed at increasing the involvement of the social partners in the negotiation process, the committee's structure mirrored the EESC's. NSZZ Solidarność and OPZZ belonged to this committee from the very beginning. Upon Poland's accession to the EU in May 2004, the Polish government gained the right to nominate 21 members for appointment by the Council of the European Union for a renewable 4-year term of office. NSZZ Solidarność and OPZZ are represented within the employees' group (group II) by three and two members, respectively. Moreover, the Trade Union Forum has sent two representatives to the EESC (see Table 12-1).

Table 12-1:   Polish Trade Union Representatives to the EESC[12]

Federation	Representative	Position	Section of EESC*
OPZZ	Rożycki, Stanisław	Vice President of the Federation of Unions of Polish Higher Education and Science Teachers	ECO, TEN
	Jasiński, Tomasz	Senior Specialist in International Co-operation and European Integration	REX, SOC
NZSS Solidarność	Krzaklewski, Marian	Member of the National Commission	ECO, TEN, CCMI
	Adamczyk, Andrzej	International Secretary	INT, REX
	Sobon-Bartkiewicz, Katarzyna	Expert in European Integration	SOC
Trade Union Forum (FZZ)	Szynaka, Edmund	Chief of the Expert Team	REX, SOC
	Siewierski, Wiesław	President of FZZ, Vice President of the Polish Tripartite Commission for Social and Economic Affairs	ECO, TEN

* ECO = Economic and Social Cohesion; TEN = Transport, Energy, Infrastructure and the Information Society; REX = External Relations; SOC = Employment, Social Affairs and Citizenship; CCMI = Consultative commission on industrial change; NAT = Agriculture, Rural Development and the Environment; INT = Single Market, Production and Consumption

The Polish trade unions' involvement in European networks and organisations can be taken as a further indicator of their engagement in EU governance. NSZZ Solidarność, as a pioneer of the free trade union movement in Eastern Europe, was immediately

---

12   Source: http://eescmembers.eesc.europa.eu, viewed on 25 August 2007.

recognised by international bodies. It quickly established various institutionalised and non-institutionalised contacts with its European and international counterparts even before the break-down of the socialist regime in Poland. In 1986, as the only East European trade union, it became a full member of the International Confederation of Free Trade Unions and of the World Confederation of Labour. It has been represented in the Trade Union Advisory Committee of the OECD since 1997. At the EU level, NSZZ Solidarność gained observer status in 1991 at the European Trade Union Confederation and became its affiliate just four years later. Furthermore, the former co-ordinator of the European Integration Commission and vice president of the National Commission of Solidarność, Józef Niemiec, was elected one of the four confederal secretaries of the ETUC in May 2003 and in the following term of office. Janusz Śniadek, the current president of the National Commission, and Andrzej Adamczyk, head of the International Department, are also Solidarność representatives in the Executive Committee of the ETUC. The ETUC is a European social partner and is recognised by the European Union as the only representative cross-sectoral trade union organisation at the European level. It works with all of the EU institutions and is involved in economic and social policy-making as well as the European social dialogue, with the stated aim of improving the European social model. Underscoring the significance of the ETUC, Andrzej Matla from the International Department of NSZZ Solidarność stated: 'Being represented in the ETUC means that our voice has influence on the shape of the European social dialogue.'[13] Nearly all of NSZZ Solidarność's branches and secretariats are also affiliated with the European Industry Federations (see Table 12-2).

Table 12-2: Affiliations of Polish Trade Unions and Federations to the European Trade Union Federations[14]

European Industry Federations	Branch structures of NSZZ Solidarność	Branch federations of OPZZ
EMCEF (European Mine, Chemical and Energy Workers Federation)	Chemical Workers' Secretariat; Energy and Miners' Secretariat	Trade Union of Miners in Poland (ZZG w Polsce); Federation of Oil and Gas Industry Workers' Unions (FZZGNiG); Federation of Chemical, Glass and Ceramic Industry Workers Unions in Poland (FZZPCSIC)
UNIEUROPA (Union Network International Europe)	Commercial, Clerical and Professional Employees' Secretariat; National Section of Trade Workers	Affiliate of UNI-Europa Graphical: Trade Union of Graphic Industry Workers (ZZPPP)

---

13   In: *Tygodnik Solidarność* 35(884)/2005, (author's own translation).
14   Sources: www.solidarnosc.org.pl, www.opzz.org.pl viewed on 25.08.2007, *Przegląd Wydarzeń Związkowych* 1(125)/2005.

European Industry Federations	Branch structures of NSZZ Solidarność	Branch federations of OPZZ
ETUCE (European Trade Union Committee for Education)	National Section of Education; National Section of Science	Polish Teachers' Union (ZNP)
EFFAT (European Federation of Trade Unions in Food, Agriculture and Tourism Sector and Allied Branches)	Food Workers' Secretariat; Rural Workes' Secretariat	Trade Unions Federation of the Food Industry Employees (FZKS)
ECF-IUF (European Committee of Food, Catering and Allied Workers' Unions within the IUF)	Food Workers' Secretariat	–
ETUF-TCL (European Trade Union Federation – Textiles, Clothing and Leather)	Textile Workers' Secretariat	Federation of Independent and Self-Governing Trade Unions of Light Industry (Federacja NSZZ Przemysłu Lekkiego)
EMF (European Metalworkers' Federation)	Metalworkers' Secretariat	Trade Union Federation 'Metalowcy'
ETF (European Transport Workers' Federation)	National Maritime Section; National Section of Sea Port Workers; National Section of Railway Workers	Federation of Trade Unions of Seamen and Fishers (FZZMiR); Trade Union of Aviation Workers (ZZ Personelu Latającego i Pokładowego)
EPSU (European Federation Public Service Unions)	Health Protection Secretariat, Public Service Employees' Secretariat	–
EFBWW (European Federation of Building and Woodworkers)	–	Observer status: Trade Union of Building Workers 'Budowlani'
EUROCADRES (Council of European Professional and Managerial Staff)	National Section of Science	–
FERPA (European Federation of Retired and Elderly Persons)	Secretariat of Pensioners	–

Thanks to Poland's EU accession, Polish trade unions have gained new channels of participation in the European social dialogue and the development of social policy. NSZZ Solidarność is a full member of the ETUC, the European umbrella trade union organisation, as well as of numerous European trade union federations and one of the social partners at the EESC. It became actively involved in the transnational decision-making process very early on and established structures for interest representation both on the national and supranational levels.

NSZZ Solidarność holds up the model of social dialogue established in the EU as a paragon for the Polish social partners:

> The experiences of the European dialogue became an inspiration for social partners in Poland even before its EU accession. Now we have gained not only real influence on the course of this dialogue, but we also benefit from its achievements. We are convinced that the quality and the intensity of the social dialogue at the European level directly influence the course of the dialogue at the national level.[15]

NSZZ Solidarność also observes that the European social dialogue is far more developed and efficient than the one taking place in Poland. Józef Niemiec pointed to a serious obstacle in this context: 'It often happens that it is much easier to reach advantageous agreements at the European level than to implement them later at the national level.'[16]

In contrast to NSZZ Solidarność, which achieved international recognition shortly after its founding and established relations with international and European structures early on, it took a long time for OPZZ to make inroads into the European arena.

In 1991, OPZZ officially left the World Federation of Trade Unions (WFTU) (to which trade unions of the Eastern bloc used to belong), but maintained a partnership with it; some OPZZ federations are still members of this international organisation's branch trade unions. The International Labour Organisation also plays an important role in OPZZ's international activities. Several OPZZ representatives are members on its committees. The federation also maintains tight bilateral relations with trade unions from East and West European countries. For a long time, however, OPZZ did not belong to any European or international trade union organisation.

Concerning the EU level, the 4th Congress of OPZZ in May 1998 set rapprochement with the European Trade Union Confederation as one of its priorities. In December 1998, OPZZ applied for membership. The general rule is for the ETUC to have one affiliate per country, usually the largest national centre, regardless of the number of union confederations there (Poland happens to have multiple confederations). Regarding new admissions, the ETUC seeks the views of its existing affiliates. The tensions between NSZZ Solidarność and OPZZ seemed to pose a significant obstacle here. OPZZ claimed that NSZZ Solidarność had hindered the development of its international activities because of OPZZ's communist heritage and the unresolved problem of the confiscated Solidarność property inherited by OPZZ in the 1980s.[17] The ETUC continually

---

15   Janusz Śniadek, President of the National Committee of NSZZ Solidarność. In: *Tygodnik Solidarność* 35 (884)/2005, (author's own translation).
16   In *Tygodnik Solidarność* 35(884)/2005 (author's own translation).
17   Ryszard Lepik, the vice-president of OPZZ. In: *Przegląd Wydarzeń Związkowych* 1(125)/2005, p. 3.

postponed its decision, and OPZZ finally abandoned its efforts for some time. OPZZ was not to become a member of the ETUC until March 2006.

In many European industry federations, the membership of the national trade union federation in the ETUC is a precondition for national branch federation to become a member. This requirement became an obstacle for some OPZZ federations. For example, the Budowlani trade union, which organises building workers, has been unable to become a member of the European Federation of Building and Woodworkers (EFBWW) despite years of good co-operation. It still has only unofficial observer status to the EFBWW. Other OPZZ branch federations have been admitted into the European structures and have scored successes (see Table 12-2), however. For example, in December 2006, the Metalowcy trade union federation finally became a full member of the European Metalworkers' Federation. Moreover, Sławomir Broniarz, the president of the Polish Teachers' Union (ZNP), the oldest and largest trade union for teachers in Poland, became Poland's representative to the Council of the European Trade Union Committee for Education in 2003. The representatives of the OPZZ branch federations complain, however, that particularly in the initial stage of their international activities, they were greeted with suspicion due to OPZZ's negative reputation among foreign trade unions. OPZZ members have therefore had to work hard to convince their international counterparts of their competence.[18]

OPZZ federations count direct access to relevant information as among the most significant benefits of their membership in European organisations and active participation at the European level. Broniarz claimed, for example, that the information the ZNP received from the responsible Polish ministries was often insufficient, and that his union therefore had no access to international research programmes.[19] The president of the Federation of Chemical, Glass and Ceramic Industry Workers' Unions in Poland (FZZPCSIC), Józef Wozny, once pointed out [in reference to the accession of his federation to the European Mine, Chemical and Energy Workers Federation (EMCEF)]: 'Analysing the situation of the branch, we came to the conclusion that we were sustaining many losses by not participating actively in the European trade union forum. We couldn't wait any longer.'[20] Despite the initial uncertainties and fears concerning the financial costs of membership in a European federation, Andrzej Chwiluk, the president of the Trade Union of Miners in Poland (ZZG w Polsce), also considers the accession of his union to the EMCEF in June 2004 as a turning point. The membership opened up new possibilities for the union, allowing it to exert influence on the European legislative processes and access information and documents to which only the Polish government had previously had access.[21]

---

18   See various interviews in *Przegląd Wydarzeń Związkowych* 1(125)/2005.
19   In: *Przegląd Wydarzeń Związkowych* 1(125)/2005, p. 4.
20   In: *Przegląd Wydarzeń Związkowych*, 1 (125)/2005, p. 13 (author's own translation).
21   In: *Przegląd Wydarzeń Związkowych*, 1 (125)/2005, p. 11.

The third Polish trade union federation, FZZ, has also managed to gain access to the European arena, especially via its membership in the Confédération Européenne des Syndicats Indépendants. Some of its members are also affiliates of the European industry federations.

Other key European activities undertaken by the Polish trade unions include the establishment of the European Works Councils in Poland and the strengthening of the Polish trade unions' participation in their work. The legislation implementing the European Works Councils Directive (94/45/EC) came into force in Poland when it joined the EU in May 2004. Polish trade unions also actively participate in campaigns and protest actions across the European Union organised by the ETUC. The most successful joint action was the protest against the European directive on services in the internal market, the so-called 'Bolkestein Directive'.

12.4. Conclusions

The Polish trade unions employ the so-called multiple strategy of interest representation typical for all European interest groups. Greenwood once elaborated on this approach as follows:

> The multi-level character of European policy process means that actors seeking to participate in European public affairs therefore have a number of so-called 'routes' of influence. At its most simple level, the 'national route' refers to the use of national contacts and national governments to influence EU decision-making, whereas the 'European route', or the 'Brussels strategy', involves seeking to exert influence by representation direct to the European institutions themselves.[22]

Due to myriad factors, Polish trade unions are seeking new approaches to interest representation and adapting their work programmes. On the home front, the trade union scene has suffered from fragmentation and the relatively weak social dialogue in Poland. The ineffectiveness of the latter has made it difficult for the unions to influence political decision-making at the national level. Meanwhile, there are pan-European challenges to contend with, such as globalisation, sinking trade union membership rates and the ever-increasing regulatory power of the EU. Faced with these domestic and European pressures, Polish trade unions have stepped up their engagement at the EU level. They are turning to the superior European social dialogue to better represent and promote their interests. As a result, their lobbying activities at the European as well as the international level have become much more significant. In the EU arena, the European Economic and Social Committee, the European Trade Union Confederation and the European industry federations are seen as strong partners for interest representation. They fulfil the eligibility criteria established by the

---

22   Greenwood, J. (2003): *Interest Representation in the European Union*, Palgrave MacMillan, London, p. 32f.

European Commission to regulate the access of interest groups to consultation processes in EU governance and are recognised as key players in the European social dialogue. Membership in European committees and organisations allows the Polish trade unions to validate their own eligibility at the European level. However, engagement in EU governance requires certain competences and expertise as well as abundant financial and personal resources, which are in short supply in Polish trade unions.

About the authors

Kristýna Bušková earned her bachelor's degree in International and European Economics Studies at the University of New York/Prague. She is a research assistant at the Research Centre for East European Studies, University of Bremen and will begin her postgraduate studies in Social and Development Anthropology at the University of Cambridge in autumn 2007.

Kristina Charrad is a member of the young researchers' group 'European civil society and multi-level governance' at the Graduate School of Politics (GRASP) at the University of Münster, Germany. Her research interests are lobbying, the development of interest representation in Central and Eastern European countries and the strategies of actors from CEE at the European level.

Redmar Damsma is a student assistant at the Law Faculty, University of Amsterdam.

Joanna Einbock is a research associate at the Koszalin Institute of Comparative European Studies (Poland) and EU projects assistant at the Research and Technology Transfer Center at Leibniz University Hanover (Germany). Her research concentrates on the activities of Polish interest groups at the European level.

Gudrun Eisele is a member of the young researchers' group 'European civil society and multi-level governance' at the Graduate School of Politics (GRASP) at the University of Münster, Germany. Her research interests are European governance, civil society and gender mainstreaming.

Gesine Fuchs lectures on Eastern European Studies at the University of Basel and works as an independent consultant and expert in the field of gender politics. Her research interests include comparative political participation and representation, gender politics and women's movements in Eastern Europe. Her new research will compare the legal mobilisation of social movements in four European countries. See also www.gesine-fuchs.net

David Lane is currently a senior research associate at the University of Cambridge and previously Professor of Sociology at Birmingham University. His current research interests are defining the social basis for reform and anti-reform in Russia and Ukraine. His recent books include *The Transformation of State Socialism: System Change, Capitalism, or Something else?* 2007 and (with Martin Myant, Editor), *Varieties of Capitalism in Post-Communist Countries* 2007.

Zdenka Mansfeldová is head of the Department of the Sociology of Politics and Deputy Director at the Institute of Sociology, Academy of Science of the Czech Republic in Prague. Her research focuses on political institutionalisation and representation of interests, in both political terms (parties and parliament) and the non-political meso-structures of social interests.

Daniela Obradovic is a senior lecturer at the Faculty of Law, University of Amsterdam. Her specialisations include European Union law and integration studies in general and the role of interest groups in European Union policy formation in particular. She has in recent years published in a number of academic journals including the Yearbook of European Law and Common Market Law Review. She is the editor of the book *Interface Between EU Law and National Law*, Groningen: Europa Law Publishing, 2007.

Silvia Payer is a managing partner of the Austrian consulting company "co.systems consulting". Her major interest is to develop supportive EU projects and appropriate project structures to benefit women and encourage their participation.

Heiko Pleines is head of the Dept. of Politics and Economics at the Research Centre for East European Studies and lecturer in Comparative Politics and European Studies at the University of Bremen. One of his major research interests is the representation of interest groups from the post-socialist member states in EU governance.

Jose M. Alonso Vizcaino is a student assistant at the Law Faculty, University of Amsterdam.

Iglika Yakova is currently finishing her PhD in political science at the Institut d'Etudes Politiques de Paris, France (Sciences Po – Paris). She has been a research fellow at the French Center for Research in Social Sciences, Prague, Czech Republic and a Fox International Fellow at Yale University. Her main research interests include interest group representation, post-communist societies and EU integration.

Series Subscription

Please enter my subscription to the series *Changing Europe*, ISSN 1863-8716, as follows:

starting with
☐   volume # 1
☐   volume # ___
    ☐   please also include the following volumes: #___, ___, ___, ___, ___, ___,

☐   the next volume being published
    ☐   please also include the following volumes: #___, ___, ___, ___, ___, ___,

☐   1 copy per volume   OR   ☐   ___ copies per volume

Subscription within Germany:

You will receive every volume at 1st publication at the regular bookseller's price – incl. s & h and VAT.
Payment:
☐ Please bill me for every volume.
☐ Lastschriftverfahren: Ich/wir ermächtige(n) Sie hiermit widerruflich, den Rechnungsbetrag je Band von meinem/unserem folgendem Konto einzuziehen.

Kontoinhaber: _____ Kreditinstitut: _____
Kontonummer: _____ Bankleitzahl: _____

International Subscription:

Payment (incl. s & h and VAT) in advance for
☐   10 volumes/copies (€ 319.80)   ☐   20 volumes/copies (€ 599.80)
☐   40 volumes/copies (€ 1,099.80)
Please send my books to:

NAME_____DEPARTMENT_____
ADDRESS _____
POST/ZIP CODE_____COUNTRY _____
TELEPHONE _____EMAIL_____

date/signature_____

A hint for librarians in the former Soviet Union: Your academic library might be eligible to receive free-of-cost scholarly literature from Germany via the German Research Foundation. For Russian-language information on this program, see
http://www.dfg.de/forschungsfoerderung/formulare/download/12_54.pdf.

Please fax to: **0511 / 262 2201 (+49 511 262 2201)**
or mail to: *ibidem*-Verlag, Julius-Leber-Weg 11, D-30457 Hannover,Germany
or send an e-mail: ibidem@ibidem-verlag.de

ibidem-Verlag
Melchiorstr. 15
D-70439 Stuttgart

info@ibidem-verlag.de

www.ibidem-verlag.de
www.edition-noema.de
www.autorenbetreuung.de

www.ingramcontent.com/pod-product-compliance
Lightning Source LLC
Chambersburg PA
CBHW071854270326
41929CB00013B/2232